To Skip & Jean,
classmates, friends, and
great summer companions. Hope
you find some entertainment and
perhaps some inspiration in this
effort.

Bill Underwood
8·20·05

ORDINARY PEOPLE: HEROES, CREATORS, SURVIVORS

Folks of San Marcos and Hays County

by

Bibb Underwood

authorHOUSE™

1663 LIBERTY DRIVE, SUITE 200
BLOOMINGTON, INDIANA 47403
(800) 839-8640
WWW.AUTHORHOUSE.COM

First published by AuthorHouse 04/05/05

ISBN: 1-4208-3539-4 (sc)

Library of Congress Control Number: 2005901718

Printed in the United States of America
Bloomington, Indiana

This book is printed on acid-free paper.

Table of Contents

Foreword

This is an accidental book. In March of 2000, I wrote a profile of a member of the staff at Scheib Center. When I took it to Linda Keese, who, at the time, was the Neighbors Editor of the San Marcos Daily Record, she asked if I could provide an occasional article for her section. I, without thinking, responded, "Sure. How about one a week?"

I had no idea what I committed myself to. It was the beginning of a thrilling exploration, exposition and understanding of the people of San Marcos and Hays County, Texas. I have often said I could go blindfolded to the phone book, put my finger on a name and find an interesting character. I still believe that, but it has never been necessary.

As I began this project, I had a few people in mind, who seemed to have unique histories, or experiences that would provide interesting reading for the general public. As the profiles began to appear in the Neighbors Section of the Daily Record, I began getting calls recommending people to write about. I have followed up on many of those calls. All of them have been worthy.

Occasionally, I have tried to link an individual to a holiday or an event. However, I have purposely avoided themes.

This book contains the profiles of "Ordinary People" who populate our mundane existence. They are heroes, creators, and survivors. Some—most—are all three. I have written about bankers, writers, mothers, civil servants, fathers, entrepreneurs, business-people, teachers, musicians, athletes, and inventors. What I have tried to capture is the essence of the person that made him or her a hero, a creator or a survivor.

It has been a fabulous journey. If the reader finds a bit of inspiration, a moment of reflection, a sense of appreciation, and a deeper understanding of all the Ordinary People we encounter in our daily lives, the book will have served its purpose.

John Edgell

This is a pain I mostly hide, but ties of blood, or seed endure, and even now I feel inside the hunger for his outstretched hand, a man's embrace to take me in, the need for just a word of praise. Carter, Jimmy, "I Wanted to Share My Father's World." <u>Always a</u> <u>Reckoning</u>, Times Books (1994).

Many of us grow up with that pain inside. The hunger for the embrace of a father too busy to offer the outstretched hand of compassion and encouragement at a critical moment. The moment is lost forever to our conscious in the backwash of time, but rests in our subconscious, goading us to sadness, loneliness, even desperation.

John Edgell is the antithesis of that father. His arms have reached out to embrace the child, to offer encouragement and praise. Not for the fleeting moment of need, not for the instant of achievement, not for the flash of recognition, but daily for every day it takes. He is a popular math professor at TxSU and the father of five. All successful, all worthy of a father's praise and devotion. Due to limited space, this article will deal with this father's relationship with only one of his children.

Five days a week they are a familiar sight at the Texas State Student Recreation Center. John unloads the wheelchair from the van and proceeds to the passenger's door where he gently and patiently assists his 34 year old son, Johnny, out of the van and into the chair. This is all a part of the commitment John Edgell sees as essential to being a father. For 17 years now, he has been Johnny's legs and arms and guide, encouraging him, praising him, assisting him in whatever way necessary.

In 1983, Johnny was ready to graduate from San Marcos High School—he was already taking courses at TxSU—when his father, in keeping with established family habits, asked Johnny how he would like to spend his spring break. Johnny chose to take a long motorcycle trip with his dad. Their destination was Leavenworth, Kansas where John grew up.

"We had a great week," John said. "We visited the Federal Prison where my dad and brother worked for years. We went to the University of Kansas and then over to Pittsburgh State where I met Lucy, my wife, when she came there on a dance tour from Texas Women's University. Johnny met a lot of his relatives; I showed him where I lived as a student and it was just a wonderful week.

"On the way back to Texas, we were in Oklahoma on an interstate highway, trying to outrun a 'blue norther.' We topped the crest of a long hill and found ourselves facing the rear end of an 18-wheeler. I drifted out

1

to the left to get around the truck and checked my rear-view mirror where I observed Johnny moving over to the left. Everything looked perfect. Seconds later I glanced in the mirror and saw Johnny go in the air. He came down free of his bike, but hit right on his head. I went back and yelled at him, 'Get out of the road, you will get run over.' He didn't move. A nurse was in the first car that came by. The second car had a physician. So, there I am with a nurse and a physician on the scene and I don't have a clue about what's happening."

Johnny was taken to a hospital in McAllister, Oklahoma where they were already trying to locate a neuro-surgeon. When the local medical facility failed to locate a surgeon, Johnny was transferred to a hospital in Tulsa. The surgeon told John, that Johnny had contusions on the brain stem.

John relates, "That is where all the nerves come together. Every bodily function is affected; temperature, heart, breathing, everything. For fourteen days we had to do everything for him. He was surrounded by machines and just changing one of those machines was a life-threatening procedure. We were desperate. To keep my sanity, I challenged people to solve complicated math problems and discussed these with them for distraction.

"Once he stabilized and they could do no more for him in Tulsa, my brother in the Department of Commerce, and the Tulsa Kiwanis Club helped us locate the best place in the country to take him. The University of Texas Medical Center in San Antonio turned out to be the place he needed to go. He was still in a coma when we flew him to Texas."

John and Lucy each had demanding jobs, but they were in San Antonio every day. John describes what it was like. "Daily, I'm forced to watch this 230 pound all-around athlete — he was ranked the number one handball player in the nation in his age group at the time of his accident—atrophy to 130 pounds of skin and bones. I got in bed with him two or three times a day and stretched every muscle and joint and limb of his body; I exercised him every way I knew how. We tried to stimulate him by creating an environment with which he was familiar. We played country music, which he loves; we put on his favorite TV shows; we used aromas and noises to try to get him out of this coma."

After three and a half months of daily stimulation, prayers, and exhortations, Johnny finally moved a toe at the instructions of his mother. The doctors shrugged it off as an involuntary reaction until Lucy convinced one of the doctors to observe the movement in direct response to her instructions. It was Johnny's first hint of awareness.

John recounted, "Not long after that, we began his rehabilitation in Lewis Bay, Massachusetts. We took an apartment near the rehab facility and I moved up there for awhile. Then Lucy took leave of absence from her job while I came back and finished teaching the spring semester. Then I moved back up there. In July of 1984 we were able to bring Johnny back home."

Johnny then transferred to a rehab facility in Galveston for about 14 months. John went to Galveston every weekend and if there was an emergency of any sort, he would go during the week. When he came home John worked with Johnny daily to continue the rehab process. He would take Johnny to the golf course for walks three or four times a day and they eventually began riding a tandem bicycle.

"He would walk 300-400 feet and fall down. But he got up, determined as ever. We went on long bike rides. It was nothing for us to ride to San Antonio or Austin on the weekend. As the years went by, he regained his feisty personality and was just doing beautifully.

"In October 1988 he and I took a short bike ride along the I-35 access road to the York Creek bridge. We had just turned around at the bridge and were on our way back home when I saw stars. We had been hit by a drunk driver in a pick-up. I hit the concrete and just rolled and rolled. I just knew Johnny was dead. In fact, when the first passersby stopped and asked who they should call, I said, 'call a priest.' Johnny had been dragged by the truck and his arms had almost no skin left."

John was taken to CTMC where he was diagnosed with a broken neck. Transferred to Brackenridge Hospital in Austin, John was lucky to have Dr. Patrick as his surgeon. The doctor had experienced the same injury. After a complex and painful operation, John wore a metal halo with screws in his skull for months, but he brushes it off as almost meaningless when discussing it in the same context with Johnny's injury. The anger returns when he tells you, "We lost five years of progress with Johnny. All that work went down the drain."

The anger doesn't linger. John smiles and determination and hope return to his voice when he tells you, "But today Johnny has once again regained his love of life, his self-respect and respect for others. He goes to church every Sunday, takes communion, and enjoys movies. He is everything you would want any of your children to be."

That is no accident. John Edgell has been with his son every step of the way. He has offered the outstretched hand to him who hungers for the man's embrace.

Bill Daniels

"On April 2, 1985, the neurosurgeon came into the room and told me, 'Son, you have the classic symptoms of ALS. There is no known cause and no known cure. Do you understand that?' I said, 'yes.' He continued, 'There is a waiting room full of people out there and I am a very busy man. I'm sorry, but I have told you all I can.' He was a cold SOB."

That is how Bill Daniels describes the moment he first knew he was stricken with the dreaded disease.

He had just been given a death sentence at age 45. Amyotrophic Lateral Sclerosis (ALS), much better known as Lou Gehrig's Disease, is normally fatal within two to four years. (Lou Gehrig delivered his famous "Luckiest Man Alive" speech in Yankee Stadium on July 4, 1939. One year and 11 months later he died.)

"Life could not have been rosier for me. My dental practice was booming. I had just completed my new house. My life was full and I was as happy as I had ever been. To get that diagnosis was staggering, to say the least. On the way home I teared up several times. My sorrow came from the knowledge I would have to tell my parents. Golly, I didn't want to do that."

Bill Daniels came to San Marcos in 1971. As he describes it, "I was discharged from the Army on August 31. I sterilized my dental tools and opened the doors to my office the day after Labor Day."

It was no accident that he landed in San Marcos. As with everything he does, he gave lots of thought to where he wanted to practice. As a youth he had often gone to the Wimberley area as a camp counselor. Later, as a salesman, prior to going to dental school, he had traveled extensively across the Texas landscape. By the time he was discharged from the Army—he volunteered for Viet Nam, but was sent to Fort Rucker where he completed his two year commitment—he had narrowed his choices to San Marcos and Marble Falls. Circumstances, as they so often do, nudged him in the direction of San Marcos. He met a couple of San Marcos doctors who had a prime piece of real estate they were willing to help him turn into an office at 715 West Hopkins Street.

His self-confidence and ability to take charge of his own life is illustrated by the route he took to dental school. As a salesman for a national company for four years, he decided the travel, the hassle of quotas and the pressure of the corporate climate were going to kill him. With a business degree from Sam Houston State, he enrolled in night school to fill in the gaps

4

he lacked in science. He was accepted by the University of Texas Dental School in Houston when only 14 per-cent of the qualified applicants was admitted. Asked *why* dentistry, Bill's self-deprecating, humorous response was, "It's inside work and there is no heavy lifting."

His attitude toward life and his determination to live it to the fullest is illustrated by his reaction to his diagnosis. "I actually got some solace from it. We have all seen people die in different ways. Some cry and whimper and become helpless. Some go with grace and courage. I started thinking, 'By golly, I'm going out with a YEEHAW like Slim Pickens in the movie, Dr. Strangelove, when he straddled that nuclear bomb as it went out the bomb bay door.' I am *not* going to confine myself to a bed and curl up in the fetal position.

"I did not tell anyone about the diagnosis for three months. But on my birthday my parents had a dinner for me and invited all the family and a friend of mine. Before dinner my friend, asked 'What about those tests you had awhile back?' At that point, I thought I might as well 'fess up. I was walking with some difficulty and I had trouble with my hands earlier and I knew it was just a matter of time. When I told my friend, there was quite a lot of emotion in the room. I knew I would have to tell my parents. I announced to my mother that I needed to talk to everyone. Detecting something in my voice, she refused to listen.

"It was a very emotional session. After hearing the diagnosis and the prognosis, several family members had to leave the room."

Reminded that the above scene occurred 15 years ago, Bill was asked if the doctors had changed their prognosis. "I don't go to doctors," he said.

"At that time the only ray of hope offered ALS sufferers was a study being done at Baylor Medical School in Houston. They were experimenting with cytoxin and cyclosporin, two drugs that attack the immune system. After four days of submitting to some humiliating tests, the doctors told me I was qualified for the study."

It was near Christmas and Bill decided he didn't want to subject himself to the treatment, lose his hair and undergo all the other humiliation the treatment entailed.

"I told them I did not want to participate and the doctors were *more* than a little bit offended. They were offended because *they* were offering me the only chance I had at life. But it just didn't seem to me I should destroy my immune system to get well.

"With that thought in mind, I went to see John Diamond, M.D. in Valley Cottage, New York. You might ask, 'What kind of doctor is he. Well, he is a very unusual doctor. He is an Australian, a psychiatrist, and he calls himself a teacher, a concept teacher. We spent 2-3 hours together the first day and he had story after story of people with terminal diagnoses who survived, not by extraordinary means, but in every case they found something, some treatment, some therapy, some system that got them over a terminal disease. The point of this is that whatever the problem, there is an answer, no matter how bad it looks. He gave me hope."

Bill goes on to explain that the most important things to come out of the visit with Dr. Diamond were the realization that he must be completely responsible for his own health and he must possess the will to live and be well. "This is not a knock on religion," he points out, "but you simply can't passively turn everything over to God; the same goes for doctors. You can't expect someone else to be responsible for your life and your health.

"It required a major change in my thought processes. When I returned, I was pumped. I went to bookstores, I read magazines, I sought every avenue of health practice I could conceptualize. I don't mind telling you, I did some crazy things. Some were stupid. But with the medical training I have I could generally distinguish pure hog-wash. I had four criteria for trying a treatment. 1)What was the upside? 2) What was the downside? 3) What was the cost? 4) What was the hassle factor. The hassle factor being, 'Do I have to fly to Tijuana, Mexico twice a week to get a shot that costs $25,000.00.' I played games with myself. For instance, I received a handicap parking tag. I refused to use it for a long time. I still pass up handicap parking occasionally."

Through his reading and studying (Bill describes the intensity of his studies as similar to studying for a final exam and hopes the irony is not lost on the listener.), he evolved 14 elements of healthy living. They are: 1)Clean air; 2) Natural clothing; 3) Proper diet; 4) Listen to peaceful music; 5) Exercise; 6) Proper rest; 7) Proper eliminations; 8) Relaxation; 9) Service to others; 10) Positive attitudes; 11) Meditation; 12) Creative visualization; 13) Creative expression; 14) Love.

Bill Daniels survival is a medical phenomenon which has brought him some notoriety among fellow sufferers of ALS and other terminal diseases. While this interview was in progress, he received a call from a concerned mother of a 50 year old man who was recently diagnosed with the disease. She wanted him to talk to her son which, of course, Bill agreed to do. That call led to his relating a similar call he received a few years ago.

"The caller, a female, was obviously smoking while we talked. I asked why she had not quit smoking. She responded she liked her cigarettes and had no intention of quitting. I told her I could not help her and had nothing further to say to her. You must be willing to do the work."

6

This interview was conducted about three years ago. Bill Daniels continues to thrive and contribute to his community.

Deanna Badgett

"I grew up in Central California and the school I went to was very small. We had enough students in each grade to fill one classroom. Not only was it small, it was also poor. For example, the bus driver also taught seventh grade. However, we had music. Each grade had a song book—like a text book—and we had a singing teacher."

That is how Deanna Badgett explains her initial contact with music.

"When I reached the fourth grade," she says, Mr. Hofer called us in individually and asked what band instrument we wanted to play. If one did not want to play an instrument, he would ask, 'Do you want to carry a flag, do you want to twirl a baton, do you want to be a drum major?' Everyone had a part in the band." Deanna recounts her interview with Mr. Hofer: When she was asked what instrument she wanted to play, she hesitated momentarily and he thrust a baritone horn in her hands and said, "How about this?". It covered half her body, but she responded, "Oh, all right." (It would still cover half her body. To say Deanna is petite is to say Tiger Woods is a fair golfer.)

He then asked what instrument she wanted to play in the orchestra. Again, she hesitated and he thrust a violin in her hands with a, "how about this," and once again Deanna responded, "Oh, all right."

"Through Mr. Hofer's influence I was in two choirs, the band and the orchestra while in the fourth grade. This was the poorest of the poor school districts. We had to provide our uniforms which consisted of white shirts and pants. The PTA bought our instruments. But as poor as we were, it was possible to have success.

"As I moved on to high school, my music teacher called my mother for a conference and said it was time for me to have my own instrument and to have private lessons. Of course, my mother would not dream of not doing what a teacher suggested. It was so hard for my mother to come up with the money for that $100.00 violin. My sister also played violin and my brother played a trumpet. Each of us would select a corner of the tiny house in which we lived for our practice studio. Sometimes, we were all playing different music at the same time. It was a wonderful part of my life, but it never occurred to me that it was something I could do with my life and turn it into a career."

In fact, Deanna had a career in science long before she turned to music as her life's work. With a masters degree in organic chemistry from prestigious Mount Holyoke College in Massachusetts, she worked as a

DNA and RNA researcher in Lawrence Livermore National Radiation Laboratory, located in the Bay Area of California.

"However, she says, "it is very lonely working in the 'cold' room alone, taking extractions, then doing the experiments with very little human contact. I later worked in the Donner nuclear medicine lab. I found myself handling extremely sensitive materials on a regular basis, so I put a dosimeter right here (she points to the general location of one of her ovaries) and I found that in two months I had received 40 per cent of the allowed lifetime dosage of radiation. I then transferred to San Francisco General Hospital. I was gravitating more and more toward working with people."

Following marriage and a couple of children, she found herself in San Marcos, Texas. Her husband, Ben, had come here to take a teaching job at SWT. She was fully occupied being a mother and a housewife, but following the pattern of her early years, she insisted her son learn the violin. She was driving him to Austin early every Saturday morning for his lessons when after three years, he rebelled against the early hours, the tedious practices, the sacrificing of little league, Saturday cartoons and all the things to which pre-teens are naturally attracted. In searching for an alternative to the Austin trip each week, she met Trudy Gildea who was teaching violin, using the Suzuki method. She describes the meeting with Trudy, "I saw teaching that I had always wanted to see. I heard things I had always wanted to hear. She put "Where Love is Deep" in my hand and she gave me some notes and announced that she was leaving in two months. She said that I could teach her students. I observed her until she left. On the day she closed out her house, I went over and she gave me one last set of notes.

"I had twelve students that first year. I did not advertise or anything. I don't know where they came from. Now I have 30 regular students plus 12 beginners at Crockett Elementary School."

"So, what is the Suzuki method?," I asked. First, she demonstrated the beginning of a lesson. She stood me up, lifted my head, squared my shoulders, checked to see if my feet were together and she said, 'At the beginning of the lesson, student and teacher bow to each other and the student and says, 'I am here to learn.'

After our formal introduction, she launched into a passionate explanation of why it is important to get children into music as early as possible. Inviting Deanna to talk about music and teaching children is like turning on a fire-hydrant to get a drink of water. She talks with deep conviction while acting out points she is trying to make. She takes the interviewer's arm to illustrate how to draw a bow. "For the first few lessons we have our students play with the bow only." she says. "It helps them understand the importance of integrating everything they do.

"Music is another language and, like a second language, the sooner we introduce children to it, the more easily and rapidly they learn it. A five month old child can recognize the music of a concerto." Then she went on to explain the importance of posture in music. "Proper posture," she said, "allows the child to release. Releasing is more than relaxing. Relaxing is a muscular thing, while releasing suggests that the child releases everything between him/her and the music."

She explained that parents were required to draw the foot charts in the first meeting she had with those whose children will be taking her course in Crockett School. This led to her explanation that the Crockett course is an experiment and the first time she has been invited to introduced her technique into the public schools. With her infectious enthusiasm she explained the importance of having parents involved with the child's learning and she emphasized that parents must be as dedicated as the child to get the best results.

In discussing the kinship of language and music, I inquired if she spoke Japanese. She responded, "No, I'm post-war. My family was in a concentration camp. They called it a re-location center, but it had barb-wire, tar paper barracks, central bathing facilities and central eating facilities. My family was in California. There were my parents, three children at the time, and my grandparents. My grandmother had rheumatic fever and was not supposed to travel. They were told they had two days to gather all their belongings and get ready to get out. This was 1942. I was almost three years old. Some people were put in holding areas, but we were put on a truck and moved directly to the camp in Poston Arizona.

"Four families were put in each barracks with no dividers, only one entrance and one stove at the end of the barracks. There was no privacy. Eventually, the grown-ups hung blankets to divide each family area. And before we left, they scrounged enough lumber to build partitions. My grandmother got worse and within a month she died.

"We were in the concentration camp two years and when we got out, my older sister went to kindergarten and one day she came home with a note pinned to her lapel which said, 'Lorraine needs to speak English at home.' My mother, who *was* bi-lingual, was born in the United States. My father was born in Japan, and came to the states when he was 13 years old. After the war, we all wanted to be *American*. My best friend was a blue-eyed blonde and I wanted to be like her.

Deanna Badgett is not a blue-eyed blonde, but her story is one of overcoming, persevering, taking chances, striving, and giving back—about as *American* as basketball, pick-up trucks and apple pie.

Darla Dees Wood

"It was February 18, 1984, the weekend of President's Day," Darla said, "and I was going to meet friends to go dancing. It was Saturday night about 9:00 PM, I was driving a little too fast on a gravel road. The weather was cold and rainy—miserable. The rabbit ran into the road, I slammed on the brakes and the next thing I was aware of was lying in a field, listening to music. I remember being thrown out of the car and I remember the radio was on in the car. I was conscious through the whole thing."

Darla Dees was a 19 year-old student at [Southwest] Texas State University. A 1983 graduate of San Marcos High, she was a fairly typical college freshman, who lived for the moment and whose primary concerns were her friends, her next date and what to wear for the social event of the weekend. She was moving into her first apartment and life's possibilities lay before her like a vast unexplored land. That she was on scholastic probation was no big deal.

The 'whole thing' to which Darla refers was the loss of control of her car on the unimproved country road (County Road 107 in Caldwell County, east of Martindale) as she attempted to avoid hitting a small rabbit. Her car flipped, she was thrown out and lay face down in a field. For 45 minutes she wondered what happened.

The rural road is lightly traveled, especially at night. No one came. Finally, her father, Ernest Dees, responding to a call from her waiting friends, set out to look for her. He was the first to find her.

"My friends called the house, wondering why I was late," Darla related. "My father's first thought was that I was out of gas. He knew I was not very responsible maintaining my car. He expected to find me walking to a service station.

"After he found me, he had to leave to get help. That was a tough thing for both of us. He must have known it was serious because I was face down, could not turn over and I was having trouble breathing. He turned me over and gave me his coat before he left.

"At that point, I remember thinking, 'I'm going to be late for the dance.' Never once crossed my mind that I had broken anything. When it did occur to me that I might be hurt, I thought more along the lines of a broken leg. "

Darla's father returned home, a few miles down the road from the accident. He summoned EMS and Darla was taken to Brackenridge Hospital. She says she finally began to have some awareness that she was seriously hurt when the EMS people would not let her father ride in the ambulance with her.

"My first realization of the seriousness of my condition came in the emergency room when the doctor told my parents I was paralyzed. However, he said that was the least of his worries at the moment. Keeping me alive through the night would be the big test.

"I thought they did not know what they were talking about. Nothing was hurting me. I suppose I was in shock and full of pain medicine, but I was still thinking I would spend a couple of days in the hospital and come home."

Even when she was put in a critical care unit where people were dying almost daily, Darla was sure she was on the wrong unit. A couple of times she was queried about donating her organs and in her shock and drug induced world of semi-conscious awareness, the real message did not register.

She remained in critical care at Brackenridge Hospital paralyzed from the neck down. She was in traction from February to May.

"That was not fun," Darla said. "They put bolts in my head and put weights on them to pull my head down flat. I couldn't move. It was crucial for stability while my neck was healing. That was probably the worst part of my treatment.

"I was still on heavy medication which created a sort of Never Never Land for me and I had never been told that I was paralyzed. One day in April, a girl whose name was also Darla, was allowed to go out with her family. She had a broken neck. I asked why she could go out and I couldn't. The nurse told me 'She's not paralyzed.' That's the first time I fully realized I was paralyzed."

Next for Darla was rehabilitation in Warm Springs, near Gonzalez. She describes rehab as a very ugly thing. While in Brackenridge, she had her family with her almost continuously. They provided her with encouragement and support from the beginning and she came to depend on their presence.

In rehab, they told her she would not see her family for two weeks. Therapists thought they needed the separation so that their treatment would not be diluted by family sympathy. The family had rallied around Darla. Her mother would have none of that separation. She quickly broke that rule.

Darla is quick to add, "My mother was and is my toughest critic. She didn't take any whining from me. She was the first to tell me to get my act together when I balked at doing what the therapists wanted. Had it not been for her I might have never come out of that stage of my treatment.

That stage is mean. For instance, I had to learn to sit up. They put me on a tilt table and gradually raised me to a sitting position. My muscles would not contract, controlling the flow of blood from my head. They raised me and left me there until I passed out. That is why they don't want the family around.

"The physical pain can be relieved with pills. But the emotional and mental pain was driving my life at that point. Realizing at 19 years old, you will never walk again, you will never go out with your friends the way you once did, you will not finish college as you planned, and that you will require 24 hour care the rest of your life—that's what puts you in the hole."

Darla was in Warm Springs from late April to August. One might expect that adjustments to her mental attitude were leading to acceptance of her circumstances.

One would be wrong. "When I got out of therapy, I said to myself: 'OK, you are through with all that. Now what? You have the rest of your life to live. What are you going to do?' I thought I was going to be a burden to my family the rest of my life. That was absolutely my lowest. That is when I really felt I might not want to live."

This feeling lasted about three weeks, according to Darla. Then she remembered discussions about going to school while she was at Warm Springs. Victoria Junior College has a small campus near the rehab center. It has designed accessibility to those in rehab and so she decided to try it.

"I went there for one semester," she says. "I hated it."

To illustrate her lingering denial, she said, "I couldn't stand it, I was miserable. There was a bunch of crippled people around me and I didn't like that. They partied all the time—they really knew how to party.

"I had to learn a whole new way of learning. I couldn't hold a book. I couldn't write and take notes. I had to listen in class. After one semester, I was determined to go back to [Southwest] Texas State.

"I was told I was nuts. I heard, 'There are too many hills on that campus and they don't have facilities for the disabled.'"

With some pushing and tugging and negotiating, Darla managed to get a dorm room remodeled to accommodate her mobility needs. She left college with a 1.3 Grade Point Average (GPA). One condition for her return to school was that she would have to bring her GPA up to a 2.0 in one semester.

"That first semester back was very tough," she said. "But after that, I learned how to study, what I needed to do to make things work for me. I learned to type with a stick. About that time a generous San Marcos gentleman bought me a voice-activated PC computer. That opened the door for me to do all my homework. I could hook up to the computer lab from my dorm room and do my programming."

Darla received her degree in computer science in 1988 with a GPA of 2.9. She always looked for the smartest person in class and asked to share her/his notes. She would then put them on her computer for study.

"I was engaged by the time I graduated. I started dating Roger in 1985 and we were engaged in December of 1986. I was not going to marry until I could support myself. So, my goal was to find a job.

"I interviewed with about 15 firms, Texaco, Exxon, Southern Union Gas—none of them would give me a chance. They looked at me and saw three things: 1) She is going to cost us money; 2) She is going to be sick all the time; 3) How the hell is she going to work?"

She answered a San Marcos Telephone Company ad for credit collection. She interviewed and was hired. She remained with the company until it became CenturyTel.

"I then went to work in Austin for CUR Systems and I work for APTIS, a telephony billing software developer. I supervise six people.

What about your marriage, I asked.

"Roger Wood and I married in 1989. He is one of the most patient individuals in the world. I am extremely blessed."

What does your story tell us, I asked.

"I don't think much has changed for the disabled. First, I don't think they have done enough for themselves. Second, it does no good to sit home and cry about your circumstances. Third, I want an outlet, and I don't know what it should be, to tell handicapped people to get off your butt and go for it."

Bruce Ingram

Bruce Ingram's manner is more that of a favorite uncle than that of an astute business man. His soft voice is spoken through a pleasant smile that puts one immediately at ease. There is a certain shyness about the man who heads a business enterprise that encompasses 24 production plants, employs 480 people, and operates 378 bumble bee colored vehicles, most of which are concrete mixer trucks.

Two family tragedies and the events that followed, greatly influenced Bruce's destiny. First, when he was five years old, his father was killed when the dragline he was operating turned over. Second, his mother died of pneumonia two weeks later.

Bruce was born to Bruce M. and Mamie Gideon of San Antonio. He says, "When my brother and I were orphaned, we were sent to Johnson City to live with our grandmother over there in the cedar breaks."

His father was working for Mr. Ralph Ingram, owner of Acme Sand and Gravel in San Antonio, when he was killed. According to Bruce, "Six to eight months after my father's death, Mr. Ingram came to Johnson City and took my brother and me for adoption. So, I changed my name from Bruce M. Gideon, Jr. to Bruce Gideon Ingram."

Bruce received no special favors from his adoptive father. He relates that he worked in the sand and gravel plants during the summers while his classmates and friends enjoyed recreational facilities such as Garner State Park.

He went to school in San Antonio where he graduated from high school at Texas Military Institute (TMI) in 1948. He then attended Texas A&M for two years until, as he laughingly puts it, "they invited me to take a leave and learn more about English."

At that time the military draft, supporting the Korean War, was in full swing. To exercise his own options, Bruce volunteered for the navy. The navy wisely sent him to the SeaBees—navy construction battalions.

"In the service, I was doing just what I wanted to do," says Bruce. "I went to heavy equipment schools and learned construction. I was stationed on the west coast, the east coast and Guantanamo Bay, Cuba. We built runways, roads and barracks. It was a valuable four years."

Upon his return from the navy in 1955, Bruce went to work for his father at the gravel plant south of San Antonio. He later came to San Marcos to work at the Hays County Gravel Company. It was an established company with a hierarchy in place and Bruce just didn't fit. One day, Mr.

Ingram called Bruce into his office and informed him that he planned to leave his business to his two natural sons.

At that point Bruce decided, "I better get out of here and do something on my own. In 1957, I managed to finance two old trucks and a portable concrete plant and started following highway construction from one corner of the state to another.

"I drove one truck myself and I had an employee who drove the other truck. We loaded our own trucks and we just went back and forth delivering concrete."

The following story may help to define Bruce and Gloria Ingram as well as illustrate the reason for the success of Ingram Readymix over the past 45 years.

While he was working at Tilden, Texas, helping build the Nueces River bridge, Bruce decided to bid on the first phase of Interstate 35 at Gardenville, just north of Cotulla. "I went down to Laredo to bid on the job. It was a Saturday and it happened to be the day I was getting married. Mr. Watkins, the contractor, told me my bid was too high, so I went home. As I was getting ready for my wedding, I got a call from him.

"He said, 'You still want that job, boy?'

"I said, yessir!

"He said, 'Be on the job Monday morning.'

"I said, but I'm getting married tonight.

"He said, 'Can you hear me, boy. You want that job, you be there Monday morning.'

"Sunday, Gloria and I moved to Dilley, Texas and I went to work Monday morning. We never had a honeymoon."

Bruce goes on to say that they moved into a *palatial* WWII barracks which had been converted into apartments. Gloria was only 18 at the time and she was afraid to be home alone when he was working late. Bruce's solution to that problem was to hire his next door neighbor to sit with her until he got home. One should understand that the next door neighbor was a six year old boy. Bruce paid him a nickel an hour.

In the beginning the business was virtually a month to month operation. Bruce borrowed money to meet payroll and he scrambled to make payments on his equipment. He had a second business, during the early years. He was a Mobil Oil agent and after working all day at his concrete business, he delivered bulk fuel in the evening to farmers in South Texas.

Today, his company is financially secure and, I suppose, a real rarity in the business world. "Way back there," Bruce says, "I got a little ahead and I began a policy of pay as you go so that in case a depression hit, I would not lose everything I have. As we have grown, we have paid cash. Because of this policy, we weathered the end of the 80's boom fairly well and, even now, things have slowed, but we are not hurting.

"We are in a great corridor between Georgtown and San Antonio. Even if the rest of the country suffers a setback, it will take two to three years for it to reach us in this area. We have seen some economic slow down in the area, but actually, it was going too fast for us.

"We couldn't do proper maintenance on our trucks, we were working over our 70 hour limit—TxDOT rules say that our drivers can't work more than 70 hours per week—but in the middle of a big pour, you can't shut down. So, we were extending our people and our equipment. Now, we are going at a good steady speed."

With 24 plants, Ingram Readymix produces 1.2 to 1.3 million cubic yards of concrete per year. In the early days almost all his production went into highway construction. He relates that he lived 12 years in Frio County, working on I-35 between San Antonio and Laredo and produced about 90 per cent of the concrete in that stretch of road. Today, Bruce supplies a variety of builders, including home building, highways and commercial structures.

All of us who drive in Central Texas have seen the ubiquitous black and yellow mixer trucks on the main highways and the back country roads. They are the most visible part of the business. Their meticulous appearance and courteous drivers would identify them even without their familiar markings and the sign on the door.

It was interesting to learn that 20 miles is about the maximum distance one of those trucks is expected to travel from a given plant. The concrete will harden if not unloaded within a relatively short period of time. Bruce pointed out that when one of his trucks breaks down his first concern is to get the concrete out before it hardens.

Spills are also a major concern to the company. According to Bruce, he and his competitors are especially concerned about spills. They are prepared to send a clean up crew any time a spill is reported, regardless of who might be responsible.

Those trucks and the drivers of those trucks comprise a large portion of the equipment and the work force of Ingram Readymix. Each truck hauls nine to ten cubic yards of concrete, weighs about 60,000 pounds and represents an investment of approximately $100,000.00. Bruce says hiring, training and keeping drivers is a difficult and crucial part of his operation.

"There has been a shortage of drivers the past few years," said Bruce. "The appearance of my trucks has deteriorated a little because if I get too demanding, they just quit. Our drivers must have one year of truck-driving experience and then we spend two weeks training them to drive for us. It is our most critical skill. About 80 per cent of our drivers are excellent employees and then we have about 20 per cent who rotate in and out and have trouble meeting our standards."

Bruce and Gloria moved to San Marcos in 1970 and continued to expand the business. In 45 years, they have added a new plant an average of every two years.

They have four children, none of whom are in the business.

Realizing that Bruce is a couple years older than I, the question of his retirement came up. "Well, I have always worked. I didn't have time to develop any hobbies and Gloria told me I could not stay around the house if I retired, so I keep coming to the office," he said. "I have 12 grandchildren and maybe one of them will eventually be interested in the business and then I can stay home a little more." weeks training them to drive for us. It is our most critical skill. About 80 per cent of our drivers are excellent employees and then we have about 20 per cent who rotate in and out and have trouble meeting our standards."

Ray & Ruth Avey

This profile is a slight departure from my usual. Normally, I write in some depth about one person and try to cover highlights of a noteworthy life. Today's story encompasses two lives, woven together like the tendrils of a morning glory vine. And while it is not intended to be a Valentine's Day story, it could be.

Not long after graduating from San Marcos High in 1936, Ray Avey decided to pursue a career in one of the leading technologies of the time. He followed his twin brother, Roy, to Los Angeles to the National Diesel School. Roy's letters told of the great opportunities available.

Ruth Holtermann Avey interjects, "We got married so he could go to California. We were high school sweethearts and he wasn't going to leave me. We were just 20 when we married."

"The school conducted lots of correspondence courses in many technical fields, radio, television, diesel engineering, etc.," says Ray. "My brother and I worked our way through the school by working in the mail room. The correspondence school even had its own printing plant.

"The machine shop at the school was a lot more interesting to Roy and me than the big diesels, and about the time we were ready to graduate, the war in Europe began. There was a huge need for airplanes and airplane parts in 1939. So, we got jobs in machine shops which were making parts for airplanes."

The United States began the draft in 1940. Ray registered for the draft and expected to be called at any time. He was required to appear at the draft board every six months, but was always deferred because his job was essential to the war effort. He was frozen in the job, consequently, he and Ruth could not come back to Texas until the war ended.

Avey Plastics is one of the oldest, if not the oldest, industrial firm in San Marcos. With the closing of Serur's Varsity Shop, it is also probably the oldest family owned/operated business in San Marcos. Ray and his twin brother, Roy, opened the plant on December 7, 1945. Initially, it was opened as a machine shop.

Ray explains the evolution of Avey Plastics, "Our machine shop customers were companies like the San Marcos Daily Record, the creamery, the oil mill, the cotton gin and any business dependent on machinery. Right after the war, there were no spare parts and no new equipment to be had, so we fabricated lots of parts for repairs. In San Antonio, a company called

Moore Plastics heard about us and started bringing some molds for us to repair or duplicate.

"We got interested in it because plastic was a big thing at that time. We decided to build our own machine where we could test the plastic molds. We built it out of surplus airplane parts and stuff like that. We still have it at the plant. The Van Dorn Company—they make injection molding machines—wants to put it in a museum back east. We may let them have it."

Ruth interjects again, "If we had stayed in California, we would probably be real rich now because they needed something like that. But we did not like California."

However, it was not until about 1959 that the Avey company found itself doing more plastic than machine work.

Asked to recount his experience in business in San Marcos, Ray tells about beginning in a basement shop across the street from the San Marcos Daily Record. The Record was in the building which is now the location of Rawson's upholstery shop. Later they occupied a quite visible site at the corner of Wonder World Drive and IH 35, now the site of a Sac N Pac. At present, the plant is located at 251 Uhland Road, near the Old Mill office complex. It is headed by Terry Avey, one of the Avey's twin boys.

"We began with a Sears, Roebuck lathe, a small drill press and lots of equipment from surplus stores. We also bought a lot of equipment from SWT when they got new equipment in their machine shop," Ray says.

To illustrate the ability of the Avey brothers to build about anything mechanical, Ruth told about their building a train engine. Roy and Ray created a replica of a steam engine for use by the Seven A Ranch in Wimberley. They even had it on a short track. Because firing up the steam was too burdensome and time consuming, it was powered by a gasoliine engine.

It is not easy for Ray to explain his plastic business. Beginning partly out of a curiosity, it developed largely by accident. They create and make whatever someone needs. Their products range from plastic parts for toy manufacturers to components of pregnancy testing kits. They developed a fishing lure and sold 350,000 to the South Bend Tackle Company. Avey Plastics also makes a huge number of weighted fishing floats for Comal Tackle. By the time you read this, Avey Plastics may have another product in the works.

Ruth reminds me that they were married 12 years before they had children, so she put her time in at the plant. Following the birth of a daughter and twin boys, Ruth directed her efforts elsewhere.

Ray chimed in that she should be known as Mrs. Volunteer. "I started my volunteer work when we were in California," says Ruth. "I worked with the Red Cross. I rolled bandages, and did whatever there was to do. When we came back to Texas, I renewed my interest in the choir of the Methodist Church, and with the children, I volunteered for everything that came along. I was in Girl Scouts, Brownies, Cub Scouts, Boy Scouts, football games, and cheer leading."

I inquired about her volunteer efforts after the children. "I have worked for the cottage kitchen. I get involved with Sights and Sounds and this year, I played my keyboard at one of the tour homes this Christmas season. I just go wherever I'm called upon to help out. There are lots of younger folks now, so I'm doing things that others are not doing.

"For instance, I go to the nursing homes and have lunch. I take my keyboard and play some pretty songs that they like. Sometimes I will go play for birthday parties. I play at Redwood Springs, Merrill Gardens, and Hays Nursing Home. Ten years ago I had a hip operation and the doctor told me I couldn't drive for three months. But I had nothing wrong with my fingers, so I went right on playing.

"I go over to New Braunfels occasionally and play German songs, the polkas, and the schottische, and they have more fun. They actually start whirling in their wheel chairs and keeping time to the music.

"I am in charge of the Adult Fellowship. Once a month we get together and have meals. Twice a year, I plan a trip and get the transportation to go see the wildflowers."

Ruth tells about having a near accident while driving to one of her volunteer appointments and explains that is how she discovered she has macular degeneration, an eye disease which destroys the center of one's vision. It took a desperate measure of that sort to get Ray to retire in July 2001, at age 83, from his full-time association with the company. He had to retire so that he could chauffeur her to her musical gigs.

Finally, I convinced her to discuss her volunteer work with the Chamber of Commerce. She reluctantly admitted that she was the chamber Volunteer of the Year in 1992. She was inducted into the San Marcos Women's Hall of Fame in 1990-91.

As I prepared to take a picture for use with this article, Ruth halted me with an enthusiastic, "I've got something else I need to tell you. Every year at Halloween we decorate our back yard. I mean we have lights and pumpkins all over the place. We have a witch and we call it the Pumpkin Patch and we invite the residents of the nursing and assisted living facilities to come and visit. On Halloween night, we open our gates and let all the children come in. That's our hobby. It looks like a bunch of kids might be living here, but we still have fun with it at our age. And then we do the same thing at Christmas. Ray and I just love to decorate. We have an attic full of decorations."

As the Aveys celebrate this Valentine's Day, they remain sweethearts who will be looking forward to their 64th wedding anniversary in May.

Denise (Sam) Brumley

Sam Brumley is one of those people about whom you ask, as you ponder the dishes in the sink, the laundry not folded and being late to the teachers conference, 'How does she do it?' Yes, Sam is a *she*. More about that later.

When I invited her to, 'Tell me about yourself,' she responded, "I'm a mom with three wonderful children."

When I insisted I could hardly get 1,500 words from that response, she reluctantly went on. "I am a military brat. Well, let me clarify that. My father was a pilot in the air force, but I lived in San Antonio since first grade and I graduated from Judson High School where I played volleyball and basketball."

I reminded her that, based on my information, she did not just *play* volleyball and basketball. "Well, I was All-City and All-District, but I was probably more accomplished in college. I did well, but when I went to college, I was an NAIA All-American volleyball player my junior and senior years at Texas Lutheran University. I was recruited for volleyball and basketball, but the first three years, I played volleyball only. I played basketball my senior year and my senior year." (That is not a typo.)

She laughed as she explained she took five years to graduate. Nevertheless, in her last two years when she played basketball, she was an All-Conference and All-District basketball player.

I wondered about the difficulty of combining college and athletics, especially when one is a two-sport star.

"It was a full-time job for me," Sam said. "I approached it that way. It is quite reasonable for people to work and go to school. That's what it was for me. My compensation was that athletics paid for my education. It was so enjoyable and rewarding and I had so much support from my parents and the coaches, I don't know what I would have done without it."

How difficult was it to maintain grades and devote the required time to practice and playing?

"I think I was on the Dean's List four or five times," she said.

I hope the reader is beginning to get the picture that this lady is faster than a speeding bullet, stronger than a steaming locomotive, and can leap tall buildings in a single bound. By this time, I am beginning to think her nickname, "Sam" is short for Samson, so I asked, 'What's your real name?'

"Denise Lynn (Sylvester) Brumley," she replied. "I adopted Sam my freshman year in college. There was another girl named Denise on the volleyball team. The coach said we couldn't have two girls with the same name on the court at the same time. My dad's name is Sam, so I volunteered the name, Sam. The coach looked at me and said, OK, we'll come up with a better name later. Many years later and we still haven't come up with anything better."

After graduation from college in 1988, Sam came to San Marcos to coach volleyball and other sports. Her first year, she was an assistant coach, and then she became head coach until 1993.

"I had the best athletes in the state," she said. "We made the playoffs every year except the first year I was here. "I also coached soccer—boys and girls soccer. In addition, I taught economics, business law, and accounting in high school. It was like having two full-time jobs.

"Kevin and I were dating at the time—he's also a workaholic—and we did not start our dates until 9:00 PM or later. He was so supportive and he understood."

Sam and Kevin Brumley celebrated their 10th anniversary last month. This month, they celebrated Brock's ninth birthday. Brock is the oldest of three. Bryce, seven, is next and Brooke is five.

Sam is organized. She plans ahead. She knows what she wants to accomplish. She and Kevin married in 1994, but only after they figured out how to get her out of the all-consuming coaching profession.

"When we decided to marry we knew we wanted a family and the coaching hours are so long, we decided we needed something that would allow me to devote more time to family. To replace the teaching/coaching, we bought Education Station, which was a small store on Highway 123."

As I sat in Sam's office, the odor of fresh paint filled my nostrils along with a little sawdust from the recent construction at 1403 IH 35. The 12,000 square foot structure is getting the finishing touches as the staff of Education Station and Scrapbook Depot erect shelves, install computers, and receive shipments from UPS. Thirty minutes into the interview Sam directed me to turn off my tape recorder and help move furniture for one of the computer stations. No doubt who's in charge here.

This is the brand new home and the third location for the business. Initially located on Highway 123, it was moved to Highway 80 to gain space. It will soon occupy 9,000 of the 12,000 square feet of the aforementioned structure.

What made the schoolteacher think she could succeed as an entrepreneur, and what are Education Station and Scrap Book Depot?

"I don't know," Sam said. "I didn't even think about it. It is a challenging business. We put everything we make back into it to improve the business. It is a supply store for teachers and parents, especially for home-schoolers and for Sunday school teachers. We can supply employers with bulletin board material, inspirational messages, that sort of thing. College kids get materials to decorate their hallways. We have a wide variety of customers.

"Four years ago I found this company that deals with scrapbooking and decided there was a reasonable crossover between that and Education Station. They are two entities, but there are many common products between the two. Scrapbooks are a large hobby. We do classes; people come here and stay until midnight working on their books. As a hobby, it is not unlike quilting. If it is a fad, it has already had a long life."

It is clear Sam is first a mother, then an entrepreneur. She credits her ability to manage a business of this size to several things. First, she hired April Sandoval, one of her former players and students at San Marcos High when April came to her in 1994 for a job reference. April has managed the store for nine years. Sam comes to the store on Mothers Day Out days and other days when the children are not at home. She does the bookwork and taxes when the kids are sleeping, napping, or otherwise engaged.

As a full-time mom and owner of a major business, I asked what she did with her spare time.

"I play a little volleyball," Sam said. "We have a lady's league and a co-ed league at Texas Health and Racquet Club. I volunteer for the fundraisers at my kids' school. And I volunteer for the Cattle Barons Ball. I wasn't as active this year as I have been in the past."

Tell me about being a mother of three children, I asked.

"I thank God every day," she said. "Brock is in third grade. He is the shy one—more like his dad. Bryce is more like me, an extrovert. He's in first grade. Brooke, my daughter, is five and is going to kindergarten next year. They have taught me a lot. I love being with them."

What have they taught you?

"Patience. A mother's love." At this point, Sam's eyes glistened as the tears crept from behind her eyelids. She hesitated, fought back the emotions and continued: "You can never understand how deep it is until you love someone as a mother."

Since this article will appear on Mother' Day, what do you want to tell other Moms? Through her tears, she replied, "I want to honor my mother and tell people how lucky I am to have her—and my dad—here. I just can't express how much I appreciate what I have. Kevin's parents passed away before we married."

Is there a reason you had three children?

"I just knew I wanted three children. I watched Kevin and his brother and sister go through a lot of tragedy and I saw how strong they were and I just knew I would have two boys and a girl. Actually, we built our house for two boys and a girl."

What's the hardest thing about being the mother of three? "Taking them for granted. Losing my temper. Letting them frustrate me. I'm getting better."

What's the best thing about being a mother? "When the kids hug you all the time. When they bring me breakfast in bed. They have such creative ways of showing love."

How much pressure is there in trying to do it all?

"Playing sports and coaching put me in a lot of high pressure situations. I became accustomed to it. My sports experience has helped a lot."

Somewhere in this story I should have told the reader that Sam has a masters degree in Education Administration and that she was TLU homecoming queen. However, she distracted me with tales of her children.

Bill Pennington

Bill Pennington was born in San Marcos January 17, 1942. He literally grew up on the square. His parents lived in an apartment above Rogers-Pennington Funeral Home which was located in the red brick building at the corner of Hopkins and LBJ. If San Marcos history and genealogy hold any interest for you, spend an hour or so with Bill. He can take you back and connect all the dots. In fact, the hardest part of this interview was getting him to talk about himself rather than early San Marcans.

Bill was delivered in the now vacant hospital on Belvin Street, two blocks from his present residence.

"I stayed there one day because it was so crowded, there was no room for new mothers. It was the only hospital in Hays County and the Air Base was in full swing and they used it also.

"I started school in what is now Evans Auditorium. Went there through the fourth grade. Moved across the street to the Education Building for fifth and sixth grade. Then went to Travis for Junior High. We went to high school at Lamar for three years and we, the class of 1960, were the first class to graduate from our present high school. We also were the first class in 20 years to win our district in football. Coach Goodnight took us to the state semi-finals.

"The high school had no air conditioning, no fans, nothing. It also had no windows because it was to be air conditioned, but the district ran out of money. Talk about warm!!

"When I graduated and went to SWT, my first class was in the Education Building. Back where I started."

That illustrates the circular nature of Bill Pennington's San Marcos. It is all connected. It is continuous. His family, by the nature of their business, stands at the center of that circle, touched by a huge percentage of the population of this town.

What is now Pennington Funeral Home began as Rogers Furniture and Coffins. It was begun by A.B. Rogers in 1897 and is probably the oldest continuous private business in San Marcos. In the 30's Mr. Rogers, in his search for a funeral director, brought Willard Pennington, Bill's father, from Austin to San Marcos.

Bill relates, "My dad came to work for the funeral home, and met my mother, Edra, there. She was Mr. Rogers' bookkeeper and ran the insurance company for him. They married, of course, and when Mr. Rogers tired of the funeral business, my father bought it in the 40's."

"My father and grandfather were killed in 1957 in a car wreck on the way to Wimberley. My father was chairman of the United Way and he was going to see Mo Smith about being the chairman of the Wimberley district. My grandfather was killed instantly and my father died two weeks later of complications of the heart.

"My mother was left with a 14, 13, and a 12 year-old and the business. I was a sophomore in high school. So, after finishing high school and two semesters at SWT, I went to mortuary school in Houston for a year and came back to the business."

At the time Bill went to mortuary school, he had to have special dispensation from the courts because the law required mortuary students to be 21 or older. He was 18 when he enrolled.

"I was the youngest student in my class," Bill said, "and, incidentally, I was the youngest Rotarian in the U.S. at one time. I have been a Rotarian longer than I have been married."

I reminded Bill that we have not always had 911, EMS, and ambulance service in Hays County. Funeral homes formerly provided this service.

"I was 13 years old," he said, "when I made my first ambulance call with my daddy. It was a car wreck on Guadalupe Street. I had never seen so much blood in my life. Three college boys drove into the train. Two were killed. One of the boys who was sitting in the back seat did not get a scratch. That experience was a real shock to a 13 year-old. I did not sleep all night."

The funeral home was the only source of ambulance service in the city for many years.. Bill recounts, "I charged five dollars a call and most of the time I didn't get paid. I had myself and twelve college boys who operated the ambulance service. We had an oxygen bottle and a first aid kit and that was about it. People don't know how lucky they are today to have the EMS and all their equipment and training."

Bill took the opportunity to say that the old hospital (where he was born) had an antiquated x-ray machine on the second floor—and no elevator. So, they often had to carry patients up the stairs for x-rays. The emergency room was, of course, on the first floor.

The funeral home gave up the ambulance business in the late 60's or early 70's following an incident where Bill's actions saved the life of an accident victim. The next day, the father of the victim came to the funeral home and informed Bill and his mother that he was suing them because they were the only ones he could determine had the money to pay anything.

I asked about the stress of dealing with death almost daily. "Auto accidents wiped out two San Marcos families within a week. We conducted eight funerals in seven days. That is about as difficult as I can remember. However, when Linda [wife] gave birth to Collier [son], my mother was in Hawaii and I got 15 calls that week."

I asked about families and survivors. "I am not a grief counselor by any means, but I have learned that, no matter how it happens, death of a loved one often makes people angry and anxious. And not all families get along. So, I and my associates are often the target for these feelings. We walk a thin line and I train my people to accept the feelings of the family and try to understand.

"We try to make it as comfortable as possible for the family. I would recommend to anyone that one of the best gifts you can give your survivors is to have a plan for your death.

"One ironic example: A veteran passed away and to claim his military rights, the family needed his form DD 214. They looked for that document for three months and finally discovered it, framed and hanging on the wall in plain sight.

"You wouldn't believe how many people don't know their grandmother's or great grandmother's maiden name. By the way, if you are into genealogy, go to the funeral home. I have records back to the 1890's."

With 42 years in the business, Bill has seen a number of changes. What is the most significant, I asked.

"The celebration of life," he said. "I don't mean to sound corny, but we used to have a church service, go to the cemetery, do the graveside service and that was it. Now, there may be a minister or there may not. People in the audience may speak; family members do eulogies. We set up tables with memorabilia and pictures. Almost all funeral homes now provide screens, computers, and projectors for "power point" presentations of the life of the deceased.

"Cremation is much more popular now than it once was. We have gone from zero to about 20 percent who opt for cremation. Many people do not understand that a service can be associated with cremation just as with burial.

"One can scatter the ashes, bury the ashes or whatever. Regardless, you can call me old fashioned, but I think there should be somewhere in this world, a relatively permanent marker that says, 'We lived. We died.'"

Bill says he has also honored requests for burial at sea. He explained that the Coast Guard will take bodies to sea and bury them. There is a significant fee involved and it is apparently done at the Coast Guard's convenience, but it is possible. Bill points out that the funeral business is keeping up with the advances of technology. "I have not done this, but there is a place in California where I can call and arrange for a space burial."

He also pointed out that the business structure has changed. While Pennington Memorial Corporation looks to the future as a family business with the third generation, Kristin Pennington Wingard, ready to continue the tradition, most of the funeral business has morphed into the corporate mold where bigger is better. Local funeral homes, like local grocery stores are becoming a thing of the past.

Bill Pennington and his family have served San Marcos professionally for more than 60 years. But that is only part of the profile. His list of volunteer activities would fill half the space available for this story. A partial listing includes: Served on the Board and the Ethics Commission for the Texas Funeral Directors Association; Past President, San Marcos Rotary and Paul Harris Fellow of Rotary International; District Chairman, Boy Scouts of America; Presented Outstanding Citizen Award by Business and Professional Women's Club; President, San Marcos Chamber of Commerce.

Bill Pennington has erected many markers in San Marcos. It occurs to me he is in his own right a San Marcos landmark.

Jerry Supple

Jerry Supple settles comfortably behind his executive desk and in a surprisingly soft voice, begins, "I was born in Boston, Massachusetts in 1936 before the introduction of sulfa drugs. During my mother's confinement, a staph infection swept through the hospital. A large number of babies and mothers died. I managed to avoid getting it, but my mother was in and out off the hospital for the first year of my life. Aunts cared for me during that time, so I became sort of a favorite son."

That was the first time Jerome Supple escaped a life-threatening health scare and potentially fatal condition. There would be another, many years later.

Jerry lived in Winthrop, a town that juts into Boston harbor and is situated across the harbor opposite Logan Airport. The first three or four years of his education were in the public schools of Winthrop. However, he was enrolled in parochial school fairly early and continued his education through elementary grades at Saint Lazarus School.

"It was run by the Sisters of Saint Joseph and they lived up to everything you have ever heard about the discipline, rules and strict standards imposed by nuns in Catholic schools," said Jerry. "They were tough, but they were also kind and made you do a little bit of work."

Education as a serious endeavor was reinforced when Jerry went on to high school. He attended Boston College High, a school run by the Jesuits, an order with a well-deserved reputation for a no-nonsense approach to teaching and learning.

His first year in high school, he attended the BC Annex because the new high school was under construction. He took the subway from suburban Winthrop to the Boston South End to school each day. His path from the subway to the Annex led through some of he seediest slums of Boston.

"This walk, which was just a few blocks, was an eye-opening introduction to urban life for this kid from suburban Winthrop. There were some interesting folks along that route every day," Jerry said.

"But I loved the high school," he said. "I tended to have a tongue that was always a few steps ahead of my brain, and the discipline kept me in check. I especially loved athletics. I played varsity basketball and considered hockey. I probably would have been killed hid I tried it. It was a good school. In fact, when I graduated in 1953, there were 222 in the class. Ultimately 222 of those students went to college."

In his characteristic style of understating for emphasis, he continued, "That was pretty good percentage."

Jerry followed in his father's footsteps and went to Boston College. His father had, in fact, graduated from Boston College High as well. It is noteworthy that his father was a writer/reporter for the Associated Press. He traveled with and covered a number of national politicians, including Harry Truman and Estes Kefauver.

During college, he worked in his father's office. Much of his work consisted of doing manually what we now do electronically. "There were machines to send photos by wire, but they also sent photos by train. Say an important event were held in the Boston Garden, I would be there to get the photographer's film, run it back to the office where it would be developed and printed and then I would run it to the station and get it on the train to get it in the New York City papers. It is hard to convince people today that it that long to get things done."

As Jerry describes it, his decision to go to college was always assumed by the family. "My sister is an awful lot smarter than I, and still is, but in those days, girls did not have to go to college. She was told she could go if she wanted. For me there were no options. I never made a conscious decision to go to college. It was a forgone conclusion."

As with so many, Jerry's fate turned on the actions of someone else. As he describes it, "As a high school senior, I had an alternate appointment to the United States Naval Academy. We had to take a series of written exams and then we had to take a series of physical exams, including strength and agility, etc. The kid who was the principal nominee was not in real good shape and he had a hard time passing those tests.

"Eventually, he made it through. I often wonder what course my life would have taken had I gone to the Naval Academy," Jerry mused.

Boston College was to be the source of his higher education. And again, like so many college freshmen, he chose to major in chemistry for no reason other than he had a great high school chemistry teacher. Mr. Collins at BC High had major influence on the young Jerry Supple.

"He was a seminarian and allowed a few of us to hang around the lab after school. It there were no athletic practice or I wasn't in some sort of trouble. He was a great guy and a great teacher. He eventually went to Africa as a missionary," Jerry related.

"I was not interested in chemistry when I was a chemistry major at Boston College. I was just going to college and taking some courses I liked. But there was nothing else I wanted to major in either."

During his freshman year at BC, he was again approached to consider a military academy. It was probably the first class at the Air Force Academy to the best of his memory. He had no desire to go through another freshman year so he respectfully declined the offer.

Unlike the 23,000 or so undergraduates he now supervises, he did not own a car until graduate school. The first car he owned was 1939 DeSoto, which he purchased for $150.00. One night late, a driver ran a red light and smashed into his car. The other car was towed away, a total wreck. "I stepped out, pulled the fender off my tire and drove home," he said.

When he completed undergraduate school in 1957, several options were open. Merck Laboratories offered him a job. He interviewed with DuPont. Graduate school was available. And the military was still shadowing—this time the draft was waiting like a gaping abyss, ready to swallow any young, able-bodied person, not exempted for one reason or another. Graduate school meant an exemption.

"In my sophomore year, I had a professor who was an absolute tyrant," said Jerry. Three people of 15 passed his course. I was one of the three. I busted his final exam and would have busted the course, but because I had a passing grade at the time, I could re-take the final. He gave us the final exam given to Harvard chemistry majors. It was the easiest test I had all year. I made 90+ on the test, but the rule was I couldn't raise my grade, so I passed his course with a D."

That professor was Joe Bornstein and he embodied at least two enigmas. First, he was a Jewish professor at a Catholic school. Second, he was a tyrant of a teacher, but a dynamo as a researcher. He supervised Jerry's master's thesis and managed to impart to Jerry his enthusiasm for research.

Jerry relates, "One day he came into the lab and said to me, 'Where do you want to get your doctorate?'"

"I'm not getting a doctorate," I said.

"Yes, you are," he said. "I have talked to people at MIT and University of New Hampshire. You are all set—they will accept you."

"I had lived at home up to this time. I thought it was time to get out of town. I opted for University of New Hampshire."

Jerry pauses to point out that, up to then, his life was like a river, flowing along with a nudge here, a push there, and that most of the major decisions that brought him to the verge of a doctoral program were made for him.

During his doctoral program at New Hampshire, his roommate was Paul Anderson who sure he would follow his father into teaching. Jerry was aiming for a career in industry.

Paul Anderson, who would later develop Zocor, a popular cholesterol drug, became president of the American Chemical Society and has recently won one of the top national awards for chemists.

Jerry describes his defining moment. "My doctoral advisor, Bob Lyle, was teaching an advanced chemistry course when he had to attend a meeting. He asked me to teach the course in his absence. I had been supervising and teaching labs, but this was a special class. Some of my colleagues were in it. I was taken by that experience. I just loved it. I was excited. I felt like a teacher. That was my turning point."

Near the end of his doctoral program, Jerry was leaning toward a career in academia. He experienced teaching as an exciting and deeply satisfying experience. But he realized post-doctoral work was a prerequisite for a decent opportunity in academia.

Jerry explains, "I talked to Bob Lyle, about post doctoral work and he suggested three possibilities: Columbia University, Michigan, and the University of California, Berkley. I thought, Berkley sounds like fun."

Jerry went to Berkley in February 1963 to work for Henry Rappaport, an internationally known researcher and teacher. Having eschewed MIT for New Hampshire, he had some concern about his level of preparation for such a high profile as Berkley. He says "I found I didn't have to take a back seat to anybody academically.

"Probably, I was better prepared than many who came from some of the more prestigious programs."

As he finished his post-doctoral program in August 1964, Jerry began looking for gainful employment. He interviewed with a pharmaceutical company and could have taken a position at their Niagara Falls research facility for $19 thousand a year. Meantime, with Dr. Rappaport's urging, he applied for a position at San Diego State.

The teaching position called for a biochemist, but "…with a lot of preparation, I could have taught a freshman bio-chemistry course."

He didn't get the job.

Dr. Rappaport received a visit from the president of State University of New York (SUNY), Fredonia. He was accompanied by one of the deans. They were looking for a chemistry professor. Rappaport set up interviews for Jerry.

"I was not impressed with the dean," Jerry said. "But the president was a chemist and he was a sharp, impressive guy."

"Fredonia is as far west as one can go in New York—snow country. Buffalo residents refer to Fredonia as the Snow Belt. Now, to digress. By this time, I had met Cathy Evans, a beautiful California girl, with a golden tan and long dark hair, who had never been out of California."

Cathy Evans entered the picture a few months after Jerry moved to Berkley. A student occupying an apartment near Jerry's left to pursue other interests and arranged for his sister to take his apartment. Cathy happened to be the sister's roommate.

As Jerry explains, "Cathy played bridge and she played the guitar. I played bridge and the banjo. It was just a natural fit."

Back to the job search. At this time, a college teaching job would routinely have 300 PhD applicants apply. Nevertheless, Jerry was hired and prepared to leave California for Fredonia, New York. Incidentally, the job was to pay $8,500 a year.

As he describes it, "I loved Cathy and didn't want to leave her even for a little while, so in August of 1964, Cathy and I married in the Newman Center on the Berkley campus. We packed the car and headed east.

There were lots of young faculty and we weren't there a week when another couple took us out to dinner and we discovered a mutual love of folk music. It was through them we met the Gilman's who were the founders of the Newton Street Irregulars.

Cathy made her adjustments to the environmental shock such as 200 inches of snow annually. Jerry zealously immersed himself in teaching and set about enjoying their historic surroundings.

" I was thoroughly enjoying teaching undergrad and graduate students. The research was a bit frustrating, but we rocked along. I am also one of those people who has a hard time saying no, so I was involved in lots of campus activities. Faculty committees, new programs and redefining the relationship between the student and the institution took a lot of my time. I helped introduce co-ed dorms and legal alcohol on campus.

"A friend, Paul Weller, who coincidentally, also became a university president, and I started writing a textbook on basic chemistry, so I was busy. But I loved to ski, so I joined the National Ski Patrol. Every weekend during the winter, we would ski. We spent 15 winters of Saturdays and Sundays on the slopes. We were on the go all the time."

The National Science Foundation sponsored a program of Science Faculty Fellowships in those days. At the end of his sixth year at SUNY Fredonia, Jerry applied through NSF to study in England with Alan Katrigky, an internationally known chemist who "…by the time he was 43 had published over 300 papers. He was dynamite. He spoke 11 languages. Never slept.

"I remember the day the letter came. I was excited for the opportunity to do some research and see if I might be ready for a change of direction. Maybe try the pharmaceuticals."

By the time he and Cathy embarked for England, they had two boys, Jimmy, two, and Andy, just more than two months. It was a busy time for the Supples. Jerry worked on a research project with Dr. Katrigky and two research projects of his own. He finished proofing his textbook, served as referee for one of the international professional journals of which Dr. Katrigky was the editor, and found time to be deeply involved with folk-singing.

Cathy's younger sister came for an extended stay and helped with kid-care. Through some creative scheduling, Jerry and Cathy were able to do lots of traveling. They enjoyed trips to all parts of Europe and the British Isles.

However, Jerry says, "With all that, I missed the academics. I missed the interruptions of students coming for consultations; I missed the conflict of demands between classroom and laboratory; I just missed the whole teaching scene."

Three or four months before he left England, Jerry was informed that, upon his return, he would be given additional responsibilities as Associate Dean of the School of Arts and Sciences.

He says, "That was the start of the slippery slope that led me out of the classroom into administration. After a year or so, there was a re-organization and I recommended my job be abolished. It was—but the re-organization created another job, Associate Vice President and Dean of Special Studies. The administration asked me to take the job full-time. I did.

"I had a lot of interdisciplinary programs. I started a music therapy program, a music sound and technology program. A whole range of innovative things were happening, such as a student advisory program. I also taught a sophomore organic chemistry class with about 75-80 students and I kept a research lab going."

Jerry was in this position for about four years when he received a call from the Provost of the SUNY system, asking him to come to Albany as an Associate Provost of the system for a one-year term. Sounds like fun, thought Jerry as he packed his family, rented his house in Fredonia and moved to the state capital.

Not long after his arrival, the Provost left and there were two Associate Provosts to deal with the system. The academic program approval for the eighteen senior institutions fell under Jerry's purview while the other Associate Provost dealt with the junior colleges.

"In this job, I found myself the first chairperson of the statewide university women's studies. There were some real activist/feminists in the state at the time. While I almost always enjoy whatever I'm doing at the time, I knew I did not want to stay in the Provost job. It was like working in a big corporation—totally different from campus work.

After a year or so in Albany, Jerry returned to Fredonia where over the next 10 years, universities contacted him about other positions. In 1978, he was a finalist for the Academic Vice President's job in Plattsburg, New York. At the same time he was asked to consider an equivalent job at the University of Colorado at Denver.

After interviewing at Plattsburgh, Jerry went to Denver for an interview. "While waiting for the President to call me into his office, I got a phone call from Plattsburgh, offering me the job. I was offered the Denver job the same day. For a long list of complicated reasons, I took the job in New York.

"For the first time, I was almost out of the classroom. I taught a five-week graduate course and changed the topic each semester. It helped me stay up with my field and I had a small research group."

The president of Plattsburgh left after a number of years and the SUNY system brought in a replacement. Because Jerry and the new president did not see things the same way, Jerry thought it was time to look for a new job or return to the classroom. "After all," he said, "he was the president and I wasn't."

In the middle of the new president's first year, the Provost of the SUNY system plucked Jerry out of Plattsburgh and asked him to go to the Potsdam campus and stabilize a volatile situation on the campus.

While in the midst of his Potsdam assignment, he received a letter informing him he was a nominee for the President's job at Southwest Texas State University.

"I was going to throw the letter away. I thought with that name, it has to be out in the middle of the desert and it had o be teeny small place. But I tossed it in my briefcase and when I got home, I showed it to Cathy and said, 'Oh, look what I got today.' She said, 'Hey, it's warm down there. You apply for that job.'

"Truthfully, I was going to throw the letter away. The school had to be in the middle of nowhere and I just wasn't interested."

With a chuckle and a dismissive air, Jerry said, "So much for the serious and studied deliberations about what we are going to do with our lives."

Following Cathy's instructions, Jerry submitted a response to the letter and promptly forgot about it. A few months later, he received a call informing him that 15 candidates would be interviewed in San Antonio. As the first of the 15 to be interviewed, he was positive he would not be remembered by the panel of interviewers.

"At this point, I realized the campus was not in Cotulla or some such place. To be honest, I had done some research before I came down and realized it was a pretty nice place. Coincidentally, Bob Lyle, my dissertation adviser from New Hampshire, was living in San Antonio. I called him from the airport and he gave me a chamber of commerce picture of the place. He said, 'You have to come.'"

After a period of time, Jerry was called for the second interview where the field had been narrowed to five candidates. One of the five dropped out before the interview. Jerry did some serious preparation this time. He researched the school, contacted people who knew the area and he felt it was a place he could fit in.

"Once I saw the campus, I knew this was the place I wanted to be," Jerry said. It made such an impact on me when I first saw it. I knew I wanted the job.

"Because of the controversy surrounding the dismissal of the previous president, there was a lot of press interest in the hiring of his successor. We were all told to be prepared to accept the position at the conclusion of the interview because an announcement would be made at a press conference at the end of the day.

"This time I was the last person interviewed. The chairman of the committee pulled me aside after the interview and told me I should be prepared to accept the job. Meantime, Cathy was in Austin with a member of the faculty and I had no way of consulting with her about the decision I was about to make."

However, the committee had certain protocol issues to resolve prior to making the normal announcement of Jerry's selection. During the interim, Cathy returned and Jerry was able to tell her that he had accepted the job before he told the press.

"We were thrilled. We, by now, knew enough about the place to know it was exactly where we wanted to be."

In March 1989, the family moved to San Marcos.

Overshadowing the thrill of accepting a new position, the excitement of new challenges, and the anticipation of a new environment, was a cloud of controversy involving the outgoing president.

Jerry says, "I read about the controversy in the national press, especially the academic press, but during my application process, I made no connection between that firing and this job. Then suddenly, like in a comic strip, the light bulb came on and I realized that's the place where they fired that fellow."

A little investigating revealed that the controversy stemmed largely from political affiliation and so Jerry determined he could navigate the political rapids because he brought no prior baggage to the position.

I asked Jerry to describe his vision for the university when he arrived on campus.

"Well, I looked at SWT as sort of a teen-ager. Gangly, big and strong, full of energy, but not all together. Not knowing exactly where it was going.

"For several years the school had been dealing with massive enrollment growth, particularly in new areas such as business administration and computer science. So, dealing with that fact occupied a lot of time and energy. How do we provide classrooms, how do we get teachers, how do we accommodate the growth?

"Growth seemed to be the foremost issue and they seemed to be doing reasonably well managing that. But they did not have time to focus on being a real university."

Citing the history and evolution of SWT, Jerry pointed out that there seemed to be a mindset, which had not fully moved beyond the concept of SWT as 'teacher's college.' There were exceptions, he noted, and pointed out that the history department recruited faculty with notable research and publication backgrounds.

"I saw an opportunity. I was excited about taking this energetic, forceful, young power and trying to help it go in certain direction. I was just tremendously excited about that.

"I wanted to form a Center for the Study of the Southwest. I was overwhelmed by the power of the culture. I talked to some people and got them interested and now it is growing. It has received national attention. I wanted it to be, and it has become, a focal point that helps bring faculty here; it provides a forum for study, exploration and preservation of this powerful culture. Getting that was easy.

"Other things were harder. Admission standards were not what I thought they should be. For an institution focusing on growth, this may seem paradoxical. But we had a problem keeping freshmen. About 51 percent of the freshman class would show up for their sophomore year. For Hispanic students that figure was 38 percent. Obviously, this affected our graduation rates.

"In 1992, we cut out the bottom 23 percent of the freshman class. Potentially, that could have eliminated almost one-fourth of our budget. Fortunately, we had a strategic financial reserve, which we thought would get through the initial decline in enrollment. And we did lose enrollment initially. Then it leveled out and finally it went up again. It went up again in part because more students wanted to come here because we were more selective, but the main contributing factor was that more students stayed.

"Now we have a freshman class that returns at a rate of about 75 percent across the board. We upset a lot of people when we did this. I was called to testify before Governor Richards' Diversity Committee. I testified before the Higher Education Sub-Committee of the House.

"Some people thought we were denying admission to certain minorities—and to a certain extent, we were. But my position was—is—that their goal might be to admit, but my goal is to graduate."

The upshot of this policy is that for the last few years, SWT has been among the top 20 universities in the country in producing Hispanic baccalaureates. Another issue where Jerry Supple's vision resulted in controversy was the purchase of Aquarena Springs by SWT.

"I was seen as going back on my word when we closed the restaurant and theme park and took the property off the tax rolls. We were actually making a little money on the theme park, but we were losing our shirt on the restaurant. In addition, had we continued to operate the theme park, several million dollars would have been required to repair the gondola and the tower ride. The place had seen better days and as a theme park, it was old-fashioned. The state auditor told us it was improper for the property to be on the tax rolls."

Fund raising, private gifts to SWT, and grant monies have increased exponentially since Jerry's arrival. But he will tell you that of all the major tasks implied in the job of a university president, he considered himself least qualified to do fund-raising.

"The year before I arrived, we received $3.5 million in grants. The year I got here, we brought in $5.2 million. I thought that should be $20 million. It is now $42 million.

"We had a young fellow in the Development Office who suggested we needed to have a major capital campaign. We looked around and found we had no up to date alumni list. So I said we have a lot of work to do before we can undertake that.

"There were some personnel changes and some retirements which allowed me to do some reorganizing of the development and advancement aspects of the university. It also allowed me to hire Gerald Hill.

"Gerald and I thought we were ready to conduct a major capital campaign and thought we ought to go for $25 million. We hired a consultant who, after some research, suggested a reasonable goal would be $60 million. The campaign raised $74 million."

One of the larger individual gifts to the university is the Mitte Endowment. When asked about obtaining these funds, Jerry digresses to explain, first, how Roy Mitte left SWT to become a high school basketball coach before becoming a multi-millionaire in the insurance business. He then defers his own influence with Mr. Mitte to Vernon MacDonald, former SWT basketball coach.

In a tone of one who can't believe this is actually happening, Jerry explains that he, Coach MacDonald and Roy Mitte were having lunch when Mr. Mitte asked what he (Jerry) would do for SWT if he had $30 million. Caught unawares, he began rolling off a list of projects, scholarships for high ability students, chairs for top faculty, and other dreams.

"When I got home, I wrote him a letter outlining these things in greater detail. As we were ready to go into a fund-raising campaign, Mr. Mitte called and informed me he wanted to fund 125 scholarships at $5,000 each. He also wanted fund five $1 million chairs. All I did was have lunch with him."

In 13 years, Jerry Supple guided that gangly teen-ager of a university to a level of maturity, which surpasses his own vision of 1989. He put the university on the road to greatness and he did it with a soft and gentle touch, melding the synergy of growth, energy, intellect, and vision.

Author's note: Jerry Supple passed away January 17, 2004. Among his accomplishments, not covered in this profile, was the name change of Southwest Texas State University to Texas State University, San Marcos. It was among his most passionate projects.

Garland Warren

We sat facing each other across a primitive antique table, the appearance of which belied its value. We sat on straight-back antique chairs, surrounded by metal grocery store signs from the 20's, 30's and 40's. To my right stood an old kitchen cupboard with a breadboard. It served absolutely no purpose except to fill the space it occupied.

We were in a back room at Center Point Station, located at 3946 IH 35 South. Center Point Station is a monument to antiquity—antique buildings full of antique furnishings. Relics such as the hand-cranked gasoline pumps out front and the Mail Pouch Tobacco sign inside bring nostalgic thoughts of childhood to those over 50. It is a stark contrast to the ever-bustling Outlet Malls just across the roaring speedway, known as I-35.

"Antiques are my substitute for golf," Garland Warren said as we took note of the surroundings. "Some people gamble, some people play golf, some people have horses. I collect antiques."

That explanation was easy to accept initially, but as the interview progressed, I came to realize the antiques are much more than golf to Garland. They are treasures that he has rescued from oblivion and they keep him in touch with his roots. Roots and rescuing are important to him.

"I was born in Seymour, Texas, southwest of Wichita Falls, and I was the tenth of 11 kids. We were all born in the same bed," he began.

Without going into great detail, Garland explained that his parents came from a ranching/farming background, but by the time he reached high school, the droughts, and other pitfalls of agriculture had forced his family into the city at Denton, where he finished high school. From high school, he enrolled in North Texas State University on a full football scholarship.

"I didn't finish college," he said. "I lacked about 12 hours, but I was actually making more money by my senior year than some of my professors. I was teaching golf and ping pong, I ate at the training table, lived at home with my parents and had a new car. In addition I had a small construction company. We built fences and a few houses.

"I chose all that over an opportunity to play football at Texas A&M under Bear Bryant and I have always had some regrets about that. My mother wanted me to go to A&M, and I have wondered how that would have turned out."

In 1959, at the end of his senior year in college, the San Francisco Forty-Niners and the Canadian Football League's Winnipeg Blue Bombers drafted Garland. He played center and linebacker in college. Influenced by a close friend, Garland chose to play for Winnipeg. He signed for what he thought was a $2,500.00 bonus. Turned out, that was just an advance on his salary and had he been cut, the team could have demanded to be repaid.

"I might have made the Forty-Niners," he said, with no remorse. "Going to Canada was one of the best things I ever did. The people there were great. We had a great team and it was fun playing there. After my first year, we won the Grey Cup (Canadian League Championship) four years in a row."

Though football paid well, Garland was not content to depend on his athletic career. "After my first season, I returned to my building business in Denton and built houses. Of course, I was beginning to know some people in Canada and so the second year, I went to the banks, borrowed some money, bought some land up there and built houses there."

As he explained, in the Canadian League, the teams began practices at 5:00 p.m. to accommodate the Canadian players who had to have regular jobs. They could not have survived on their football salary. He mentioned his first year salary was $12,500.00 plus incentives.

Garland's football career came to an end when he had to miss one year due to a knee injury. When he went back the next season, he played only six games before the team cut him.

"I thought I could live and work in Canada, but it just got too cold," he said. "I came back to Denton and took up my construction business. My dad taught me about building. He could do most anything. He gave me a strong work ethic and everything I am today, I owe to my dad."

His stay in Denton would last only a couple of years. Garland describes his coming to San Marcos: "We had a couple of friends who were coming to San Marcos to visit friends at Gary Job Corps and they asked if we wanted to ride down with them. When we got here, we liked what we saw. The river, the trees, the college were appealing. One evening, the children of the family we were visiting needed milk. We went out and finally found one little store where we could buy a gallon of milk.

"Back in Denton, I had friends who owned convenience stores. They were always on the golf course, and some of them owned racehorses. You don't play golf and run racehorses without some money. I came back to San Marcos with one of those friends and after looking around, he said this is the place to open some stores.

"I wasn't tied to Denton, so I came to San Marcos and in 1965, I put up my first Sac N Pac store on Ranch Road 12."

"How did you know you could make a grocery store work?" I asked.

"Well, my daddy taught me to work and those guys in Denton were spending lots of time on the golf course, so I thought it couldn't be that hard. I asked lots of questions before I started.

"I had some money saved from football and I paid $21,500.00 for the lot where the Ranch Road 12 store is located. I thought I had bought downtown Dallas. But my friend who came with me said this is the location. This is the place. Within a couple of months after that store opened, I had paid for most of my grocery stock."

Since location, location, location has been cited as the three criteria for selecting a business site, I wondered how he determined his future locations. "First, it should be on the going-home-side of the road," Garland said. "You never take a gallon of milk to work, but you often take one home. And I like to be on a corner so that the driver can turn in and drive out with minimum traffic problems.

As his business began to expand, Garland followed his Denton friends into the racehorse business. After buying a farm on Center Point Road, east of the Outlet Mall, he gave horse breeding a whirl. His stable produced one horse that showed promise by finishing with the 12th best time in the All-American Futurity Trials. When he found he couldn't make money with horses, he gave up trying. The only people who make money on racehorses, according to Garland, are the veterinarians, horse-shoers, trainers and jockeys.

Almost 40 years ago, Garland Warren and family put the first Sac N Pac store on Ranch Road 12. Today, there are 42 stores throughout the San Marcos/Hays County area and beyond.

In describing the evolution of Sac N Pac Food Stores, Garland says, "Our goal was to put up one a year. Some years we put in two, some years, none. We didn't know how many we ought to build at any given time. I spent a lot of time driving the countryside looking for going-home locations. I took enough money out of the business to live, but I put a lot of money back into the business to make it grow. I have been lucky to find good locations and I always tried to buy extra space anywhere I put in a store. Our real estate decisions have been good for us."

Garland now suffers from early onset of Parkinson's disease and two years ago, he solidified the family's involvement in the corporation when he sold the company to his three children, Blair, Blake, and Cheryl. Each plays a crucial role in the operation of Sac N Pac Food Stores and Warren Fuel, with Kevin Brumley as CEO.

Garland has made an impact on San Marcos in areas other than the business community. He served two terms as president of the Greater San Marcos Chamber of Commerce, Chair Person of Chillympiad, and has supported, at some level, almost every charitable event, athletic endeavor, and fund-raiser held in San Marcos in the last 40 years.

Not as well known as his support of public charities and civic endeavors is his support of the Walk to Emmaus Movement, an ecumenical spiritual retreat. He has sponsored more people on the Walk than he can remember and he has been a team member on nine or ten of the three and a half day events.

I asked what message he wanted this article to impart to the citizens of San Marcos.

"I want people to know that I care," he said. "I care about people. I care about their lives. And I want people to know I have had a lot of help. People in this town have been great to my family and me. We have had a lot of luck.

Cornelia Cheatham

Cornelia (pronounced Cor nell ya) Cheatham ushered me into the living room of her home at 400 Centre Street, San Marcos. The wall on the right is a tapestry of medals, plaques, ribbons, certificates, and pictures. And so is the wall on the left. More about that later.

Cornelia's selection for this Mother's Day profile was neither random, nor accidental. While I recognize that motherhood is unique and all mothers are special and today is set aside to commemorate that fact, she is featured because she gives a whole new meaning to the concept.

She begins her story, "I contacted breast cancer about 13 years ago at the age of 30. Even when the doctor found a lump in my breast, he said, 'Oh, there's no way it's breast cancer. You are way too young.' A few days later, he called me to come into his office. When he wouldn't tell me the test results over the phone, I knew something was wrong. I burst into tears when I heard "breast cancer." I was scared. I thought I was going to die."

That would have been terribly inconvenient. She had three girls, eleven, seven and three. I am convinced that this deeply religious woman said to God, 'You must have something I can do to make this world a better place.' He gave her an answer.

"I took chemo every two weeks for six months. It is about the worst thing you can go through. Following my chemo, I became a volunteer in the Road to Recovery Program and drove patients to chemo or radiation appointments.

"I also was convinced that if I could go through six months of chemo treatment, I could do anything. We were watching Wednesday's Child on TV and my husband and I thought 'Why don't more people become foster parents?' There are lots of children out there who need a place to live."

Coincidentally, Cornelia and Lionel happened upon a newspaper ad, announcing classes for foster parents. They signed up. They spent four hours every Tuesday in the classes, at the Department of Human Services (DHS) on Dutton Lane. This program is not an easy one. The dropout rate is high and it requires commitment and determination.

Cornelia describes some of the requirements. "You must have a certain number of hours of instruction. The paper work is a real pain. First aid and CPR classes are required every two years. You must pass a house inspection. The state also does a background investigation. Often, my husband and I didn't want to go. We were tired or busy and we had a hundred excuses. But I am so glad we finished the course and became licensed for foster care."

That was seven years ago and she says having the kids has made it all worthwhile. The kids to which Cornelia refers are Shileta 20, Jessica, 16, Maria, 14, Kody, 11, and Jakob, 8. Keep in mind that she has three daughters of her own, one of which is still at home and in high school.

Just to insure she doesn't while away her time eating bon-bons and watching daytime soaps, she also baby-sits three children. The 18 month-old slept in the back room as we conducted this interview.

"I stay busy," she says. "I go to all the meetings—I have to go to court a lot; I attend the Permanency Planning Team (PPT) meetings and I go to all the parent-teacher conferences. One child is a junior, my own daughter is a sophomore, another is in the eighth grade, one of the boys is in fifth grade and the other is in second grade. I go to a lot of different schools...and a lot of different meetings."

Shileta who was the first child to come to the Cheathams spent almost six years with the family. She is now an army airborne soldier at Fort Bragg, NC. According to Cornelia, she is doing "really well. We are proud of her."

Cornelia describes the other children. "The girls came about four months after Shileta. Maria could not read when she came, nor would she raise her head to make eye contact. However, she is now doing well in school and has moved beyond special education classes.

"Jessica, Maria's older sister, is a junior at San Marcos High and makes straight A's. She is just doing great. She is in Upward Bound, and the Academy at the high school. When Jessica and Maria came to us, they were not in school. They had been abandoned by their parents and were homeless. Even now, we are the only family they know. There are some aunts, but for their own reasons, they choose not to be deeply involved with the girls.

"Then we have the two boys, Kody and Jakob. Kody is enrolled in the Duke University Talent Search and will be going to a math camp on scholarship this summer. Jakob is at the top of his reading class. He is a second grader reading on a fourth grade level. I am really going to miss them when they leave."

The boys have been with the Cheathams almost a year. Their situation is somewhat different than the girls. Their mother is getting help and is trying hard to straighten herself out so that she can get her boys back.

Cornelia elaborates, "There are ups and downs. Everything is not peaches and cream, you know. But, we figure someone has to do it. There are stressful times. For example, one of the girls really tries our patience at times. But, I think she sees herself as a failure and she thinks she can prove it. I don't accept that. I don't give up on them. We expect them to follow the rules and perform. I tell them it is part of life, like it or not."

Cornelia admits she is the calm, laid back parent, while Lionel is the better disciplinarian. They work together and demand their children, whether foster or natural, meet certain standards.

Jessica and Maria will be not be eligible for foster care when they reach 18, and they have no family who is interested. The likelihood they will be adopted is remote. I asked what might happen to them.

"Oh, this is their home. They can come back here any time," she said. "They are like my own children and I have told them that."

The children call her Mrs. Cheatham in her presence, but they call her Mom when in conversation with their friends. The children choose the name most comfortable for them.

Because Jakob and Kody's mother is attempting to rehabilitate so she can reclaim her children, she visits her boys at the Cheatham household and she and Cornelia have a friendly relationship. While she is from out of state, she now lives in San Marcos and keeps close contact with her children.

Fostering can be highly sensitive to many factors and race is one of those factors. I asked if the children are African-American.

"No," Cornelia replied. "Two are white, one is Hispanic and one is Hispanic and African-American. I take any color. Doesn't matter to me. There is no problem at all. They do not even see color. Kids have to be taught that kind of difference."

The Cheathams are a rarity among foster parents. They will take children of any age, gender or race. Many foster homes take only infants.

Resources for foster parents are not abundant. The only medical coverage available is Medicaid. Foster home regulations require one doctor's visit and two dental visits per year. It has been important for Cornelia to locate medical and dental facilities that will see her foster children under Medicaid.

It would be unfair to Lionel and Cornelia not to elaborate on their natural children. Dynisha, 24, is a corrections officer at Wackenhut while her fiance is deployed to the Persian Gulf.

Remember the walls, I mentioned at the beginning of this story? One is devoted to Tanya, 20, a scholarship student at Notre Dame who habitually makes the Dean's List. She was preparing to compete in the Big East Track Meet. The second wall is devoted to Chelsea, 16, an outstanding student-athlete at San Marcos High.

To spend time in the Cheatham home and feel Cornelia's love for the children, hear of their successes, and observe her enthusiasm for the program, one could get the impression that all is well and no child is left behind. Sadly, statistics belie that picture.

In the state of Texas, there are almost 4,000 children awaiting adoption. In the 30 counties comprising the Central Texas area, there are almost 500. Texas has more than 15,000 children in foster care placements. The Central Texas area has 2,200.

In light of the above statistics, one is reminded of the story of the boy walking along the beach, tossing starfish back into the ocean. When he is confronted by an older, wiser person who informs him he will never save all the starfish, he replies, "I will save this one."

The statistics are overwhelming, but Cornelia Cheatham and her family are saving kids…four or five at a time.

Jimmy Cobb

"Easter is hope. Hope for all of us. But the hope must be accompanied by faith. Christ had no guarantee of his resurrection, even though he announced it to his followers. His certainty was based on the certainty of his faith." This is how Dr. Jimmy Cobb, pastor of the First Christian Church of San Marcos describes his feelings about this important Christian celebration. His own faith has led him to the place he is supposed to be, though there have been some moments when he wondered what God had in store for him.

Jimmy Cobb (seldom does anyone refer to him as Dr. Cobb) has the studious appearance of a professor. Maybe it is because for a good portion of his life that is what he intended to be. In a pleasant voice with a measured tone he is quick to let you know that he once "hated to preach. It was just such an ordeal. When I was in seminary, I never sought the weekend preaching assignments as did most of my colleagues because I intended to teach when I left seminary."

Family history may have influenced his teaching aspirations. Born in 1941 in Lubbock, Texas, Jimmy was the youngest of five children. His father was a professor at Wayland Baptist College in Plainview, and when Jimmy was six, the family moved to Corpus Christi where his father was the first faculty member hired at Corpus Christi College, now Texas A&M at Corpus Christi. After finishing public school, Jimmy enrolled at Corpus Christi College with his father as his primary professor. Not a good formula for a carefree, rip-roaring, gentleman's C, college experience. "He graded me harder than any of his other students. I know that."

He met Sue, his wife of 38 years, there and married right after his graduation and one year before she graduated. Jimmy worked one year for Humble Oil while waiting for Sue to finish. Then it was to seminary in Fort Worth.

Jimmy finished seminary and came to San Marcos as the chaplain at San Marcos Baptist Academy in 1966. He served the academy until 1983. During that time, he was able to take a two year sabbatical and get his Ph.D. from Baylor University, with the idea that this would enhance his chances of realizing his goals in the teaching profession.

However, chance would dictate a future not foreseen by him.

According to Cobb, "Rod Coleman, pastor of the First Christian Church, and I were very good friends. He was a chaplain reservist with the military, so during his two week summer training and vacations, he invited me to sub for him in the pulpit. Rod decided to resign in 1983 and move to a church in Austin. Following his resignation, the search committee asked me to fill in while they sought a new minister. This in itself was unique because they had asked someone outside their denomination to be their interim minister. In most Christian traditions [denominations] that would have never happened. Nevertheless, I preached my first sermon as interim minister on the first Sunday in February 1983.

"It is strange how the Lord can change things around for you. For five years before that, Sue and I had conversations with more than twenty pulpit committees of Baptist churches and I never received a call from a single church. I guess they didn't figure I had any experience because they didn't think chaplaincy was really ministry.

"I was beginning to wonder what is going on here. When the Lord gives you the opportunity to get an education, there are obviously some skills, but you don't get the opportunity use them. There were just no opening in parish ministry for me. But as I look back—the rear view mirror is always a lot more focused than the present or the future—I can see the Lord was preparing me for something else.

"It was made easier for us by our love of San Marcos and the fact that we did not have to move. Our children were settled in school, we knew almost everyone in town and I was wonderfully received by the congregation."

Elaborating about his children he said, "We have three children, Chris, the oldest, graduated from San Marcos High and attended SWT. He is married and lives and works in Austin. The middle one, Melissa graduated from SWT. She is married and lives in Austin with her husband, Tom Lacy, and our two grandsons. Stephanie, the youngest, also graduated from San Marcos High. She finished Baylor University and has her masters degree from Yale Divinity School. At present, she is finishing her Ph.D. at the University of North Carolina at Chapel Hill, NC."

When asked if she would follow in dad's footsteps, he replied, "She is an extraordinary preacher, but she says she wants to teach." Might there be some genetic wiring influencing the youngest child?

When reminded that his initial distaste for preaching seems to fly in the face of the extraordinary talent he exhibits weekly, he replied, "My not preaching in seminary allowed me to be in the congregation of a brilliant preacher in Fort Worth who showed me you could have intellectual integrity with the scripture and move people at the same time. Intellectual integrity, to me, is a tough faith issue. There are those who want to go to church and be fed a little pablum. I believe it is important to have intellectual continuity in our lives. I don't think we can segment our spiritual life from the rest of our life."

A thoughtful pause followed a query about the stresses in the life of a pastor. "There are so many issues. When you know people so well, it is very difficult to see families in distress; to see children of good families doing crazy things; to be closely associated with people experiencing prolonged tragedy; to bury young people who have struggled with disease or have become accident victims. Sometimes our role is misunderstood. There are those who see us on Sunday morning and seem to think that is the extent of our service to the congregation. They are rare, but they are there.

"When I accepted this job, I naively assumed I would dictate my own schedule and be where I wanted to be when I wanted to be there. This week is Holy Week, perhaps the busiest week of the year for me. I have absolutely no control over my schedule."

That brought up the question of who ministers to the minister. "I don't have a minister. Our area minister advises us to take care of ourselves, reminding us that we can't properly serve our parish if we are not well and to call on him when needed. Meanwhile, I know he has as many responsibilities as I and so it is difficult to find someone who might be appropriate.

"On the other hand, I often turn to Sue. When I accepted this pastorate, I told the congregation they were not getting a 'twofer.' I am your pastor. My wife is not. She would be a member of the congregation and participate as she chose. I think that has been important in our marriage as well as my ministry. She has always been an extraordinary companion for me. She has supported my decisions; she has been there for me in time of need; and yet, she has created a life of her own. She is a reading specialist in the San Marcos school system."

While Jimmy has somewhat overcome his dread of preaching, he has invited guest speakers every Sunday during Lent. Though he has been in the pulpit, some of his guests have been Pilate, Barrabas, Judas and Mary Magdalene. Maybe one day the dread will disappear.

Betty Beard

Betty Beard and Gene Sutphen were high school sweethearts at Ballinger High in the early 40's. Gene graduated in 1942, while Betty finished in 1943. World War II would separate them for 50 years.

Though Gene is not the focus of this profile, he is responsible for it. His email said he had a good subject for my column. Turns out, he did.

Though born in Fort Worth, Betty grew up in Ballinger and says of Gene, "We went steady for two years. He lived on one corner of the block and I lived on the other. He graduated from high school and joined the navy. I saw him once when he came home on leave and I did not see him again for 49 years.

"There was an air cadet training center in Ballinger and I met a cadet, Earl Beard, who became a bombardier/navigator and flew with the B-25 squadrons off Okinawa in the bombing of Japan. He and I corresponded during the war and in 1945, when the war was over, we married."

Upon returning to the states Earl wanted to be a teacher. He got his bachelor's degree at Baylor University, then went to the University of Iowa where he obtained a PhD in history with the notion of pursuing a career in academia.

His first teaching job was at the University of Maryland and for the next 38 years, Betty lived the somewhat itinerant life of the academic wife. Earl would eventually become vice-president of Southern Illinois University. They lived in Alton, Illinois and in about 1970 Betty, replied to a summer recreation program which offered classes in swimming, golf, tennis, ceramics and hand weaving.

That was the beginning of a life-changing experience as described by Betty. "I had dabbled in art at Texas State College for Women—that will tell you how old I am—and so eight or ten of us signed up for the six weeks course in hand weaving. When it was over, we signed up again. We organized a local hand weavers guild and discovered there was a large guild across the river in St. Louis. The St Louis guild is the second oldest in the U.S. The Boston guild is six months older."

Through the guilds, Betty expanded her association with weavers all over the world. From the St. Louis guild, she became associated with the Mid-Western Hand Weavers Guild. That led to an association with the Hand Weavers Guild of America.

"The Hand Weavers Guild of America attracts some 2,000 people to its conferences," Betty said. "The year I went to Atlanta there were participants from 27 countries.

"My own progression in the art has been through workshops and self-teaching. I am largely self-taught. I knit, knot, needle point, crochet, dye, quilt, spin and weave. What I enjoy most is designing and weaving one of a kind materials for very special garments. I also enjoy teaching workshops and weaving classes.

"In 1980, Interweave Press published my book, *Fashions from the Loom*. It went through seven or eight prinitings. At the time, I thought I was still a novice, but people at my workshops kept asking me to put my instructions in a book. So, with my mechanical Remingtoin typewriter at the dining table, I cranked out my ideas and sent it off to Interweave."

With the publication of the the book, Betty began to get even more invitations to present workshops on weaving. She has presented throughout the United States—Illinois, Wisconsin, Iowa, Indiana, Missouri, Georgia, Tennessee. Many of these workshops were by special invitation of the various guilds and some were presentations at state and national conferences.

She also has an international reputation. She has made at least 25 trips to England to teach or attend weaving classes.

"The guilds of England are very large and well attended. I was envious of them because the weavers there have a wonderful opportunity to learn about the technical aspects of the art. My experience has been largely do-it-yourself and trial and error. I attended Scottish School of Textiles for two summer sessions at Gallashiels.

"I have conducted workshops at Oxford, Hatfield, London, Taunton and others places.I can't even remember. The most memorable experience was attending and teaching at the East Sussex Guild. At that time, I was doing my Ritzy Rags series."

Please explain, I said.

Betty brought out a luxurious hand woven evening jacket, she called a cocoon, and explained with an anecdote.

"The program chairman introduced this odd-ball American to the large guild audience and explained that, 'she uses rag strips as weft' (the horizontal material of the weave). In the front row was a lady dressed in a hand-woven, tweedy outfit, accessorized with real pearls, who remarked in a voice heard throughout the hall, 'Well, I certainly wouldn't want to wear clothes made out of rag rugs.' How to welcome an already nervous speaker!

"I pulled out what I call my hoop-de-do, New Years Eve outfit (a sexy, bare-shouldered cocktail dress one might expect to see in a Nieman-Marcus collection) and said, 'Does this look like a rag rug?'"

To make her Ritzy Rags, Betty cuts expensive yard goods into strips, then weaves the strips into one of a kind fabric. From that fabric, she then creates the garment for which she designed the new cloth. This technique allows her to create unique patterns in the cloth.

"I really stretched the parameters of hand weaving," she said. "By the way, the workshop went great. I was later invited to participate in the British Textile Festival and this is what they wrote about me."

The ebullient Betty Beard is an American who travels the world, teaching under the name, Ritzy Rags. Betty specializes in producing the most individual and beautiful garments using a technique of rag weaving. They not only look different, but they have a soft and unusual handle and drape to them. The before and after of the strips of rag to couture garments achieved by Betty and her students, literally need to be seen to be believed.

As she leafed through magazines where her work has been published, she pointed out that most of her pieces were designed to illustrate a particular weaving technique. She told me a whole lot more than I could understand about weaving.

Betty's work has been published in British and American magazines. She has won blue ribbons in a number of guild exhibits. And she was elected to the board of directors of the Hand Weavers Guild of America for a two year term. She could have served longer, but it was at about that time that her husband was quite ill with cancer.

In 1992, Gene's Ballinger High School class was having its 50th class reunion. Betty attended and saw Gene Sutphen for the first time since 1943.

"All those years, I really did not know where he was, even though we tried to keep up with each other through assorted cousins and acquaintenances," Betty said.

In 1993, her class had its 50th reunion and Gene was invited to present a program. I have to interject that Gene is a professional photographer who is as creative with a camera as Betty is with a loom. That is another story for another time.

By 1993, Betty's husband, Earl, had passed away and following the '93 reunion, Betty and Gene, who was divorced, began a correspondence. He made a few trips to St. Louis to visit her.

"We had lots to talk about," Betty said. "We had the same roots, knew each other's families and we were quite comfortable together. So, we decided to get married. I never dreamed this Texas boy would move to St. Louis, but he did."

The courtship lasted through most of 1994 and they were married in 1995. They lived in St. Louis for three years before moving to Texas. At first, they came to Austin, but found the location inconvenient for their purposes. In addition, they have a very important connection in San Marcos. Paul Sutphen, Gene's son, is owner of Grins Restaurant, but even more important, Paul has provided them with two grandchildren.

As I thought I was wrapping up the interview and preparing to get a picture, Betty casually mentioned, "This is my coat made from hand-spun Samoyed dog fur."

A coat made from dog fur? She's kidding, of course.

She is not kidding as she relates that she saved the fur as she brushed her pet Samoyed and spun it into yarn, then wove it into a beautiful snow white coat.

So, you can go from the raw material to a finished garment, I asked.

"I can spin it, weave it, design it, cut it, sew it, and occasionally, I get to wear it," she replied.

"I spin wool, vicuna, silk, several kinds of dog fur, and camel. I love to spin. I don't spin cotton and I don't spin linen."

Though she is a bit shy, Betty says, "I can talk about the things I know and love and it is such fun to exchange ideas with people who want to learn. The greatest thing I can do is inspire someone to be creative."

Creative, industrious, innovative, persistent, artistic, ingenious—all apply to Betty Beard. But inspirational is the one word that comes closest to capturing her and her work

Janette Ramsay and Jan Stark

Out of the night that covers me,
Black as the pit from pole to pole,
I thank whatever gods may be
For my unconquerable soul.

Death stands at the door and motions for them to follow. They refuse. Two women. Two stories. One foe. Cancer. It lurks like a hungry predator in the lives of Janette Ramsay and her daughter, Jan Stark. They accept its presence, as you and I accept the traffic on the Interstate Highway. They are equally vigilant and respectful of the need for caution and perseverance.

In a quiet, controlled voice, free of anger or fear, Janette says, "Between 1986 and 1987 I felt bad for about a year. I kept going to the doctors and complaining about my symptoms, but none of my doctors detected anything. I finally went to a psychiatrist friend of mine and asked, 'Could all this be in my head?'"

The psychiatrist scheduled a complete battery of tests for her. Among those was a CBC/CBS. If that test provides results of 10 or above there is a high likelihood of cancer. "My body hides cancer," says Janette. "When my cancer was at its very worst, the CBC/CBS test result was 2.5."

Nevertheless in 1986, Janette was scheduled for surgery, but because of her blood tests, the surgeon did not expect to find cancer when he operated. Her medical history led him to suspect a recurrence of endomitriosis. During the procedure, he saw her perilous condition and decided to do all he could. He removed 85 per cent of her colon and 27 lymph nodes and discharged her with the prognosis of a five percent chance that she might live six months to a year.

"I didn't hear that," Janette emphasized. "My mind was protecting me."

"My mother insisted I get a second opinion. I saw this well-known doctor who looked at my records and said, 'Well, Ms. Ramsay, there's not much I can do for you. You are not going to live a year, anyway.'" As she laughs out loud at the irony she is about to reveal, she says, "And that is the first time I really heard it. My poor mother's face was ashen. We did not say a word, just went down the elevator and got in the car."

In the fell clutch of circumstance
I have not winced nor cried aloud.

Under the bludgeonings of chance
My head is bloody, but unbowed.

In spite of the dire predictions, Janette chose to do the painful, debilitating chemotherapy treatments with the notion that it would be stupid not to give herself every chance. Every two weeks for two years she subjected herself to the ordeal. In 1987, she had an exploratory operation to determine, as the doctors put it, 'how far the cancer had progressed.' There was none.

For nine years she lived a normal life, if a normal life consists of working 14 hour days hustling real estate, getting your kids married, tending your grandkids, surviving a broken pelvis, and subjecting yourself to prodding and poking by the medical profession. In 1996, following one of her regular check-ups, the doctor informed her the cancer had returned. This time, it was in her lung. The doctors removed most of her left lung.

Casually, she remarked, "Then in 1998, it returned to my colon. I had that operation in June and no more than three weeks later, I received this call from Jan." The call informed Janette that she, Jan, had a brain tumor.

Beyond this place of wrath and tears
Looms but the horror of the shade.
And yet the menace of the years
Finds and shall find me unafraid.

Unexpectedly, Janette volunteered, "I have always felt that cancer was a blessing to me. It forced me to look at some relationships that I needed to heal. You begin saying things to your children that you, otherwise, think you have plenty of time to say. And so, it has been a gift. I have done nothing miraculous to recover. I have just had some marvelous people around me."

Jan begins her story. "I was having lunch with a recruit we were courting for the law firm. I was talking and all of a sudden, no words came out. I felt so weird. I almost wrote on a napkin, 'Take me to the hospital.'"

This occurred one week after she knew her mother's cancer had returned for the third time. The first doctor, an internist, thought she might have a seizure disorder and so ordered a CAT scan. Reflecting her selflessness, Jan says, with pity for the doctor, "The poor man calls and says 'I need to see you.' It's the first time he has met me and he has to say, 'You have a brain tumor and I have scheduled an appointment with a neurosurgeon tomorrow.' I guess I was in shock. I thought I better get a second opinion and with the help of the law firm, we found this neurosurgeon whom I really liked. He saw me on Friday and operated on Monday. It was a primary brain cancer."

Jan's surgeon warned her not to look at the Internet, don't listen to other people's war stories, realize everyone is different. "I didn't want to know," she says. "For six months I did not want to talk about it, but I started radiation and after seven months, I started chemo. I had about a year of that. And right now, I'm pretty stable."

Janette: "She's beat the prognosis of 18 to 24 months [to live]."

Jan: "It was tough. The prognosis. I did not fear for myself, but as the mother of two children, five and two, at the time—I said, 'I gotta live.' My doctor was taken aback when I told him I'm going to see my grandchildren."

Janette: "I sometimes get trapped when I speak for my adult children, but I think we both believe in God and prayer. We had all sorts of people rallying around us."

Jan: "We become aware of changes we need to make. As the cobbler's children go barefoot, I was a lawyer without a will. Really."

Janette: "The second important thing I have gained in living with cancer is laughter. Years ago when I was doing chemotherapy, I always believed in getting dressed up to go. I wanted to look good. I saw people coming to treatment in robes and looking downcast and sad. I have always believed if you are a pleasant person to be around, people will respond to that. And I believe maybe those who don't care how they look have given up. Everybody lives with something."

Jan: "My sister said, 'Maybe you got a brain tumor because you needed permission to take care of yourself.' In some ways, she is right. I was trying to juggle a stressful job with two small children and when the doctors told me I couldn't go back to work, I admit, I felt some relief. I don't know if I will ever be cured, but I'm hoping to be healed. I have re-ordered my priorities."

Janette: "I was at the Relay for Life last year and I was deeply moved. I didn't really expect to be. I wasn't sure I would make the survivor's lap because I was having trouble from an accident which affected my hips and legs. But the medals I got that day are the last thing I see before I go to bed and the first thing I see when I awake. It was the first time I had publicly announced and admitted to myself that 'I am a survivor.' I just don't want to boast about it. It was so moving. When they lit all those luminaria, and I went around and read all those cards…"

Tears began to form as it became obvious it was time to end the interview.

It matters not how strait the gate,
How charged with punishments the scroll.
I am the master of my fate;
I am the captain of my soul.
(The poem is <u>Invictus</u> by Henley)

Shirley Lehman

Shirley Rogers Lehman was born in San Marcos to the family who developed and, for years, owned and operated the business most often associated with the city. The mention of San Marcos still evokes questions from other Texans about the status of Aquarena Springs. As one of the last connections to the passing landmark, Shirley shared her recollections of the early days of the development and operation of the Texas tourist destination.

"As a child, I lived on the banks of the San Marcos River at what is now known as Rio Vista Park. At one time, I understand, it was known as Rogers Park, but I always knew it as Rio Vista. All the cottages had clever names. The one we lived in was called *Linger Long,* as I recall. My grandparents, who owned the park lived in a small rock cabin nearby called *Idlewild.*

"My grandfather, A.B. Rogers, gave the land to his children, my father and his sisters, and eventually, my father purchased their shares and ended up with all of it. It was later sold to some families from Houston who finally sold it to the city."

Shirley related that her grandfather built the Aquarena Springs Hotel and the golf course at the head of the springs in 1929 on land he bought from the San Marcos Electrical Company. He operated the hotel two years until forced by the economic conditions of the depression to close. She explains it served as a hospital for a few years and then was leased by the Brown Schools for 20 years until they purchased the land up on the hill northeast of the hotel.

"My father was Paul Rogers. He left San Marcos and went to Corpus Christi to pursue the oil business after my mother died. I was about three when my sister was born and my mother died in childbirth. She and I lived with my aunts in Houston until my father remarried and moved back to San Marcos.

"He had a dream of a tourist attraction in San Marcos. When I was very young, we moved back here from Corpus Christi where he had been in the oil business. Not long after we returned, in August of 1947, he launched his first little 16 foot glass bottom boat. He was so amazed with the beauty of the plant life and the fish and the make up of the springs, he became more determined than ever to make his dream a reality."

Paul took his family to Florida for what was ostensibly a vacation to Silver Springs and Weeki-Wachee Springs. Actually, he went there to study tourism in the state and explore the possibility of doing something similar in Texas. When he returned, he set about creating what was to become Aquarena Springs. The first thing he had to do was dredge what is now the lake.

When I asked for the origin of the name, Shirley explained that her father wanted something that would describe his vision. He imagined an entertainment arena on and in the water. After meeting with his backers, some of whom were from Florida, they decided *Aquarena* was a suitable name which aptly described its venue and activities.

According to Shirley, "Aquarena opened as a tourist attraction and center in 1950. We were really the first tourist attraction of its kind in Texas. When it first opened they brought in a seal act. It was wonderful and we had some great seals. They would climb ladders and dive into the lake and do all the balancing acts expected of seals, but that soon had to be disbanded because it was discovered the seals could not live in the fresh water.

"The show changed many times. At one time we had a high diver and other acts. It just evolved over the years. My dad did not want rides or anything that smacked of a carnival atmosphere. There was no drinking of any kind. It was to be a family oriented facility which retained as much of the original attractions of nature as possible. We wanted to share this beautiful facility with the people of Texas. It became well known for the underwater theater which was advertised as the 'world's only submarine theater'. Life magazine ran a feature on an underwater wedding in 1954. And of course, Ralph, the Swimming Pig got national publicity in a couple of magazines."

Shirley recounts that she was involved with Aquarena in many aspects since its beginning. She laughs as she tells about her and her sister defying her father's orders not to swim in the theater productions.

"He did not want his daughters performing in front of the public. We saw it quite differently. Margaret Russell who came to Aquarena with her husband, Don, was a professional swimmer in Florida. She taught us all the routines and we enjoyed performing three or four shows a day."

Florida made a significant contribution to the success of Aquarena. Don Russell was piloting one of the glass bottom boats Paul Rogers and his family rode while on the initial expeditionary trip. Mr. Rogers offered Don a job as general manager of the embryonic Texas tourist attraction if he would have it. Don accepted.

As Shirley explains the evolution of Aquarena Springs, "Don was a promoter and my father was a promoter. What they needed was a business man. In the early 1960's Gene Phillips was getting ready to close his business with Mobil Oil and move out of San Marcos because of a great deal of controversy with the school board and other issues. My dad asked him if he would consider coming to Aquarena Springs as the business manager.

"My father died of leukemia in 1965, not long after Gene came to work for him. The board of directors later appointed Gene general manager. In the mid 1970's Gene's wife, Betty, died of a heart attack. I had just been through a divorce and since Gene and I knew each other well as friends, we began going out. We were married in 1976 and Gene continued to run the facility until 1985 when it was sold to the Baugh family."

The Baugh family kept the hotel and the park open for a few years until they sold it to Southwest Texas State University.

When asked for her feelings about the demise of the park and SWT's proposed use of the facilily, Shirley responded, "I don't allow feelings to come into it. Things change. I think I'm pretty open-minded about it. I hated to see it end as a tourist attraction, but in reality, it no longer had a place in the tourist business. The gigantic parks such as Sea World, Fiesta Texas and Six Flags have made it obsolete."

Nevertheless, Aquarena is still remembered, even in the metropolitan areas. The Houston Chronicle did a feature on the water park last month.

"As much as I hate to see it change, I'm not sure it is a negative change. If the University in coordination with Parks and Wildlife can manage it in a way that it benefits people and the state of Texas, maybe it is best. I *am* concerned about what they are going to do about the dam. Time will tell."

Shirley assured me that the sale of Aquarena did not end her connection with the tourism industry. She is deeply involved with one of her step-sons, Bill Phillips, in the Ripley's Believe It or Not museum in San Antonio. In fact, she informed me she is supporting Bill in his latest venture, Ripley's Haunted Adventure, to open in San Antonio next June if all goes well.

Shirley, with her husband, Jim Lehman, stays busy, traveling aboard their boat, seeing after her business interests and keeping up with her family.

"Time is going too fast," she responds to a query about her regrets. "I can't get it all done—all that I want to do."

So, what accomplishment is missing from her life? "Have a career, I guess. I was educated to be a teacher. But I took a year off after graduating from the University of Texas and by the beginning of the next year, I had already begun having children. So I never taught full time. One of the things I would like to do is write. I do a lot of journaling on the boat and I thoroughly enjoy it.

If her journal is as interesting and delightful as the woman who writes it, it will be a runaway best-seller.

Terry Serur

Serur's Varsity Shop, the oldest business in San Marcos, will close around December 1st, bringing to an end 110 years of service to this community. The closing symbolizes more than the end of a business's long run. With a finality we all dread, the curtain rings down on an era. It was an era characterized by intimacy—store personnel not only knew your name, they knew your shoe size and your inseam length; it was an era of neighborly trust—one's promise to pay when the cotton was sold was money in the bank; it was an era of simpler ways—utility and durability outsold style.

That era of intimacy, trust and simplicity has been trampled underfoot by sterile, impersonal shopping malls, prairie dog towns of factory outlets, and super stores which cover more ground than a sharecropper could farm with two mules and a cultivator. All this in the name of progress, and efficiency.

"I literally grew up in the business," says Terry Serur, owner, operator, head clerk, fitting specialist, main greeter, and special order man at the Varsity Shop for more than 30 years. "As long as I can remember, I was always around the store." His soft, reflective voice is calm and steady and reveals no sign of anger or regret as he talks about his years in business.

"When I was real young, San Marcos was a lot smaller, of course, but I can recall during cotton-picking season, the town would be loaded with people. "We were supposed to close at eight o'clock, but at that time of year we often could not get out of the store before 10:00 PM. I would be in the store, until all hours. I often would go to sleep in the back until my dad could get away and go home."

By the time he was 13 years old, Terry Serur was working around the store, helping his dad, Dempsey, with chores, running errands and doing whatever was necessary. In high school, he worked at the store when other activities did not take him away. During his college years, Terry says he worked in the store every minute he was not in class.

"I just feel as though I have been here forever." Terry says.

Actually, Terry spent four years in the Air Force from 1966 to 1970. During the height of the Viet Nam war, he enlisted, even though he lacked one year for graduation from Southwest Texas State. At the end of his enlistment, he returned to finish his degree and, like slipping your foot into an old shoe, Terry found himself back in the comfortable and familiar role of helping his dad at the store.

By the time Terry had his degree, his father was beginning to lean on him more than ever. It was Dempsey who asked Terry what he planned to do after college. It was also Dempsey who provided an answer to that question when he suggested Terry stay in the store.

"I had no idea what I was going to do," says Terry, "but during that year, I pitched in and helped around here and I could see my dad was getting tired of the demands of the store. I loved the business, so it made sense to me to stay here. As time passed, we became partners and eventually, I took over the store completely."

Serur's Varsity Shop has occupied several locations in San Marcos— as one might expect of a business with a 110 year history. For the past 41 years it has been on the same block. It has been at 326 North LBJ for the past 15 years. For the twenty-five years prior, it was located in the store next door.

Terry remembers his early association with the store, "Prior to moving to LBJ, we were in several locations on the square. The most notable one that I can remember was on the north side of the square. Back then, all the best businesses were on the north side. We were separated from Hilburn's Drug Store by the alley on that block.

"Before that, my grandfather had a big department store on the south side of the square where the Scanio Brothers law firm is located. That was back in the 1920's. Later, he had a location on the east side of the square."

Gabriel, "G," Serur, came to San Marcos in 1892, accompanied by his brother, Sam, "S," Serur. They immigrated from Bierut, Lebanon to New York and made their way to Texas in a horse drawn wagon by peddling merchandise along the way. They established homes in San Marcos upon arrival, but did not immediately establish businesses. They continued to purvey their merchandise on the road, concentrating on the route between San Marcos and Laredo.

Once the brothers settled in a location and established their businesses, they sent for brides from the home country. The brides happened to be sisters, so the Serur brothers married sisters. "G" Serur, Terry's grandfather, had nine boys while "S" Serur had three sons and one daughter.

Though they were brothers and traveled to Texas together, and were in the same business, "G" and Sam were not partners.

As Terry relates, "They were friendly competitors. And the 13 offspring of the Serur brothers were double first cousins, so they were close as a family.

"My dad was the second youngest of the nine boys in his family, so there was quite a gap between the oldest and youngest. Older brothers,

Ellis and Tom, eventually took over the business from my grandfather, "G." They were the principal owners until after World War II. When my dad came home from the war, (note: Dempsey Serur distinguished himself as an Army Air Corps pilot in WW II) he and his brother, Edmond, bought out brothers, Ellis and Tom. Eventually, my dad bought out Edmund and that left just the two of us."

Terry shared his memories of an earlier time in San Marcos when the pace was slower, traffic lights were a rarity, and the merchants on the square gathered at Hilburn's Drugs for coffee twice a day. "The square was like one big happy family," he says. "All the commerce was done right there on the square. There were no shopping centers or malls. While we were all competitors, it was friendly. There were two main hang-outs, Hilburn's and Miller's Drug store. By the time we moved down to LBJ in 1960, things had begun to change a little.

"But even then, my dad, Jack Kercheville, and Mo Mauldin would go next door to Manske's and drink coffee."

The name Manske prompted the question: Is that where the Manske roll came from?

"That is it and I ate the very first one Roland Manske ever made. It was accidental, but one day he picked up the scraps from the dinner rolls he was making, rolled out the dough, added some cinnamon, sugar and butter, plopped it in the oven and about the time they were ready, I walked in for coffee. He sat a roll in front of me and told me to taste it. Man, it was delicious! My friends and I encouraged him and the Manske Roll was born. He first sold them for a nickel apiece."

When asked what he would like San Marcos to know about him, Terry replied, "For the thirty years I have been in this business, I could hardly wait to get here in the morning. I love clothes, I love to see people dressed well, and I love to sell quality. The worst part of leaving is I'm going to miss seeing all the wonderful friends. I have always considered my customers as friends and tried to treat them that way. But Carol (his wife) and I have been planning this move for some time. My son, Ash, is playing in some good golf tournaments as a member of the SWT golf team and we like to watch him play."

For 110 years the Serur family has played a major role in the growth and development of San Marcos. (Note: Ellis Serur, Terry's uncle, was mayor in the 60's) Except for a cousin, John Serur, who will be moving soon, Terry is the last Serur to call San Marcos home. As such, he is a scion of history, an icon of the past, a testament to family loyalties, and a living definition of what it means to put down roots.

Dan O'Leary

He is a big bear of a man who stands over six feet tall and weighs more than 200 pounds, all of it pretty well placed. His life is driven by crises, danger, loss and destruction. His ever present smile and gentle welcoming eyes seem to belie the reality of the job he holds. His voice is firm and commanding, but far from obstreperous and dictating.

Dan O'Leary has been a San Marcos fireman 21 years and San Marcos Fire Chief 12 of those years. That statistic might lead one to assume he began early in life with a design to follow a family pattern or to answer an unrequited call to destiny.

Not so. O'Leary is an accidental fireman. His career as a fire fighter was initially motivated by money, good working hours and the benefits associated with public employment.

Dan says, "I lived all over Texas as a kid as my family moved around with my father who worked in the oil business. He started out on the bottom rung in a refinery for Continental Oil Company and wound up as plant manager. Later on, he traveled around the country building refineries. I even lived in England for a year and a half during my high school years. I graduated from Kermit High School and came to San Marcos to go to Southwest Texas State and never left."

Moving around the state and living in England did nothing to get rid of O'Leary's West Texas drawl nor the confidence inherent in a denizen of the oil fields.

"I came to San Marcos in 1973—Gosh, has it been that long?—to go to school. While in school, I was in the roofing business to make a little extra money. I sort of lost interest in school and quit after about a year and started my own roofing business in Austin, but I had a buddy here in the fire department who kept after me to take the civil service test and become a fireman.

"The way he put it was, 'You can be a fireman and still work at your business on your days off.' That sounded good. My wife, a San Antonio girl, whom I met while we were students at SWT, was pregnant and the idea of a steady paycheck and benefits sounded pretty good, so I took the test, and got the job."

In spite of his gentle, laid back demeanor, it doesn't take long to grasp Dan's desire for excitement, his thrill at being in charge of a crisis and the confidence that he can handle any situation. It lies just below the surface of his public persona and as he talks, he admits—almost as if he just discovered this about himself—these things are a major factor in his love for his job.

"That's a good question," Dan responded when I asked how he became the Fire Chief after only nine years with the department. "First, I became active early in my career in other city activities other than the fire department. I got to know the people at city hall, the city manager, and the administrators. I used to volunteer for city committees. I really enjoyed the functions of city government. I watched the department heads and I thought, 'That is not so difficult. I could do that.'

"When the position opened up, there was an assessment process. They ran us through a battery of tests and I did pretty well on that. Plus I knew the city staff. A.C. Gonzalez was the city manager at the time, but he was leaving just as these decisions were being made. Larry Gilley replaced him and for some reason, he hired me. I was at the right place at the right time. It just sort of fell in my lap."

Getting the position is one thing, but keeping it is quite another when the power structure at City Hall changes as often and occasionally as drastically as it does in San Marcos. Dan O'Leary avows a non-political stance. He proclaims his department stays out of the politics of the city; he refuses to endorse candidates; and he refuses to espouse political rhetoric. While realizing there is some danger in not endorsing candidates, he says he chooses to remain free of any political identification and tries to provide the best services he can for the citizens of San Marcos.

"I work with whoever is in office, but I think doing as good a job as we do is what keeps people off my back. We have a good reputation in the community. Statistics bear us out as for as being able to do our job in comparison with other fire departments."

Chief O'Leary emphasizes that he keeps statistics to help him determine if his department is meeting performance standards. Among some of the more important comparisons he gave are: 1) Average annual loss by fire in dollars per capita in San Marcos has been below the state average for the past 12 years. 2) For the past 10 years 85 to 90 per cent of all structural fires have been confined to the room in which it started. This compares with the state average of 60 to 65 per cent. 3) Response time throughout the city is expected to be five minutes or under. We meet that about 75 per cent of the time. 4) The fire department responds to an average of 1,400 calls a year.

Asked about the rescue mission of the fire department, O'Leary stated, "This has sort of evolved over the years. When I first started, rescue was pretty much an afterthought for the fire department. We would go to a wreck and do what we could, but we were not expected to be experts or to do a whole lot. But over the years that changed.

"I'm not sure why that changed, but we got better at it. We spend a lot of time training our fire fighters how to get people out of unusual situations. We teach them how to use specialized equipment such as the Jaws of Life; we train our personnel to rescue people from raging rivers; manholes; caves; trees; any kind of hazardous situation, to include dealing with hazardous materials.

"It seems to me the expectations have grown. People just expect us to do more, but it was never mandated as our job. We have become much more professional in our approach and every man in the department is trained in all these rescue operations."

Chief O'Leary went on to explain that his department is too small to have any sizable number of experts in any one of these specialized missions. He may have one or two highly trained individuals and they then train *all* the other fire fighters in that specialty. This provides a capability throughout the fire department, so that no matter who responds to whatever situation, there is some capability to provide some level of help. He was quick to point out that training is an ongoing thing.

He was quick to point out that training is an ongoing thing. "If we are not responding to an emergency, we are training to respond to an emergency."

This is an implementation of his philosophy that the more broadly trained a fire fighter is, the better fire fighter he will be. "He needs to be exposed to a lot of things rather than being narrowly focused. My people love the training. They enjoy this work and I think they know we try to become the best we can possibly be.

"We are also part of *first responder* policy. We send a unit from the nearest station if a medical emergency comes in. We don't wait for EMS. All my firemen are trained in CPR and can perform emergency first aid while the ambulance is on the way."

In addition to being the fire chief, Dan is the city's Emergency Management Coordinator. In this job he found his greatest challenge since he became a fireman, the flood of October 1998. Space prevents a full explanation of his vivid description of the Fire Department's part in that disaster, but suffice to say more than 7,000 people, one-fourth of the city population was evacuated during the period. He has prepared an amazingly detailed 32 page history of events, arranged chronologically. This typifies the degree to which he attends to the details of his job in order to improve his department.

I pointed out to Chief O'Leary that walking into his fire house one is struck by the absence of minorities and females. He was eager to respond.

"There are several factors which contribute to this," he said. "First, these positions are under civil service regulations. People take the test and we hire the people who get the highest score. There is no flexibility. At one time that was good because it prevented the hiring of political cronies and the practice of nepotism. But today, I would love to hire some of my reserve firemen who are members of a minority. Second, we have very little turn-over and that is good in one sense, but it presents us with another problem. They are not as young as they were when we hired them and this is a young man's profession. Third, we don't have to recruit. I just hired a young man who was with the Lubbock fire department. He has a degree in economics from Rice University and was a Southwest Conference champion athlete.

"I have taken this problem to city hall, but there has been no action. Everyone in the chain of command is aware of the situation and would like to see some changes."

To those of you who have been reading this and relating the Chief's name to a famous fire in Chicago, I can assure you, had it been his cow who kicked over the lantern, the fire would have been contained in the milk shed.

Author's note: Since this interview, Dan O'Leary has moved to City Hall where he is the City Manager.

Vicki Fruit

In a couple of weeks when you drive across the Hopkins Street Bridge, you will be greeted by a galaxy of lights illuminating the San Marcos River and its banks. Colorful tents will be spread across the area. One can find entertainment, food, crafts, costumes, Biblical scenes, and Santa Claus to set the scene and evoke the feeling of the coming holidays The Sights and Sounds of Christmas will once again delight San Marcos children of all ages.

Many individuals, businesses, and organizations are responsible for the scope and beauty of the displays and activities. They function like the spokes of a wheel which radiate from a hub. That hub is Vicki Fruit. For the fourth consecutive year she has the monumental responsibility of coordinating this unique and joyful event.

"My coming to San Marcos was completely tied to the move of The Mensor Corporation in July of 1978" she said. "The turnover of employees in Houston was so great, we were looking for a more stable work force that San Marcos seemed to provide. Jerry and I spent a lot of weekends and vacations in the Hill Country, hiking, camping and doing all the wonderful things people can do here," says Vicki as she explains how she got to San Marcos. "When the company moved here, 33 families from Houston accompanied us. Only two chose to stay in Houston. It was just a wonderful move for Mensor and for us personally."

Though she is a native Houstonian, she is quick to admit she has 'been there, done that' and has no desire to repeat it.

Discussing her formative years, she begins with the surprising, if not shocking, news that her grandfather had a museum in the attic of his home.

"It was called Hyde Park Miniature Museum. He was a master of hobbies. He could do so many things. He did short-wave radio; he did lapidary work; he began making model airplanes when he was bedridden for two years with tuberculosis of the spine. He was written up as the King of Hobbies. His reputation put him in contact with many people and they would send him unusual and historical items which he insisted on displaying. People would come to the house and go through the attic and be entertained. Somehow, that soaked into my brain and had an influence on me."

Vicki's parents were professional photographers who lived in a modest Houston neighborhood near Rice University. She went to Lamar High school where she was heavily influenced by the theater group there. She began by doing set design, but found that acting and directing was where she really wanted to be.

As Vicki describes it, "There were some wonderful people in the group. In fact, my senior year I had the privilege of directing *Bye Bye Birdie* with Tommy Tune. I was the student director and he was the director. He came back as a favor to our drama teacher. Jaclyn Smith of *Charlie's Angels* fame was in school with me. I remember she played a harem girl in one of our productions.

"The theater was key in my life at that time. When I graduated from high school, I had a wonderful scholarship to the Royal Academy of Dramatic Arts in London. Wouldn't that have been a good idea?" says Vicki as she laughs it off.. "But I was falling in love at that time and, like a kid, I let it go."

After attending the University of Houston for a short time, she found work in the real world with Channel 13, the ABC affiliate in Houston, doing public relations work. Among the memorable moments of that job were squiring Peter Jennings around Houston, picking up David Hennings from the airport, and driving the *Outer Limits* monster—in full costume—down the Gulf Freeway.

"Actually, my time at Channel 13 had a significant influence on the direction of my life. Times were so different then. It was a privately owned television station and they could do anything. The management, Willard Walbridge, was a great supporter of the arts. One of the directors there was very interested in Shakespeare and he did what was probably the only full length TV production of *Romeo and Juliet*. It was on tape, totally unedited—not one word was cut," according to Vicki.

"I played Juliet and served as production assistant. We did a number of other major productions where I had the opportunity to learn the production/direction end of the business as well act. I found the experience invaluable and I suppose that has some effect on what I do now. The anxiety of knowing the curtain is about ready to go up and you better have everything in place is always a high for me."

After coming to San Marcos Vicki and her husband, Jerry, chose to live in the country near Staples where they bought a farm, but that did not keep her out of the civic affairs of San Marcos. Initially, she became active in the Heritage Association, helping organize and manage, with county participation, the restoration of the Kyle Log House. As an offshoot of that effort she found herself involved in Fest Affair, an event where a lot of the history of the area was recreated through demonstrations of the pioneer skills needed in the early days to survive and flourish.

"I was not a part of the first Sights and Sounds of Christmas which was held in 1986, but I have worked on the other 13. As spectator at the first one, I was amazed at what happened. So, I became involved and because I had been involved earlier with the pioneer demonstrations, I worked to bring that element to the event."

When it was suggested that getting it all together involved a lot of persuasion and maybe even some arm-bending, Vicki deflected any credit for herself with, "We are very lucky to have in this area such a cooperative and diverse group of people. All one has to do is provide the opportunity and they respond.

"We have a working board of directors. Every member of the board has a specific task to accomplish and I am only the conduit through which they operate.

Always quick to give credit to others, Vicki pointed out that Kelly Franks, director of Main Street San Marcos, organized the early versions of Sights and Sounds and held the affair around the court house square. Its growth over the years continued until it could no longer be accommodated there. Since the event is free there is no way to accurately count the attendance, but two years ago police and fire department officials estimated approximately 30,000 people in attendance Saturday night. That approximates the entire population of San Marcos.

Vicki says, "There have been numerous changes in the board of directors, but there has always been a core of experience, knowledge and willingness to make things work. Each year there is more decentralization. Not to say I am not deeply involved, but we know, for example, San Marcos Electric is going to put the lights where they are supposed to be and Robert Cotner of Robert Cotner Electric, Inc. is going to make them work.

"My dream, and Rodney Cobb, director of Parks and Rec, will scream, is that Sights and Sounds will eventually extend all along the River Walk so that people can just wander the whole river."

What made you think you could manage this project, I asked. With the intensity of a TV evangelist, Vicki replied, "I watched Kelly and saw that she had the structure in place. And the energy of this town is so great! When you see something like this take shape, you just want to be a part of it. It is such a thrill to see the lights go on...and stay on! There are so many opportunities in San Marcos to participate. Those who don't are really missing out. It is truly a two-way street. I look at pictures of families, kids, all kinds of people attending Sights and Sounds and the glow on their faces—it's just worth every hour of effort I put into it."

Maybe it is true that old actors never die, they just exit stage left. I asked what no one knows about her and she said, "Very few people are aware that I still do voice-overs for commercials occasionally. Once," she says, "I was the voice of a blouse in a soap commercial. That had to be the low point of my career."

Asked, if she had it all to do over…the actress surfaced once again as she did an almost perfect impression of Saturday Night Live's Garret Morris, "Beezball been bery, bery good to me" she responded with a hearty laugh. All these little bits have led me to where I am and I am happy. I would like to do more grandmothering. This is the second marriage for Jerry and me and we have six children between us. We have an 11 year old granddaughter in Pennsylvania and a year-old grandson in San Marcos."

For Vicki Fruit Sights and Sounds of Christmas is almost like another child. She would welcome your visiting the "child" she is nourishing this month. Your volunteer hours, your money or your talent are always needed and welcome. Her producer/director talent will put it to productive use.

Buddy Mostyn

It is 100 years old. Actually, it is more like 100 *million* years old. And for the last 30 years Buddy Mostyn has been the owner, operator, caretaker, promoter, and expander of Wonder Cave, the central attraction of Wonder World, a Texas Natural park.

Buddy was 10 years old when he came to San Marcos with his family in 1957. They moved here from Galveston where they owned and operated a number of souvenir shops on the piers and along the causeway. Hurricanes in the late 50's were primarily responsible for the family's move.

As Buddy says, "It was a family business. My uncle, my granddad and my dad were in the souvenir business together. Then along came the hurricanes and disrupted the family business—and the family.

"When we arrived in San Marcos, Wonder Cave was owned by the Rogers family. The Tula Townsend Wyatt collection contains an account of Mr. A.B. Rogers purchasing the cave from Judge Barger in 1916 for $50.00 and a gray horse and saddle.

"At the time we moved here, it was leased by Mr. Ralph Marker, an energetic entrepreneur, who built the Stuckey Stores, a once familiar sight along the highways.

"My father, T.J. Mostyn, was a buddy of Paul Rogers, son of A.B. Rogers. Texana Village at Aquarena Springs grew out of their close friendship."

When Ralph Marker decided to move on, T.J. Mostyn purchased the cave from Paul Rogers in 1958, and Buddy Mostyn began his 44 year association with Wonder World. Though T.J. died in 1967, Wonder World remained in the family.

Buddy remembers, "I began working here when I was eleven years old for twenty-five cents an hour. I probably made more money then than I do now. I have worked all my life at this business with the exception of two years."

The two year hiatus occurred after Buddy completed public school and college in San Marcos. He left the area for a couple of years.

Buddy describes how he came back to San Marcos. "After I graduated from SWT, I went to Houston with Reins Printing Company as an outside salesperson. In the early 70's, while I was in Houston, my mom and step-dad called and asked if I would like to buy the business. I told them I could do it only if they financed it. This December I will make my last payment to them on the loan. Next month I plan to present them with the check during the cruise I'm taking them on."

When I asked about the evolution of the park and the town, Buddy recalled his introduction to San Marcos. His family lived on Sycamore Street and cabins still stood on the banks of the San Marcos River in the Rio Vista area. San Marcos was a tourist destination because of the river, Aquarena Springs and Wonder World.

Beginning with its opening in 1903 and for the next 90 years, Wonder World and Aquarena were cooperative tourist attractions that helped put San Marcos on the tourism map. Wonder World's web site describes its early history. It was known initially as Bevers Cave and the owner, Mr. W. S. Davis, offered tourists a candle and a guided tour for 10 cents. Other attractions at the cave at that time included a medicine show and a tent that housed a South American anteater.

Buddy says, "Aquarena Springs and Wonder World operated almost as one. We advertised and promoted together. Those were the glory days of our operation. We had no competition. The huge theme parks did not exist, the water parks were unheard of and no one else had developed other natural underground attractions.

"People came to Central Texas for Aquarena and Wonder World and we were world famous. One of the pleasures of being in charge of an establishment that has been here 100 years is that I hear stories from families who represent the sixth or seventh generation to have visited the cave. They come here with their small children and tell me, 'Oh, I came here when I was a kid,' so I am happy to be a part of that. And I plan to be here another 100 years."

The cave was out in the country when it first opened as a tourist attraction, but today it is surrounded by family residences and suburban streets. In addition to the cave, attractions today include Texas's largest petting park, stocked with animals native to this area, notably white tail deer. The Tejas Observation Tower provides a panoramic view of San Marcos and the drop-off point of the Balcones Fault Line. The Anti-Gravity House provides a humorous optical illusion as a diversion for travelers.

In addition, Buddy has reached back into his family history and revived the souvenir business. He has a 6,000 square foot store filled with mementos, bumper stickers, silly hats and the like. It also contains a Mexican import shop.

"We had record crowds and continued to grow until about three years ago," said Buddy. "But now we are feeling competition from other attractions in the area. The outlet mall, the water park in New Braunfels, other caves in the area, and the big theme parks in San Antonio are taking their share of the family's entertainment dollar. We advertise as the most heavily visited cave in Texas and that is based on 100 years of operation. The best we can estimate, there have been about four million visitors to the cave since its opening in 1903.

"We get visitors from Mexico, perhaps as a result of the mall. We can conduct an entire tour in Spanish. It is recorded by a professional and provides a complete summary of the cave and the area.

"But the truth is, San Marcos tourism is changing," Buddy added. "Several factors contribute to this. Among those factors, the outlet mall is the most obvious, but the lottery, IH-35, and closing of Aquarena have changed the face of tourism in San Marcos."

Promotion of the cave has evolved from emphasis on pure entertainment to a greater push toward education. Since it is the only commercially operated dry cave in the country—a cave formed by an earthquake, as opposed to a cave formed by an underground water system—it offers a unique opportunity for students to study the earth's crust, earthquakes, and fault lines. The Wonder World web site (www.wonderworldpark.com) contains up to the minute information on earthquakes worldwide, it links to the international library of geology and it describes the Balcones Fault Line which runs from the vicinity of Ardmore, Oklahoma into Mexico. The web site averages around 1,100 hits per day.

One of the often overlooked contributions Buddy Mostyn has made to the San Marcos community is the number of high school and college students he has employed over the years. When I asked him how many he thought it might be, he escorted me to the souvenir shop and pointed to the ceiling. Dollar bills with names, comments and messages covered almost the entire area.

"I have been putting those up for the past few years," he said. "I don't have any idea how many are up there. During the summer, I will have a staff of 80 to 100 kids."

I confronted Buddy with a rumor that floats around San Marcos occasionally. I asked him about his reputation as an excellent racquetball player. "That is a lie," he responded adamantly. "That is a lie. I can beat Clarence Miller because he no longer has any knees, but I can't beat Wallace Dockall. Bill Taylor and I have been playing each other three times a week for over 15 years. At 14-14, he got the final point this morning, so I guess he is ahead of me. Anyone who can get up at 6:00AM is welcome to join us."

The Mostyns stay in San Marcos has not been without its trials. Their home of 23 years was struck by lightning in June 2000. As Buddy describes it, "A huge bolt of lightning struck the back of the house and in 18 minutes, it was gone. Everything in the house was destroyed.

"It was an event that changed our lives, obviously, but it also changed our lifestyle. We have a smaller place. I don't own a lawn mower or a weed-eater and I do lots of fishing."

Wonder World is truly a San Marcos Natural. Buddy Mostyn, for 30 years, has been the promoter, caretaker and protector of this natural treasure. While progress and technology is changing the face of our city, Buddy believes there is a place for history, especially history that can take us back 100 years or 100 million years.

Lisa Dvorak

She is petite. Her attire, gray turtle-neck and dark slacks, seems more appropriate to the design director of a major department store. Don't be fooled by appearances. When she makes eye contact, it is as if one is looking down the business end of a double barrel twelve gauge. Her piercing gray eyes and the intensity of her message get your attention.

Lisa Dvorak occupies the number two position in the San Marcos Police Department. Officially, she is the Assistant Director, Operations Division. As such she supervises the Patrol Division, Detective Division (investigations), Bike Patrol, and Parking Enforcement. Additionally, she manages the finances for the Drug Task Force. Twenty-three years ago she began her law enforcement career as a civilian on the lowest rung of the operational ladder. In 1977, she was hired by the San Marcos police department as a dispatcher.

Lisa explains, "I was beginning my graduate studies in sociology at Southwest Texas State. Though I was a graduate assistant, I needed a job that paid more. I was interested in law enforcement, even in high school, so I found a job as the dispatcher—now known as a telecommunications operator—on the midnight shift. It wasn't long before I found I could not work a full-time job at night and go to school during the day. The graduate program was really my second choice because SWT had no masters program in criminology at the time."

Lisa opted for her deeper interest, police work. It has been her consuming pursuit ever since. During the next three and a half years she worked as a dispatcher and strengthened her determination to become a police officer.

The silver badge was not handed to her on a silver platter. With no bitterness or rancor in her tone, she describes it this way: "I flunked my first physical test in 1979. I was very overweight and not in good physical condition. People in law enforcement depend on each other and you have to be willing and able to do whatever it takes to come to the aid of a fellow officer. Women in law enforcement at that time were a rarity. There just weren't that many."

Recognizing that it was and still is a traditionally male domain, Lisa explains, "It was hard to break into this male dominated business, especially when you look at my stature. People who were accustomed to seeing me in the role of dispatcher had lots of trouble seeing me in the role of police officer. So I left the department for nine months to get some distance and to get myself in physical condition."

Meanwhile, the police department came under civil service regulations. Lisa relates that Karon Guenther had applied many times to the San Marcos police department and had been told she would not be hired because she was a woman. However, once the civil service regulations went into effect, Karen was the first woman hired. Still, no woman had ever passed the physical test required by the department.

"One had to scale a six-foot wall as part of the test," says Lisa. "You had to have a lot of upper body strength to accomplish that. Women normally have less upper body strength than men, but I had learned to approach the problem differently. I determined I needed to use my entire body to get over the wall, especially my leg strength.

"I can still remember that moment, being at the very top of that wall, because I was the first woman to do that. I went over the wall and came back around to the other side. I had mixed emotions about doing it because there were some men who did not want me in the organization—being a woman, personality, whatever it was—they did not want me. They made that very clear. I had one person in the administration let me know directly that we already had one woman and we did not need any more."

Balancing that attitude, however, were a number of male officers who were supportive and welcomed Lisa as a full and bonafide member of the force. One of the more influential members of the hierarchy made it clear that all members of the department would be treated fairly, regardless of who or what they are. This gave her a chance to show what she could do and for two years she was assigned street patrol.

Lisa explains her feelings about patrol duty. "I loved working the streets. I tried to recognize the balance required to be a good patrol officer. There were situations that required strength and physical skills, but my goal was to use my communication and interpersonal skills to handle volatile situations. When the position of Crime Prevention Officer, a newly created program, was offered to me and I really did not want to do it. I had some notion it was a 'girly' kind of job to get me off the streets."

She laughs when she relates, "I can remember answering calls and seeing 'When are the real police going to arrive?' in the eyes of people at the scene."

Lisa recalls that one of her supervisors called her aside and told her to get her act together and go for the Crime Prevention job. He assured her she was not being 'put in a pigeon hole' and informed her she would be learning essential skills needed to realize her potential. It was in Crime

Prevention that Lisa learned community building, public speaking, grant writing, fund raising, and how to administer a program.

As she describes it now, "I loved that job. I gained skills that I would have never otherwise had an opportunity to learn. One of our larger accomplishments was the McGriff Puppet program. We managed to get a puppet in every classroom of K-6th grade in San Marcos. That took a lot of fund raising. We were one of a very few Texas cities able to accomplish this. We also did the Helping Hand program throughout the city—a hand decal on the rear view mirror of a vehicle indicates a safe haven for a child."

In 1986 Lisa was promoted to sergeant and got a new title, Crime Prevention Coordinator, where she supervised crime prevention activities, a juvenile officer, and worked in criminal investigations. From there she moved over to administration. Her skills were put to use on special projects, research, and community liaison.

Lisa's promotion to lieutenant came in 1989. "I was the first woman on the force to make lieutenant. I was in charge of Support Services Division. That job encompassed supervising records, communications, data processing, animal control, parking enforcement and building maintenance."

Sounds safe enough, but with a wry grin Lisa reminds me that she was supervising animal control during the SWT cat controversy. It was during this 'crisis' Lisa had to use all her communication skills to negotiate this political minefield. Seems an individual on campus who was particularly fond of the feline creatures had accumulated a veritable herd of Garfields by feeding them generously. They became a general nuisance to a large part of the citizenry. There was considerable debate as to who might or might not be responsible for their welfare or removal. It provided letters to the editor for a couple of weeks.

In a change of direction, Lisa interjected that in 1986 she attended a Psychological Profiling class and when she returned, she met with Karon Guenther, who along with Lisa, had maintained an abiding interest in San Marcos's most infamous cases, the Bertha Martinez case. It had all the elements: mystery, tragedy, pathos, suspicions, frustration, and futility.

Bertha was an eight year old girl who disappeared from her home. Her body was finally discovered only a short distance away several days after her disappearance. She was a victim of sexual assault before her brutal murder.

"We started from scratch," Lisa says. "We asked to work on the case on our own time. From the beginning we knew it had nothing to do with Lisa Dvorak or Karen Guenther. It was something bigger than either of us. We were being led by a force much greater than ourselves. We take no credit for solving this case. It was a God-driven quest where we pulled together everything we could find. We worked with DPS, the Wichita, Kansas police department, retired sheriff, Ed Richards, of Georgetown, Mike Wenk of the Hays County DA's office, and anyone who had any thing at all to do with the case.

"We became sick of each other, our families became sick of us, and we felt lots of frustration. We were consumed by the case. A case like this forever changes you. I reached a point where I had to say to myself, 'Get a grip!'"

Lisa says the Broughton family and Doil Lane had long been suspects. The case she and Karon constructed helped put the pieces in place when detectives from Wichita, Kansas arrested Doil for Nancy Shoemaker's murder. Even then it took a year-long investigation to tie the two cases together. Eventually, Doil Lane was tried in Hays County and received the death sentence for Bertha's abduction and murder.

When it was suggested to Lisa that her rise through the ranks was most remarkable because she had largely come up through the operational path, rather than the administrative path, her response typically gave credit to others. "Who I am is not only the result of efforts that I have put into it, but…it is also the result of other people in this organization and the mentoring and support they have given me. I have been afforded lots of opportunities and I've been fortunate to use them wisely."

Billy Moore

He looks like a former football player whose most recent workouts have been at the dinner table. He weighs over 300 pounds, but carries it well on a frame towering six feet seven inches. He is athletic, played a little college basketball. But do not let the frame and the bearing fool you. While he is a big man with big appetites, five minutes with Bill Moore and you are much more likely to compare him to Thomas Wolfe (yes, *the* Thomas Wolfe of Look Homeward Angel, etc.) than Thomas (Hollywood) Henderson, late of the Dallas Cowboys. (*If you will kindly move your great hulking frame away from the sink...* Thomas Wolfe, A Biography, Turnbull, p. 135) It doesn't take long to realize it is the size of his intellect and the heat of his passions that are much more interesting than the size of his body and the volatility of his moods.

"My Ph.D. thesis was that the influence of Marx, Freud, James Joyce, and Einstein changed not only the world we look at, but the way we understand the world we look at."

That is the way, Bill begins to explain why he is not an English professor today. Stay with me. This is a complex man, who under the prism of the interview has many more colors than ordinary light.

He was born, appropriately, in Littlefield, Texas where the view is from horizon to horizon and the space gives one plenty of room for expansive thoughts. It likewise provides an opportunity to visualize the world the way we would like it to be. At the time of his birth his mother lived with her mother.

Bill relates, "I remember my father walking up the sidewalk in 1945 in his sailor suit, home from the war. He opened his duffel bag and gave me a can of Planters Mixed Nuts and a pocket knife. I still have the pocket knife.

Our family from that point on became extremely tumultuous. My father was a world class alcoholic, a violent and angry man, and we moved and separated many, many times. (*Less cheerful were the memories of W.O.'s* (Wolfe's father) *rampage, of his distant lion's roar as he reeled home from the square, with his head held .high to keep from falling on his face....*op. cit. p 6.)

"On my tenth birthday my parents re-married. We lived in Littlefield, Pampa, Borger, Lubbock, Brownfield, Plainview—all kinds of places." (*It was an epic misalliance. Two people more temperamentally unsuited could scarcely be imagined.* op. cit. p.5.)

Work in the oil fields eventually took the family to Odessa where they stayed for about five years. By this time Bill was a teenager and the family was no less tumultuous. He was having major problems with his father. Their efforts at communication became bloody contests of survival.

"It was like I lived two lives. One life was at school where I was an honor student and where things were OK. The other life was at home where things were not so OK. I did well in high school and loved high school." (*From the outset, books and learning filled him with an almost sensuous delight.* op. cit. p.12.)

Bill's academic acumen, after a stint at a junior college, earned him entry to the University of Texas. However, he ran out of gas, literally, in San Marcos. Teachers and coaches in Odessa had planted seeds of awareness and curiosity about Southwest Texas State. Bill said, "While I was filling my car, I looked across the street at the majestic Sam Houston Oak and the cool freshness of the historic San Marcos River and said to myself, 'This will do.'

"I drove immediately to the gym and talked to the athletic director who told me to talk to the basketball coach, Vernon McDonald. He said, 'If you can stick, you can stay.'"

He enrolled in 1963 and finished his undergraduate work in 1965. In 1967, he completed his masters degree.

After teaching a year as a full faculty lecturer in 1968, Bill went to Louisiana State University to pursue a doctoral degree in English. After two years, he had completed all the academic work with a near 4.0 average. His dissertation became a matter of contention when his advisor questioned his ability to incorporate the intellectual diversity of Marx, Freud, Joyce, and Einstein into a coherent theme which could be understood by his dissertation jury. (*All creation is to me fabulous...experience comes into me from all points, is digested and absorbed...until it becomes a part of me.* From a letter from Wolfe to Margaret Roberts around 1929 when Look Homeward Angel was published.)

"After a major struggle and working two more years on the dissertation, I failed to complete it to the advisor's satisfaction and I finally gave up and returned to San Marcos. I worked three years at the Colloquium Book Store before Dean Oscar Dorsey came to me and said, 'I would like you to come to work for me half-time and spend half-time in English. I jumped at the chance.

"I walked into the classroom on January 20, 1979, spread out the student roster and five years evaporated like water droplets on a hot wood stove. Absolutely amazing to me. Remains amazing today."

I asked him to explain. As tears dripped like a melting icicle, Bill's voice took on a determined, almost urgent quality: "I was born to be a teacher, I was trained to be a teacher, I am bound to be a teacher. I am proud of the people I have turned out as a teacher."

In 1980 Bill became interested in city politics. Actually, it wasn't just an interest. It could more aptly be described as an uncontrollable passion, resulting from an out of control party which saw a multitude of young people urinating in front yards, disregarding private property and abusing the sensibilities of the community. "When one of them entered my front yard and leaned against my front porch and started to urinate in front of my mother-in-law, I carried this souvenir of my youth (he presented the bottom 20 inches of a pick-axe handle, filled with 10 inches of lead) outside and I was just about to jump over the railing when my wife stopped me. We called the police and they said there was nothing they could do. They were outnumbered."

In 1981 he was appointed to the Planning and Zoning Commission where he was chair for eight years. While a member of the commission, he was exhorted by a number of people to stand for city council.

By 1988 Bill was getting a great deal of encouragement, if not outright pressure, to run for city council. That year he ran, was elected, and served three 3-year terms on the council.

"In 1996," Bill said, "there were people who were asking me if I would be willing to serve as mayor. I discussed this with my superiors at the university. Their response was: We will never ask anything of you; we will never expect anything of you; we will never tell you to do anything. All we want to know is which hat you are wearing when you talk to us."

With a certain air of resignation and regret, Bill continued: "Much to my dismay that got lost in translation. There were a good many people in the community that objected to my doing both things because they didn't believe I could be objective.

"I was elected in 1996 and again, by a scant 39 votes, in 1998. I believe I could have run again and won. But I think another term, coupled with my full-time university job, would have killed me. The longer I served the more stressful it became. In the last year of my term, I had a job change, my mother died, and I had health problems. Further, I was willing to turn over the reins (or reign, if you will) to David Chiu because I think he is wonderfully qualified and passionately eager to lead us where we need to go in the most exciting time of our existence."

I asked Bill to describe his agenda during his term as mayor. Once again, a well of tears flowed as he began to describe, "a teenage female of an ethnic minority in a dysfunctional environment who finds herself

at a crossroads with a choice of dropping out of school to encounter all the pitfalls this implies or staying in school and becoming a productive citizen with hope. My agenda, then and now, is the training and education of those people. The bottom line, however, is education, and training for productive and sustainable jobs. Right below that is affordable housing. There are young people in this community who are renting and paying two-thirds of their income for housing. My passion lies with young people and giving them opportunities." (*He surprised his friends with sympathy for the downtrodden; already this stripling seemed Atlaslike in his assumption of the world's burdens.* op. cit. p. 19)

When Bill speaks of his passion, he speaks of it passionately. His feelings for San Marcos run deep. He devoted 20 years of his life to doing what he always believed to be in the best interest of San Marcos. His progression up the administrative ladder at SWT has not prevented Billy Moore from continuing to serve his passions—youth, volunteerism and the pursuit of knowledge.

John Navarrette

For a real live, walking around, in the flesh Horatio Alger story, one need look no further than the local telephone company. John Navarrette, the Area Operations Manager for the Texas Market of CenturyTel, epitomizes Alger's "bottom-rung-to-the- top-of-the-ladder heroes."

After two years at Temple Junior College, John with wife Chloe came to San Marcos from Belton as students at Southwest Texas State University. During his first semester, relatives informed John that the phone company needed temporary help delivering directories. That was in November 1975.

John relates that experience with a trace of awe and surprise as if he still has trouble believing the outcome.

"My aunt and uncle called and said the phone company needed student help delivering directories. I was just waiting for the semester to end, so I went to work. Back then, the directory was about 6" x 8" and contained about 40 pages. We scotch-taped it shut, put a mailing label on it and threw it in a mail sack. That took only a couple of days.

"Then they (the phone company) asked if anyone was willing to help the pay station collectors deliver directories to SWT dormitories, the hotels and motels and to Gary Job Corps. I was the only person who volunteered."

John's pay station collector and supervisor was a veteran of WWII who had bad knees. He did the driving and John did the loading, unloading, and delivery of the books. When the job was finished, his supervisor recommended to Mr. H.Y. Price, owner of the telephone company at the time, that John be hired permanently.

"I applied for a job and almost immediately after I was hired, I went to Texas A&M for a telecommunications course. The course was put together by the Texas Telephone Association," says John. "It included construction, climbing, installation, splicing, maintenance—just about every aspect of telephone technology."

John returned from training and began work as an installer. He recounts that often people around town remind him that he installed their phone. He also emphasizes that during this era, Mr. Price reinvested heavily to improve technology of the phone company. Without his (Price's) foresight and concern, the recent storms would have meant major interruptions of service and tremendous overtime stress on the staff to keep the city's phones in service.

John likes to emphasize that Mr. Price was always looking for ways to improve the San Marcos phone system through innovation, better servicing systems, and new technology. (I had to remind John that I was there to interview him, not learn about the Price family.)

"But I can't talk about myself without talking about 'who brung me,' he said. "I like to think I learned from him to be passionate about the community, putting the customer first and giving back," says John. "He did it in his own way through foundations and did not seek a lot of publicity. He was concerned that his employees had a living wage and that the less fortunate of the community had opportunities. He built some of the first low-income housing in San Marcos and from his foundation made it possible for many people to get home loans.

"Today, we are more open. We sponsor a great number of local activities. Since our parent company is in Monroe, La., many people think we are not local. Well, we are. San Marcos, Port Aransas and Lake Dallas are all separate and autonomous companies."

John's progression up the company ladder was largely through hands-on grunt work. After about a year and a half as an installer, he was given responsibility for telephone maintenance for all of SWT.

John says, "In that job I did it all. I installed all the phones on campus—offices and dorm rooms—and I did all the repair. I was responsible for the entire system. Of course, there were only about 10,000 students at the time."

After about a year, the company turned the system over to the University. At the same time in 1979, there was a vacancy at San Marcos Telephone Company for a supervisor. John applied for the job and in spite of competing with people with 15 to 18 years seniority, he was promoted. He gives part of the credit for his success to the managerial experience he gained while a full-time student at Temple Junior College.

John says, "I did retail outlets when retail outlets weren't cool. Right out of high school and while attending Temple Junior College full time, I managed three clothing outlet stores—that's when outlet stores were literally in the back of the factory. There was a store in Temple, one in Waco and one in Dublin. I think that experience was a factor in my selection for the installation/maintenance supervisor's job."

One morning in 1985 John says he awoke and realized he did not have a degree. Ten years had passed since he left school to work for the telephone company. He determined he would go back and finish his undergraduate work. Attending classes at night and whenever he could, he continued his full-time job while going to school. In 1987, he graduated from SWT with a bachelor's degree in business.

Upon graduation, a new job, Director of Operations, awaited John. "Mr. Young Price told me I was to be the Director of Operations. He said he was going on vacation, but that he would return and give me some on-the-job training. When I finished all my academic requirements, I reported to Jim Pendergast, then company president, that I was ready to begin my new job and I would like to go to work with Young.

"Jim said, 'Oh, he's not coming back.' I felt as if I had just left the frying pan for the fire. But I have always been a self-starter and easily motivated, so I jumped in. I supervised operator services, central office, splicing, installing, warehousing, and maintenance."

John continued as Director of Operations from 1987 to 1993 when San Marcos Telephone Company was purchased by CenturyTel. Following the tradition established by Mr. Price, the company introduced a number of innovations during this six year period. John points to the 911 system as an example. In addition to installing and operating the system, the company prepared a mapping system to accompany it, so that emergency services could locate the source of calls.

Technology changes were moving at a break-neck pace during the early 90's. San Marcos Telephone, to remain up to date, was installing the newest equipment and innovations, such as wireless and cellular communications.

In 1993 San Marcos Telephone Company was sold to CenturyTel. Again, John avows, Mr. Price had the community's interest in mind when he selected a buyer. CenturyTel was headed by a close friend of Mr. Price and he knew there would be minimum turbulence in San Marcos.

"A lot of our administrative and executive duties were absorbed by the corporation, but we have the same people in operations," said John. "Jim Pendergast and I helped with the transition.

"January 1, 1994 is a day that I will never forget. Jim called me into the office. I couldn't imagine why he would be calling me in on Sunday. He told me that he had decided to move on to other pursuits and that he was recommending me for Region Vice President."

Since that day John Navarrette has been extremely visible in the local community and the telephone community. He unquestionably learned well from his Price family mentors. John is as intense and concerned about doing *good* in the community as he is about doing *well*.

He has been a board member of the Texas Telephone Association since the early 90's. Twice he has served as president.

His involvement in San Marcos encompasses the entire range of civic activities. John has been active in the Chamber of Commerce, serving as chairman; served on the Economic Development Council; the Small

Business Council; the Central Texas Higher Education Authority Board; and the Bobcat Athletic Foundation. His involvement with SWT athletics includes sponsorship of the CenturyTel/SWT Bobcat Classic Basketball Tournament.

He is one of the founding members and former president of the San Marcos Education Foundation, a non-profit organization that provides scholarships for students to attend SWT. Other boards on which John sits include: The SWT Development Council; Wells Fargo Community Council; Gary Job Corps Community Council and the telephone company supports Students In Free Enterprise.

John and the telephone company and employees support the Price Senior Center, bought and donated by Mr. H.Y. Price, by volunteering time and talent to modify, improve and maintain the facility.

Space restrictions limit my elaborating on the full extent of John's and the telephone company's involvement in community affairs. For more than 50 years the telephone company in this city has been an essential public utility, striving to provide the best possible service. It has also been a source of major community improvements.

John closed this interview with the following: "Each morning, I say to myself, 'I want to give something back today, I want to learn something, and I want to treat others the way I want to be treated."

Horatio Alger could not have created a better hero.

Barbara Tidwell

"I hated it! I hated to retire!," said Barbara Tidwell, who founded the Strutters and directed them for 38 years. For those of you who arrived in San Marcos yesterday, the Strutters are the world-renowned Southwest Texas State University dance team. Formed in 1960, they have performed in seven states, 18 foreign countries, 22 times for the Houston Oilers and made the cover of Newsweek over the last 40 years.

Barbara Guinn was a little East Texas girl from Rusk, born at the beginning of WWII, for whom a trip to Dallas was a major undertaking. Her early ambition was to go to Kilgore Junior College and be a Rangerette.

"They were the first dance team in the country and they had a big impact on my life," she says of the Rangerettes. "The director was a fabulous, dynamic lady, but it was the choreographer, Dennard Haden, who influenced me more than anyone. He taught me how to choreograph. He taught me showmanship and, though I didn't know it at the time, he prepared me to do my life's work."

Barbara finished two years of college at Kilgore Junior College where she taught with and for Mr. Haden before she went to the University of Southern Mississippi in Hattiesburg. After finishing her degree in history at USM, she embarked on a teaching career in the public schools. She grew disillusioned with teaching in the public schools when she discovered that not all high school students had the same passion to learn history that she had to teach it. Reared in the era where professional women could pursue nursing, teaching, or clerical work, Barbara decided she might find more attentive students at the college level, so began her quest for a masters degree in history.

After applying to several schools to enter their masters program, she was interviewed by Dr. Flowers, the president of SWT, when he noted her extensive experience with dance.

"Our football games were not too well attended," says Barbara, "and he wanted to increase attendance with some half-time entertainment. In addition, he wanted a group on campus who could entertain visitors and who he knew would represent the school well.

"I had no intention of making San Marcos my home. Nor did I intend to teach dance for 37 years. I wanted to get my masters degree and this way I wouldn't have to ask my parents for help.

"I arrived on campus in August of 1960 and in September we performed at our first football game. We had no money. We were as poor as Job's turkey. Dr. Flowers gave me a condemned gymnasium for work-outs. I drafted a few injured football players who liked to girl-watch and they scrounged some lumber and made our first props."

Barbara recruited her first girls at a student body assembly. At that time the whole student body would fit into the auditorium. According to Barbara, almost every girl in school tried out for the dance team. She spent the short weeks available eliminating those who could not walk and chew gum at the same time, teaching a few basic dance steps, a low-high kick, and how to line up in formation. Her first team of Strutters was made up of 67 energetic and dedicated young women. And, oh yes—she eliminated gum-chewing among her dancers.

"I gave Margie Martin, a fantastic artist, an idea of what I wanted in the way of uniforms and she put it on paper. One woman made the first uniforms for us. She farmed out some of the sewing, but we were still sewing buttons on our home-made uniforms one minute before our first performance.

"Our first year was magical. Today, there are drill teams everywhere, but in those days, there were, at most, small drum and bugle corps or pom pom squads, so I had no talent coming to me out of high school. My girls were largely from tiny Texas towns. They had never performed. However, today, probably every town in Texas, no matter the size, has provided me with a girl, or I have gone there as a teacher. Name a town, no matter how remote, and I can tell you a story about some girl from there.

"It was great. We went to Washington, D.C. for President Kennedy's inauguration and we went to the Sugar Bowl. It was the first time Southwest Texas was represented at that level."

Barbara is also responsible for the name of the dance group. When asked how she chose Strutters, she explained, "I didn't want to have anything with 'ettes' on it, because I didn't want to copy anyone. I didn't like BobKittens—not for me. There were two or three songs that emphasized the 'strut' or 'strutter' and there was an old tune used in twirling schools, called The Strut, and I just liked the name, so I chose Strutters."

The sound-track from the movie Giant is the signature tune of the Strutters. Every time they have gone on a football field, that tune has played. Why? Because Barbara liked it. Her unique stamp of individuality and independence does not end there. While the school colors are maroon and gold, the Strutters, during her years, wore red and white.

"Mr. Haden, my mentor at Kilgore drummed into my head to use bright colors for showmanship, so, I chose red and white. Maroon and gold are wonderful colors, but they are not good show colors. The Board of Regents had to approve everything I did and I told Dr. Flowers, I had to do it my way. He said OK, and got it approved. He wasn't too keen about our short skirts, but he went along with us."

SWT almost lost Barbara to Angelo State University. The president of ASU visited the SWT campus and was so impressed with the Strutters, he invited Barbara to come to Angelo State for a lot more money. Speaking of money, Barbara relates that her beginning salary was $87.00 a month.

When ASU offered her the job, she was preparing to marry Howard Tidwell. She says she had a choice of leaving SWT for a lot more money or staying for not much money and marrying Howard.

Since she was the first Strutter director, where did she fit into the academic scheme of things? "The first 19 years, I was in the music department. The second 19 years, I was in the athletic department. The salary was never that great. After a few years, I formed a company called Half-Time USA and what a lot of people never knew is that great deal of the money from that company went to buy props and to cover other expenses of the Strutters.

"I got hooked on kids. I loved them. I loved my kids and about the mid-70's I started working more on the girls than I did the team. I saw more and more girls having more and more troubles. Many times I probably had no business doing what I did, but I took my responsibilities seriously. I tried to provide a well-defined structure for those young women. On trips, I checked their rooms and they better have wet hair. Once on an overnight ferry while going from Russia to Sweden, I stayed up all night checking the girls' rooms. There were so many good-looking young Swedish and Norwegian males on the ship, I was afraid to go to sleep. I checked rooms every 30 minutes.

"Another time in Nice, France, our hotel was full of good looking young men and I let the history teacher in me handle that situation. That evening, I loaded all the girls on buses and took them for a late night tour of Cannes. The girls were furious with me."

Did you ever have a routine completely unravel, I asked. "We made mistakes, but I never had a complete failure. The girls knew what to do when they went on the field. We would begin rehearsals around 3:30 PM and it was often near midnight when we quit. They gave up lots of time and holidays to perform for the University. When we performed for the Oilers, it was always Thanksgiving and for years, I never had a Thanksgiving break.

How did you come up with a new routine each week? Barbara said, "The best thing I did was patterns. The girls were all over the field. I watched old movies and searched all over for ideas. To this day, I dream about patterns and where I am going to put each girl. We had no way of drawing them out and giving a copy to each girl, so I taught each routine from the platform. I can't tell you how many platforms I have fallen through."

Barbara is extremely proud of the Strutter Alumni. among their number are women who have become CEO's of national organizations, women who have become doctors, lawyers, mothers, and teachers. Some may be waitresses, she says, but you can bet they will be a good one. She is quick to point out that dancing was never the primary goal of her work with the Strutters.

"I wanted my girls to be well educated. I wanted them to be able look someone in the eye, smile, shake their hand, and say something meaningful. We have a Strutter network all over the nation and they are more than willing to help each other.

"From August 1960 to July 1997, lots of little girls. Lots of tears and lots of sad stories. A lot of happy stories. I have nothing but fond memories."

Angus McLeod

"As an educator, I think it is important that we teach kids the great choral music and bring them into that art form. That should be the core of the program and then we can bring in the musicals. When I was in the Fort Worth area, the musicals seemed to be the core of the program instead of choral music." This, from Angus McLeod, the man who has produced 19 Broadway musicals over a 27 year span at San Marcos High School.

In spite of the fact that he is producing the last musical of his 27 year career at San Marcos High, Angus exudes the enthusiasm of Mickey Rooney's character in the old B movies when the solution to every problem was 'let's put on a show.' Bye Bye Birdie will be performed at San Marcos High January 25, 26, 27 and February 1, 2, and 3.

Before we get into the musicals, probably the most visible part of the choir program, it is important to hear Angus discuss 'great choral music.' Using visual art as an analogy, he says, "It is as if you could walk into the Louvre, take a Mona Lisa off the wall, go to the National Gallery and take a Picasso, then get a Rembrandt and share them with a group of 15 and 16 year old students and talk about lines, faces, shadows and all the things I'm sure visual artists talk about. Well, great choral music is like that except it is a temporal art form. Every performance is different.

"Great choral music for me is that which speaks of the greatness and goodness of human-kind…like any great art."

Before you conclude that Angus is a musical snob, he hastens to add that there is greatness in all forms of music. Our pop culture has produced wonderful tunes, he says, but there is good music and bad music and as an educator, it is important to help young students understand both.

"We often have to hook them with the more popular music, because that's where they are, to lead them to the great."

So, when did he become interested in music and decide he would teach high school choir? "I grew up in McAllen, Texas where we had a strong program. Our choir director was a national figure in choral music. We went on five to ten day tours, sang at national music conventions as far away as Colorado Springs, CO and St. Louis, MO. At that time, all we did was the high brow sort of stuff. About the time I was a sophomore in high school, I knew what I wanted to do."

Angus came to San Marcos in 1975 and, as a 25 year old teacher, two years out of Texas Christian University, took his current job. It was a few years before he produced his first play. According to Angus, he followed an excellent choir director and it took him awhile to work through the reputation established by R.B. Doyle and feel confident that he could put his own mark on the department.

He began small. His first play was You're a Good Man, Charlie Brown in 1979. With a cast of five or six, he double casted to get at least 10-12 students involved.

"One of the things you can do with a musical," says Angus, "is draw in those students who are not into the classical choral music. You can captivate those who are into the pop, light stuff, or the dance, or the visual, or the drama of the show. That's the beauty of the musical. It combines all of these art forms. It allows the kids to cut loose and entertain and be entertained."

Angus diverts the conversation to recall some of the summer musicals produced by the San Marcos community in the mid-80's. While he performed in a number of them, he says he felt like an apprentice to Ron and Marie Jager. It was from them that he learned to build sets, to do stage design, and to direct diverse talents.

I wondered how he chose his material. "I stick to the well-known, popular musicals which almost everyone knows. The kids would love to do Grease, but it would be difficult to re-write and eliminate all the dirty words. Second, I want a large cast. I want as many kids to be on stage as possible. I want those kids to experience the magic of performing. It is a delight to watch the kids experience that for the first time.

"Most people single cast a musical, but I almost always double cast. To double cast is insane, but that is how I get my kids on stage."

To verify his insanity, he showed me his January calendar. Beginning January 4th, it shows no days off for the entire month. I mean, there are no free Saturdays or Sundays. The earliest any day is scheduled to end is 6:00 PM. Most are scheduled until 9:00 PM and a few do not end until 11:00 PM.

To further complicate his balancing act, there is no time set aside during the school day for rehearsals, set building, lighting, or staging. It is an extra-curricular activity. And no school money is used to fund the productions.

As Angus points out, "I start all my shows with zero money. For example, Fiddler on the Roof cost us $15,000.00 to produce. I have to generate all that income from ticket sales. We pay for the sets, the lights, the programs...the myriad of expenses involved in doing a show. The students must provide their own costumes as well.

"What makes all this possible is a lot of parental help. There are parents who spend hours and hours building sets, painting, helping us with lights.

Some will spend up to 400 hours helping us get ready. I even have some parents working nights until midnight, who have no kids in my show—not even in my choir program. Their kids have graduated, but the parents just stay involved."

I pointed out that his department and those involving the arts are often the first eliminated when the financial crunch hits. Angus agreed and voiced concern that the recent mandate for 30 minutes of physical education for each child would cut into time available for music and art programs.

Angus points out that the choir and the performances, including the musicals, are major public relations activities for the entire school district. "There will be 3,000 to 4,000 people who see Bye Bye Birdie over the coming weekends," he says. "It isn't as if there were 14,000 fans watching a football playoff game, but we do touch a lot of people."

While Angus is as committed to his program as a nun is to her vows, he also recognizes priorities. He has lost star performers to other academic demands. He points out that graduating and getting the diploma is the first consideration. Second, he wants to help them to understand and enjoy music.

"But, like any teacher, my job goes beyond that. I have an obligation to teach these kids about life. Teaching kids how to appreciate, how to define, how to plan is part of that. Through music, I teach teamwork, dedication, and the pleasure of doing a thing to the best of your ability and then to be happy with what you have done."

I wondered about students with exceptional talent and their eventual destiny. Angus turned the question around. "My pleasure is getting those students who do not recognize they have outstanding musical talents. In fact, they may have many talents. I can think of kids who have gone into music as a career, but could have become heart surgeons. The other side of that is the kid who could have gone into music, but chose another field. Two in that category have PhD's in nuclear physics. But they still retain their love of music and performing."

Angus reflects that, perhaps, he could have gone to another place and enjoyed a different level of success, but, "The kids here are so special, so unique. They are wonderful, hard working kids who want something of quality. They are just great kids. They are the reason I have stayed so long."

This may be his last year, but Angus McLeod's passion and heart will fill the San Marcos High choir room and auditorium stage long after his body has departed.

Jake Sullivan

It is that time of year when the mail bags get heavier, the lines at the post office get longer and the route carrier is still making his rounds as darkness settles. The holiday season involves a lot of heavy lifting, figuratively and literally, for postal workers. Jake Sullivan spent 39 years doing a lot of that heavy lifting.

J.C. Sullivan was born in San Saba, Texas in 1923 where he lived until his senior year in high school. His mother passed away when he was just more than two years old. The family then lived with his grandparents until Jake came to San Marcos to live with his brother, and finish high school. In 1940, he enrolled at Southwest Texas State.

Jake is a part of the rapidly vanishing "greatest generation." After attending SWT for two years, he and three friends left college in January 1943 to join the Marine Corps. One of those friends, coincidentally, was Patty Sherrill's older brother, Malcolm. More about that later.

Jake was assigned to the 4th Marine Division after boot camp. The division was shipped to the Marshall Islands where after extensive combat, the division returned to Hawaii to retrain before deployment to Saipan.

On July 1, 1944, Sergeant Sullivan was leading a patrol on Saipan when a Japanese sniper opened fire, hitting Sullivan in the chest. According to Jake, "It was a bullet from the sniper, but I had my rifle in front of me (I don't think you need to put all this in the paper, Jake cautioned.) and it took everything he fired. It saved my life. Nothing went through me. My lung collapsed and I was evacuated for a 10 month stay in the Naval Hospital in San Diego."

His wife interjected that the shrapnel is still in the lung and they must inform medical personnel what they are seeing every time Jake has an X-Ray.

By Christmas of 1944, he was well enough to be granted leave from the hospital. He returned to San Marcos for two weeks and during that time, Malcom's mother invited Jake for dinner.

"I had been in their home a lot with Malcolm and knew the family intimately," said Jake. "After a lovely dinner and a pleasant visit, I noticed Malcolm's little sister, Patty. She had grown up while I was gone.

"I invited her to go to the show with me—which was the only thing to do in San Marcos at that time. She made every kind of excuse in the world why she couldn't go with me. Finally, her sweet mother said, '*You...go to the show with him.*' And that was our first date."

Jake returned to the naval hospital to be medically discharged in May of 1945. From December to May, there was lots of mail going between San Marcos and San Diego as Jake and Patty cemented their relationship by correspondence.

Upon returning home, Jake sought to reestablish old ties. One of his passions before the Marine Corps was the San Marcos Volunteer Fire Department. Lew Haynes was the Fire Chief, as well as the Postmaster. He was one of the first persons Jake visited.

Jake relates, "He suggested I come into the post office to help him out. Most of the young men were still in the service and Mr. Haynes could not get enough help. My plan was to go back to college, but he insisted I work until the fall semester began. That was the beginning of my postal career."

So, in June of 1945, Jake began his 39 year association with the Postal Service. He tosses out a few facts. First class stamps were $.03; air mail was $.08; and Jake's part time wage was $.65 an hour. The post office was open from 8:00 AM to 6:00 PM: Saturday was just another workday and the only day of the year that the post office was completely closed was Christmas Day: clerks arrived at work at 5:00 AM and the last clerk stayed until 9:00 PM. Though there was no window service on Sunday, box holders received mail on Sunday.

"Our mail came by train," said Jake, "and we had eight passenger trains a day. Each train had a mail car with clerks aboard, working the mail. The mail was picked up from the depot before 5:00 AM. Clerks then sorted and routed it properly. All outgoing mail was postmarked in San Marcos. We hand stamped a lot of it."

There were three star routes out of the San Marcos post office. One went to Martindale, Staples, Fentress, Prairie Lee, Luling and Gonzalez. The second star route went to Maxwell, Lockhart, Lytton Springs and Dale. The third star route included Wimberley, Fischer Store and Blanco. Mail was delivered to and picked up from those post offices. They then sent mail out by carriers who served the rural routes.

"At that time," says Jake, "we had four city routes. People who lived on those routes had door delivery. There was no such thing as a mail box out by the curb. We also delivered mail to the university dormitories."

Jake never made it back to college. "I found great satisfaction at the post office. I knew all the guys, most of whom were volunteer firemen, and I loved the work. When September came, I thought I would just put off going back to college for a year. The post office was good to me and on October 19, 1946, Malcolm Sherrill's little sister, Patty and I got married."

Over 22 years, Jake rose from a part timer to clerk, to superintendent of mails, to postmaster. When he was appointed postmaster in 1967, Jake was an anomaly among postmasters. The job was a political plum, handed out by successful politicians to supporters or contributors. The postmaster did not have to know anything about the postal service. This practice went all the way to the top. The job of Postmaster General was normally awarded to the successful presidential campaign manager.

"When Mr. Haynes retired, Patty insisted I submit my application and Mr. Haynes encouraged me and recommended me to Representative Jake Pickle. With a lot of luck and a lot of help from my friends, I was named Postmaster."

Reflecting on the way things used to be, Patty and Jake showed me a picture of the post office where Jake began. The picture shows a classic example of Spanish Renaissance architecture. "With today's emphasis on restoration and preservation, it would never have been torn down," said Patty.

"State Bank and Trust (now Frost Bank) wanted that location badly," said Jake, "and so, in 1960, we opened the new Federal Building and demolished the old post office and the bank built on our old location. Those palm trees were there when the post office was there. They have probably been replaced several times."

I asked how he managed the Christmas season while he was postmaster. "The main thing we were interested in was giving service to the customer. I made sure all our windows were manned all the time and our customers didn't have to stand in line. I had outstanding employees who knew our mission was to serve the public.

"The area behind the windows was all open and I spent a lot of my time back there observing. If we needed to reinforce the window staff, we put somebody up there.

"Today, however, they have so many customers to serve. This town has grown so much in the past few years and almost all the business still goes through the main post office. We need another post office or we need a larger one."

Patty interjected that Jake still gets calls from friends who have a complaint about the postal service. "It doesn't matter that he hasn't been there for 18 years," she said.

One of Jake's proudest accomplishments is that his post office made money every year. "I didn't have a year that we didn't pay our own way."

I asked if, in light of email, UPS, FedEX, faxes, etc., post offices would become obsolete.

"I don't think so," Jake said. "People are always going to need to send letters, invitations, thank you notes and other personal items. We will always have a need for the post office."

Jake Sullivan's latest accomplishment required all the courage, tenacity, and stamina that he exhibited as a U.S. Marine and San Marcos Postmaster. In July of 1999, Jake was diagnosed with cancer of the bladder. To get a second opinion, Patty and he went to M.D. Anderson Hospital in Houston. Surgery was performed and aggressive chemotherapy was initiated.

Following the surgery and treatment, Jake visited the hospital every three months for check-ups. In May, 2002, he was told he was all clear and that he was not to return for a year.

"That was the best medicine they could have ever given me."

Jake Sullivan is an icon of The Greatest Generation. about which Tom Brokaw writes: "They came of age during the Great Depression and the Second World War and went on to build modern America—men and women whose everyday lives of duty, honor, achievement, and courage gave us the world we have today."

Kathy Morris

"Daddy was killed in an automobile accident when I was eleven," Kathy Morris said shortly after we began this interview. "Mother, who had just survived cancer, was left with a two year old, an eight year old and an eleven year old. I was the oldest, so you can see that it all fits."

Kathy was referring to her compulsive personality, "…which I work on all the time," her need to be busy, and her natural gravitation toward responsibility.

She related that her grandfather came to San Antonio from Savannah, Georgia in 1918, went into business and settled his family there. She graduated from Alamo Heights High School and came to Southwest Texas State Teachers College in 1965.

In 1968, she met Randall and they were married in 1970 when she graduated from SWT, a university by this time.

"It never occurred to me that we would not go back to San Antonio when he graduated. Initially, we lived at Clear Springs apartments, then bought a small house on Moore Street and in 1975, we bought this home on Belvin Street.

"Randall had a masonry and construction business until 1980 when he sold it and went into real estate. And here we are."

I reminded her that she skipped a few chapters.

"After getting a degree in sociology—there was no social work degree at SWT at the time—, I went to work in Austin for the Texas Department of Welfare, now Department of Human Services," Kathy related. "Then, I took a job with Urban Renewal here in San Marcos. My job was primarily helping families relocate from sub-standard housing to more desirable housing. Many were moving out of the flood plain to safe housing. I put the families in touch with social services to which they were entitled, medical facilities for example. I did social work until 1974 when I had my first child, Christopher."

I asked how she became so deeply involved with the Scheib Opportunity Center.

"It was a time of de-institutionalization of mentally ill and mentally retarded from the state hospitals and state schools. Nicci Harrison, Eleanor Crook, and Dr. Leland Burgum began an effort in earnest to create something concrete with a bequest left by Dr. and Mrs. Scheib. At the same time, Josephine Mann and Joyce Bostwick were providing mental health services through the county health department from the courthouse.

"There was an emerging need for a place to provide services for mentally handicapped adults. At least, we needed to provide a day care so that parents could have some relief. Urban Renewal had houses. So, I became involved. The first Scheib Center was on Cheatham Street. Later we acquired land on Georgia Street and moved two buildings down there and patched them together. At that time, we combined mental health and mental retardation."

Kathy continued to work with the Scheib Center as a volunteer long after she left Urban Renewal. She also became involved in other social service organizations. Early and mid-70's was a time of huge drug awareness and she was involved with the establishment of the San Marcos Drug Center, which became the Crisis Hotline. She also became active in the Interagency Council and helped put together the city's first social services directory. She was also involved with the formation of the Heritage Association and the Bi-Centennial Committee.

As Kathy searches her memory for her contribution to organizations that have contributed so much to San Marcos, she is quick to laud the contribution of others—Frances Stovall, Nettie Serur, Helen Van Gundy, Tula Wyatt.

"I continued to work on a number of boards and commissions," Kathy said. "In the mid-80's I was appointed to the Central Texas Higher Education Authority (CTHEA). In 1987, CTHEA became involved with the city in a disagreement about the use of the Authority's funds. We were in a major battle with the city, there were a number of things happening with the government that we didn't like and the economy was tanking.

"San Marcos was in a state of decline. There is no such thing as 'growth v. no- growth.' You have growth or you have decline.

"We were having a Belvin Street luminaria party at my house when Bill Crook showed up with "Kathy Morris for Mayor" bumper stickers. I took the bait and ran for mayor and was elected in 1988."

What was it like, being mayor?

"It was great fun," she said. "I had experience interacting with city, county, state and federal government through my volunteer work and I had experience with the bond market through CTHEA. I knew about those funding levels and I knew about intergovernmental relations and I enjoyed all that stuff.

"I ran for mayor because I found myself being very critical of the city government because of the CTHEA experience. I have always believed one is either a part of the problem or a part of the solution and one has to get in there and try to make a difference if one is to be a part of the solution."

Kathy says that about a week into her decision she began learning more about the processes of government. She was looking at businesses leaving town. She was asking why no new businesses were coming to town, why was our tax rate high and what was wrong with our tax base?

"With the help of some very good people, we identified our mission, we identified our goals and we moved forward. Our city was not diversified, we had no growth, and people were not working together.

"Basically the city as a government is responsible for certain health and welfare issues of its citizens Those include water, electricity, sewage, garbage, traffic, fire and police. Extras include libraries, community centers, park land, ambulance service and other amenities a city may enjoy."

Kathy said her initial goal was to upgrade basic city services. The city faced a water crisis. Surface water was acquired from Guadalupe Blanco River Authority (GBRA). She worked to upgrade the fire department and the police force. Traffic lights were added. Utilities were upgraded by the purchase of our power source.

What vision prompted building the Activity Center, I asked.

"The same thing that brought about the library," Kathy said. "We had a real need. We did not have a meeting space large enough to accommodate our requirements. Our basketball courts were all outside and in dangerous locations. We needed a year round swimming pool and we needed a pool which could be used by adults.

"We began upgrading the parks. Certainly we had a wonderful staff, but it is council that sets policy. Councils and school boards are generally volunteers and, at times, it is hard for others to realize the responsibility of policy setting."

Should [the volunteer status] change, I asked. "Absolutely not," according to Kathy. "It makes a lot of sense to have volunteers. It was always important to me to pick up the phone and call someone or talk to someone on the street or in the coffee shop and get input on matters of public interest. It is possible to become so focused on an issue that one forgets to ask others.

"It is especially important to get input on unpopular decisions. Many people won't agree with what you are doing. Many still disagree with some of the decisions we made, but our goal was to meet the basic needs of the majority."

What will be your legacy as mayor, I asked.

"Oh, who knows? Well, we have a crackerjack wastewater system; a great water distribution system. We expanded the tax base and provided lots of jobs. I don't know what my legacy is."

As mayor how did you deal with SWT?

"I was mayor only a couple of months when President Hardesty left. Mike Abbott, the acting president, and I met frequently. When Jerry Supple came in, he and his cabinet met often with me, the city manager and staff. We had a spirit of cooperation and certainly tried to keep open lines of communication."

What was it like after you were diagnosed with breast cancer?

"Hard! I was diagnosed in the summer of 1993 and started chemo in September and continued to summer of 1994. I ran for office in May of 1994 and it worked out fine. I managed to schedule everything around my treatment. It was hard and I got very tired.

"The cancer was a blessing and a curse. It is a gift that keeps on giving. It is a blessing because it forces you to face your mortality. When you do that, you begin to make decisions about how you want to live your life. Most of us go through life thinking we will live forever. Once you accept the reality that you might die, you get your house in order, but you also look at ways to live. I made up my mind I would survive, but if I didn't I was going out in a blaze of glory. You realize there is so much to do—for your family, for yourself.

What about the curse?

"It is scary! The situation is frightening and uncertain. No one will give you a definite answer. Am I going to live? Maybe. Am I going to die? Maybe.

What is the future of San Marcos?

"It lies in the education system. But it will continue to grow and prosper, and..."

Kathy Morris has a great deal more to say—and do. About a lot of things. Space precludes our including all of them.

Jack Fairchild

Some would describe Jack Fairchild as a pesky gadfly who pokes around in stuff and tries to raise a stink. Others would describe him as a conscientious, determined, intelligent watch-dog of our precious natural resources. It depends on where you are on a given issue, especially if it concerns the San Marcos River.

Jack is a former navy fighter pilot; has a PhD in aeronautical engineering; has designed an airplane which has been accepted by the famous aerial pioneer, Burt Rutan; has built his own airplane; and has been instrumental in effecting change in Texas laws affecting effluent dumped in our rivers.

In an off-hand manner and with the beginning of a mischievous smile in his eyes, he explains his long love affair with San Marcos and its river.

"My great-grandfather came to San Marcos from Canada in 1873. I trace my family back to the Pennsylvania Dutch. It seems during the Revolutionary War they were Tories, and so the outcome of that affair caused many of them to move to Canada. My grandmother was born in San Marcos. She married a building contractor and moved to Austin where they lived north of the university at 2009 Avenue B, which was considered way out of town. But they had trolleys that ran out that way. Light rail was in vogue in those days.

"My mother entered the University of Texas about the time World War I started. She met my father there. He was a Connecticut Yankee whom the army had sent to the university for ground school to prepare him to fly airplanes in the War. She was also a 'river rat' who always enjoyed the San Marcos River.

"The story I heard is that after they left the university, my father was in the insurance business in Houston, but my mother refused to move to Houston with him until he reassured her she could spend summers in San Marcos. So, every summer we would come to Rogers' Park—it is Rio Vista Park now. There were about a dozen screened cottages on the river and we leased one every summer. All the cottages had names and ours was called Rio Vista. Because of gas rationing and other difficulties associated with traveling during WW II, our last summer to stay in San Marcos was 1942.

"I spent all the summers of my youth on the San Marcos River, swimming, fishing, exploring. That's how I came to know and love San Marcos and the river, and it has always been my favorite place."

Jack went to the University of Texas for one semester before joining the navy in 1945. He volunteered for flight training and was trained as a carrier pilot. In 1950, as a money-saving measure, the navy decided to discharge a large number of pilots. He was in the separation center, just hours away from discharge, when the Korean War erupted. His squadron was ordered to Korea. The squadron commander pleaded with those soon to be discharged to volunteer for a six month extension.

Jack says, "Being young, eager fighter pilots, we all extended our tour. We went to Korea in August 1950 aboard the carrier, *Philippine Sea.* We flew close air support and interdiction missions for the army and marines as they moved north to the Yalu River, then all the way back to the Pusan Perimeter.

"After Korea, I went back to school at the University of Texas and got my degree. A job with Bell Helicopter in Dallas followed. At Bell, I worked on what was to become the Huey helicopter, the workhorse of the Viet Nam war. Later, I moved over to Ling Temco Vaught for a few years until I heard that University of Southern California was looking for someone with military experience and an engineering degree to teach aviation safety.

"It seemed a good opportunity to get a master's degree and earn a living at the same time. At about that time the army aviation program was getting cranked up and they offered to send me through helicopter training at Fort Rucker, Alabama. After completing their training, I returned to USC. I found I was beginning to like teaching, but I knew if I was going to continue at the college level, I would need a PhD.

"The opportunity to teach and get my PhD came at Oklahoma University. I was there for four years. When I finished my degree at OU, I went down to the University of Texas at Arlington to initiate an aeronautics department. I established the first program for a degree in aeronautical engineering at UTA."

Jack spent 25 years with UTA from 1964 to 1989 when he returned to his favorite place, San Marcos. Among the highlights of his tenure at UTA were his selection as a Visiting Professor for a year at the United States Military Academy at West Point and his designing and building an airplane as a teaching aid. It was constructed from original design. This was no model from a pre-fabricated kit.

During his stay at UTA, he followed his mother's pattern and spent as much time on the San Marcos River as work and other obligations would permit. He made up his mind he would buy property on the river, and in 1979 he was able to do so.

"I initially wanted to build a summer cabin, sort of a temporary thing we could use on our vacations, but now that we had the property, I began to think that maybe I would want to retire here, so why not build something a little bigger.

"It was a family project. The kids, my wife, Marie, and I built it. The only thing we did not do was pour the foundation. We sawed every board and drove every nail."

Jack's involvement with the San Marcos River Foundation began shortly after he started building his house.

"We met a few people when we started building the house and we heard they were thinking of starting a River Foundation. This is around the mid 80's. In 1985 the River Foundation was formed and I became a charter member. But over the next few years I never heard anything from them. No newsletter, no activity, nothing. I guess it really wasn't that active. Oh, the Heritage Association, the Lions Club and some of the interested citizens had supported it financially and we had a board of directors, but nothing was happening.

"I attended my first meeting of the Foundation after I retired in 1989 and opened my big mouth to complain that I had not received one communication from the group in four years. At which point, I was immediately made the editor of the newsletter. I later served as president for five years.

With a seriousness a bit foreign to him, Jack explains, "We had several issues. First, we didn't think there was enough river awareness in the town, so we initiated River Awareness month as a public education program. And then the Foundation people began to get educated on the river. Old timers would tell us they used to be able to see fish in water 10-12 feet deep where, at the time, you could not see one foot below the surface. Most people dismissed it as 'that's the way the river is.'

"We began looking into the situation and we could see the yucky stuff being put in the river at the city waste-water plant, at the Gary Job Corps discharge and at the state fish hatchery. A little bit of inquiry led us to places where effluent pollution levels had been reduced 20 to 40 times less than we were experiencing in our river. Chesapeake Bay in Maryland had lost the crab industry due to pollution and they had to come up with a solution. We figured if they could, why can't we?

"In 1993 or 1994 the city wastewater plant was coming up for certification renewal with Texas Natural Resources and Conservation Commission. We saw they were applying to continue dumping their garbage in our fragile and pristine San Marcos River.

"The Foundation had been told there was no way to successfully affect the city's application; that they would eventually get what they wanted. We knew we didn't want to organize a bunch of protesters, and make a bunch of signs and go around shouting and screaming. At this point my scientific and engineering background came into play. We began measuring water quality in the river. We also contracted with Professor Groeger at SWT to do a river impact study of the waste-water plant.

"The city got their permit approved, but we had enough data, we thought, to file a protest and demand a public hearing. The TNRCC granted our hearing and to get the city's attention, the Foundation hired Bill Bunch, a well known environmentalist attorney. We even went so far as to investigate the computer models TNRCC was using in arriving at potential damage effluent will have on a given river. We looked at their variables and data, much of which was assumed and so we decided to get real data. When we provided the TNRCC with real data of the river, the outcome was significantly different than their original model showed. The commission finally approved a permit for the city waste-water plant that seemed to meet standards which would allow the river to flourish.

"The upshot of all this is that after much haggling, and wrangling with different figures and standards, the TNRCC has begun to require waste-water to be four times cleaner than it was in the mid 90's."

Jack concludes by saying, "We found that to get a seat at the table it is sometimes necessary to be the bad guys and protest the things that are not right."

Though Jack is 'around 70' years of age, he is as dedicated to his causes today as he was ten years ago. It is reassuring to have a person with his brains, energy, and determination protecting one of the greatest resources of our home-town.

James Polk

James Polk's neatly trimmed gray beard gives him the look of a professor. But he has not always haunted the hallowed halls of academe. He has served his apprenticeship in the band halls of segregated high schools, he has experienced the wall of open hatred that blocked the path of a black person; he has spent months at a time on the road with an international music star. He has been a trailblazer and a pioneer—not always by choice.

The accident of birth that stuck him in the 60's generation also thrust him to the forefront of change in a number of instances.

James grew up in Corpus Christi, Texas where he graduated from high school in 1957. Following graduation, he immediately went into the army and served two years. After his military obligation, he enrolled in Huston-Tillotson College in Austin.

"I graduated with a degree in music in 1962," he said, "and, at that time, there wasn't much for a black kid to do except teach school or some sort of sports. I taught school.

"My first teaching experience was in Elgin, Texas. The schools were segregated and I taught at Washington High in Elgin for six years," James related. "In 1968, the school administration decided to integrate the high schools. I knew this would happen, eventually and so I had talked with the band director at the white high school and we agreed that he would retain the high school band and I would teach the middle school and the two elementary schools.

"He was around 60 at the time and he knew he would be there for only a couple more years and I would then move up to the high school. But when integration came, I was fired. They said it was duplication of effort. Then they hired another band director—a white man."

James admits that earlier, he might have been a bit outspoken and assertive for a black teacher—somewhat ahead of his time. At the black high school, there was no field where his band could practice precision marching routines. After coordinating with the white band director, he took his 50 or 60 black kids up to the white high school football field to practice at night under the lights.

In James' words, "All hell broke loose the next morning. My principal called me in and told me I couldn't do that.

"I'm 22 years old and hot-headed and full of energy and I said, 'what do you mean?'

112

"He said, 'They don't want you up there.' At that, I marched right up to the superintendent's office.

"I pointed out that we were part of the school district and I had permission to use the field. The superintendent said the town didn't want that many black kids up there at night. I stood my ground and said we use the football field at night or the district provides facilities for my band to practice.

"The very next morning, workers from the city of Elgin were at the vacant lot behind the black school digging holes to put up light poles.

"I didn't have a football field, but I had lights. I used string to mark the intervals in the vacant lot and when we went to state that year, we were recognized as a number 1 band. Those kids had never experienced that."

From Elgin, James sought a drastic change in scenery. He went to Bedford, Massachusetts as the director of the music program for Rodman Job Corps Center. IBM had the franchise for the job corps where they taught data entry. Under the terms of their franchise, James was an employee of IBM.

"I had a small band and a choir and we went up and down the east coast, putting on shows and promoting the job corps program. Many of the small job corps like this one closed, but it was policy of IBM that they did not lay anyone off, so in 1969, I was offered a chance to go to work in the just-opened IBM plant in Austin, Texas."

For James, that was like throwing Br'er Rabbit into the briar patch. He had a home in Austin and was eager to return. However, the transition was not glassy smooth.

"The pay scale in Bedford was so much higher than Austin that I was making management level pay when I came back, but they weren't going to make me a manager because they didn't have any black managers in Austin.

"I became a production analyst making more money than my managers. The result of that is that I got no raises for over three years. Finally, the salaries began to level out and the next promotion out of production was buyer. Well, they eventually had to promote me, so who do you think was the first black buyer for IBM in Austin?"

After 10 years with IBM and a divorce, James was sitting in his cubicle one day and decided he couldn't stand his job. The walls were closing in. He was not playing music. He quit.

He sold his house, took his severance pay, along with his savings and for eight months, he played golf. Every day.

He finally took a happy hour job playing piano to remain solvent. The money was not terribly different than the money at IBM.

"One day I got a call from a friend with whom I played in the 60's," James said. "He was with Ray Charles in San Antonio and they would be playing the Country Dinner Playhouse in Austin the next night. He invited me to the show. After the show, I met the bandleader and gave him my name and number.

"A couple weeks later, my phone rang and Cliff, Ray's bandleader, said they fired the piano player, would I like the job? He said someone would get back with me.

"Monday morning, just before I left for the golf course, the phone rang. It was Ray Charles and he offered me a job immediately. I said I would have to give notice, but two weeks later, I joined Ray Charles in Valley Forge, Pennsylvania. I stayed with him for 10 years. This was in 1978. I came back to Austin in 1988.

"During that period, I not only played, I did a lot of the arranging, and conducting. We did studio work when we weren't on the road. I wrote, arranged and conducted his entire Christmas album."

In 1989, James enrolled in graduate school at SWT and fulfilled a promise made to his mother years earlier. He obtained his masters degree in music in 1991.

To discuss graduate school, we need to flashback to 1963 to James' initial effort at obtaining a masters degree. He decided to pursue that worthy cause while teaching at Elgin He enrolled in, then, Texas A&I during the summers, and found himself, in his words…"the only black spot in the entire music department. No black person had even gone through the undergraduate program and here I am in graduate school.

"I had a rough time. I was trailblazing and it was during the height of the civil rights movement. There were people dead set against integrating white schools.

"My major professor taught a course in classical music. Our class notes had to be turned in at the end of the semester and he announced that if they didn't weigh a pound, he did not want them. He brought a scale to class. I knew mine had to be two pounds. They had to be typed and organized in book form.

"After several weeks of attempting to get my notes back from the professor, I went to the dean of the graduate school. He wasn't much help, but when my notes were finally returned to me, the prof had scrawled an 'F' across the front. He told me they were too well done and therefore, I must have copied from my classmates.

"In an education course, the professor called me a nigger in class. His excuse was that he was trying to prepare me for integration and let me know what it would feel like when someone used that word with me. In another education class, I had to write two term papers. Even though I turned in the first paper the third week of the course, the professor held it until the fifth week of the six weeks course to tell me it was unsatisfactory—because I had not alluded to 'supervision' enough. I had to write another 35 page term paper in the last week of the semester."

At that point, James decided it wasn't worth it. Getting a masters degree was like wading in molasses. In 1963 white people did not want a black man educated in a white college.

James now speaks enthusiastically about the Jazz Studies program at SWT. He points with pride to the fact that he is now a teacher at a university which, 40 years ago, he could not have attended as a student. He also holds an honorary doctorate from his alma mater, Huston-Tillotson. However, he assured me racism is alive and well, perhaps just more subtle these days.

I asked about highlights of his travels with Ray Charles. "Being nominated for a Grammy Award. Ray Charles was nominated, but it was all my arrangements."

What's it like working for Ray Charles? "Bittersweet," he replied. "Ray Charles is a perfectionist and demands that everything be right. The only thing that Ray Charles can not do is see. I learned a lot from him."

James Polk is a teacher. He has been a trailblazer and a pioneer. He has waded through lots of molasses so that those who come after will have a somewhat easier path. He is walking the walk to help Martin's dream come true..."[We] will not be judged by the color of our skin, but by the content of [our]character."

Lewis Gilcrease

Dear Mrs. Fricks:

. . . . .

Lewis is the type of boy we are looking for to attend this school Mrs. Fricks. Mr. Meyer speaks highly of him from the standpoint of character and his ability to make his work in school. I am convinced that he has definite possibilities as a college basketball player and track man.

. . . . .

This scholarship will pay his tuition and fees, room, board plus $7.00 a month...

This scholarship will continue as long as he makes his grades, which I know that he can do, or unless he becomes a case for the dean to discipline for violation of college regulations, which neither you nor I fear will happen.

The above is excerpted from a letter written by Milton Jowers May 21, 1949 to Lewis Gilcrease's mother. It should be noted that the day Lewis worked out for Coach Jowers in pursuit of an athletic scholarship, he had to hitchhike home to Woodsboro, Texas.

Ten days after coach Jowers' letter, Lewis wrote back:

Dear Coach Jowers,

I am sorry about my delay in writing to you about my attending San Marcos, but I wanted to think it over.

I have decided to attend San Marcos and to take the full scholarship you offered me. If I would participate in basketball and track.

I will try and do my best in athletics and keep up my other work.

With the exception of two years military service, four years coaching in McAllen, and four years to complete his dentistry training, San Marcos has been home to Lewis Gilcrease since the 17-year old high school graduate responded to Coach Jowers.

"I was born in Bayside, Texas, near Rockport," said Lewis. "Because my parents divorced when I was quite young, I lived a great deal of my school years with my grandmother out in the country. I rode the bus 18 miles one way to school each day. When I was in about the third or fourth grade, my mother and grandmother took over the school lunch room in Woodsboro. They ran the school cafeteria until I graduated."

Lewis explains that Coach Meyer, his high school coach, became something of a father figure to him, so athletics was a huge part of his high school years. Just as Coach Meyer coached all sports, Lewis played all sports. While he was captain of the basketball and football teams, his talents went well beyond the athletic field.

He was also president of his senior class, received the All Around Student Award, and was elected King of the All-Stars of South Texas basketball for his academic and leadership achievements. He was a class officer throughout high school as well as assistant editor of the school's first yearbook.

"My senior year we went to the state tournament in basketball and lost to Big Sandy. But I remember during that year, we lost our own tournament to Bishop. We played them later in the regional championship game and beat them 50 something to 35. It was my night. I scored 36 points. More than the opposing team. It was exciting.

"It was an exciting career and Coach Meyer turned me on to SWT because he was a graduate of SWT. My mother wanted me to go to Abiline Christian, but they did not offer me a scholarship."

At Southwest Texas, Lewis was an all-around athlete, playing basketball, football and track, but basketball was his first love. His 24.8 points per game for the 1952 season is still a record that is now 50 years old. In four years of freshman and varsity basketball, his team never lost a home game. In three years of varsity play, the team won 78 games and lost seven. All losses were on the road. Two of those losses were in the national tournament in 1952.

In 1953, they were 21-3. Lewis says, "We lost one game in Kansas City, one to Lamar Tech one to East Texas. East Texas won the conference, but we beat them in Bobcat gym the last game of that season. They went to Kansas City and won the national championship."

When Lewis graduated in 1953, he was subject to two drafts. As an All-American basketball player, the Boston Celtics of the NBA drafted him. The US military also had designs on his service. He elected to pursue a masters degree and remain in ROTC while he took a teaching job in Prairie Lee. He taught every subject to the seventh and eighth grade. There were 15 eighth graders and 10 seventh graders, all in the same classroom. He coached six-man football, girls and boys basketball, and took six hours of work toward a masters degree. After practice, he took the kids home if they needed a ride. He earned $24 hundred a year.

The next year, Lewis taught at Luling and coached the basketball team. By now, he had a 2d lieutenant's commission in the Air Force and in 1955, he was called to active duty at Victoria, Texas. He served two years as a special services officer.

Upon his discharge from the military, Lewis took the basketball coaching job at McAllen High School where he taught and coached for four years. Lewis' high school coaching record stands at 143-36.

While at McAllen, Lewis attended summer school in preparation for dental school. "I always wanted to go to dental school, but I couldn't see how I could get the money and I thought you had to have Latin to get in. I didn't think I could ever pass Latin. Then I found out it wasn't required."

He accepted his appointment to the University of Texas Dental School in Houston only after turning down an offer from Coach Jowers to coach *football* at SWT. With wife, Linda (Cliett) teaching, and Lewis working part time, he made his way through school. By 1965 when he completed school, they had two of their three boys.

Lewis and Linda returned to San Marcos to establish a practice. With all his accomplishments to this point in life, one might expect that Lewis would be content to quietly pursue his dental practice and kick back. One would be wrong.

Among his first efforts to give back to the community was his election to the San Marcos Consolidated Independent School District Board. "That was the biggest mistake I ever made, "says Lewis. "People wanted me on the board because they thought I could get things done. Then I was criticized because I had too much control of the board. We got a lot done, but my dental practice suffered by almost half."

His nine varsity letters at SWT may be what he is best known for, but Lewis Gilcrease has been a quiet star in this community for many years.

"Four of us founded the Bobcat Club in 1971. It was something that we needed. And the University eventually took it over. In 1970, I was president of the SWT Alumni Association and have been on the board of directors since 1966."

He has also been a deacon of the University Church of Christ since 1971. Lewis was a founding member and chairman of the board of Balcones Savings Association, now Balcones Bank. He was a long time member and one time president of the Rotary Club. He continues to serve on a multitude of boards, foundations, and associations. His honors are too numerous to list, but when asked what is important to him, Lewis replied, "My religion and my family."

His success as a father deserves recognition. He and Linda have three boys, Greg, a dentist who practices with Lewis, Glenn, a science teacher in New Braunfels, and Gary, an M.D. in Austin. They also have five grandchildren. Linda says, "He is still an all-star. He is a better grandfather than he was a basketball player."

Carol Powers

The billboards outside San Marcos proclaim "Paper Bear, a Texas-size Gift Shop." With that introduction one might expect to find a continuation of advertising bravado such as the garish banners of a used car lot, along with an inflatable gorilla atop a building festooned with signs suitable for a roadside snake farm. And one could further stereotype the owner as a loud, overbearing, purveyor of Texas Tacky memorabilia.

Nothing could be further from reality. Paper Bear is an 8,000 square foot understated emporium of the most serendipitous merchandise found under one roof in the state of Texas. And its owner-creator is, likewise, a major departure from the imagined stereotype. Carol Powers' shy smile, soft voice and deep blue eyes belie the entrepreneurial mind behind this San Marcos landmark.

Lest you believe Carol is kicking back and surfing on the wave of her financial success of the last twenty-three years, I should report I found her in a red apron, hoisting a huge box of candles from which she was stocking shelves.

Carol describes her early childhood as the unlikely combination of military brat and a farm girl. "My father had a career in the air force and when he retired, during my early teens, we moved to a farm near Mexia, Texas. That is where I graduated from high school. I rode the bus to school; we had cows—the whole bit."

Paper Bear may have had its embryonic formation when the farm girl received a degree in art from the University of Texas in 1971. More about that later. It was also during this time that Carol met Leo Ellis, a musician to whom she would be married for thirteen years and with whom she would have one child, Melody. She confessed she met Leo while hitch-hiking. With her penchant for understatement, she remarked, "Things were a lot different in those days."

Following graduation, she went with Leo to Mississippi where she discovered a practical application for her art degree. She began making jewelry and pottery and selling it to supplement the family income. In 1977 Leo's parents, who lived in San Marcos, became ill and she and Leo moved here to look after them.

"That's when I decided to open the store. Actually, I couldn't get a job. Nobody would hire me, so I thought I might set up a small outlet for my jewelry and pottery. I think maybe, it was all just meant to be," Carol said with diffidence.

Carol laughs gently, and with an inflection of disbelief, expounds on how Heartworks, the precursor of Paper Bear, came into existence. "I couldn't get a loan. I thought I needed at least $200.00 to start and no one would lend me the money. They wouldn't lend money to women back then. Leo was able to get a $400.00 loan and promised me $200.00. We were trying to rent our first store (the present location of WesRay's restaurant). During the negotiations, Leo became very impatient with the way things were going and we were about to walk out when Jory Vanderburg, a freshman at SWT who was also negotiating for the space, came over and asked if I might be interested in sharing the space with him. He was looking for a place to sell Hawaiian jewelry made by his mother. I took his phone number and said I would get back to him."

She and Jory worked out the deal and Carol, artist that she is, could not have designed a better arrangement. Jory went to class in the morning and ran the shop in the afternoon. Carol took the morning shift and spent the afternoons with Melody. "It was a great partnership. When he graduated, he just left his part of the store with me."

For those of you who think it is easier to drive the streets of Nuevo Laredo in an eighteen wheeler than to sidle down the aisles of Paper Bear, listen to Carol's description of Heartworks. "You had to come in sideways. Actually, it seemed no one could get in. I remember people sort of stood at the door and looked. We were so crowded we thought we would limit our stock to Texas handmade items. Then a lady wanted us to sell custom-made greeting cards. I thought, 'I need to call her and tell her not to ship the cards because they will never sell.' They were a radical departure from Hallmark and others and they were like seventy-five cents each—nobody's going to pay that for a card. But I procrastinated and it's a good thing I did. The order came in and they sold really well. That got us started thinking about other items."

Though Heartworks grew and evolved into Paper Bear, Carol did not let success destroy her naiveté about business finance. In 1987 when she met David Powers, an accountant, he was appalled at the financial operation. At that time she was keeping all the bills in paper bags. She had a storage area full of stock with no inventory and it took a week to write all the checks by hand. In fact, David put the first file cabinet in her office.

"It's a good thing he came along when he did. We decided to incorporate about that time and David helped with that. He put us on the computer. I hired a lawyer and an accountant, but David set up our business operation. Oh, and we got married a couple years later."

Carol laughed when she recounted the creative way in which she financed the early operation of the store. "When I would go to Austin to buy stuff I would write a check and it would take a week for it to clear the bank, so I would go to the bank just before I thought the check would clear. You could do that with sales tax money as well. The taxes were collected on a certain day and you could use the tax money to buy stuff. But those were the good old days. The bank people were so sweet back then. I would go a whole week before I could get over to make a deposit. I would get a call from one of the clerks, 'Carol, you better get over here and make a deposit. Your account has no money in it.' The first year I was incorporated I couldn't pay income tax because I had no money in the corporate account. The banks would not loan the corporation money even though I had money in my personal account. They wouldn't let me pledge my own money, so my mom paid my corporate income tax."

Carol delights in laughing at herself when she reveals that, "I have been used as an example by the SWT business school as how not to run a business."

Asked what she gets out of coming down to the store six days a week after 23 years of success, she replied. "It's fun, it's still fun after all these years. I get to go out and buy everything I ever wanted to buy. Satisfies my need to go shopping. The displays are fun because they are sort of an artistic outlet. And I really like to make people happy. It is so cool. We try to keep a fun environment."

Carol recounted that people seem to enjoy coming into the store. Many have told her they come to relax and to find peace. She says she has observed many people coming into the store to pray. Carol's own spiritual persona permeates every nook and seems to hang as heavily in the air as the aroma of the ever present incense.

The store in its growth and evolution has never lost its uniqueness. It is the tangible statement of Carol, the artist. She has taken the diverse materials of commerce, brushed them with loving strokes of innocence, talent, creativity and hard work, made order out of chaos and constructed her masterpiece. Paper Bear is no less a work of art than a great portrait, a stunning sculpture or an architectural classic.

Mark Burroughs

"I don't want people to judge me for what I can't do. I want to be judged by what I do." That is Mark Burroughs' answer to my question concerning his limitations. Mark suffers from retinitis pigmentosa, a degenerative eye disease that has left him blind. It soon became apparent that Mark seldom thinks about what he can't do.

He is a special education language arts teacher at Goodnight Junior High School. The immediate image that came to mind was a chaotic classroom populated by a dozen behavioral problems who have learned, over time, to be extremely manipulative. To handle this special challenge, we put a blind man in charge. Whoaaa!

Mark, whose father completed a career in the Air Force, was born in Dover, Delaware in 1962, and lived in various locations around the country, as well as Europe. He finally put down roots in Geronimo, Texas when his father retired there in 1971.

He graduated from Navarro High School in 1980 and began college that summer at Southwest Texas State, but after a couple years, he decided college was not for him and left the academic setting to go to the oil fields in Luling. A number of jobs, most of which involved truck driving, followed his stint in the oil fields.

"I was diagnosed with the disease when I was about 12 years old and I knew I would eventually go blind. It has a genetic component and so I was not surprised. At this point, it is a little like looking through a cheese grater which is constantly moving. There are lots of holes in what I perceive. So much of my vision depends on lighting and other circumstances."

I asked why, as a blind man, he wears glasses. "If I take the glasses off, there is not a whole lot of difference," Mark said. "I wear them because they make me look stately. In addition, I have scratched lots of lenses, broken them on tree branches, and had other incidents, so the glasses are also a safety measure for me."

I noted that he appeared to be looking at me and making eye contact. "The glasses help me focus and so I will always wear glasses for the comfort of other people," he said. "I try to maintain habits I developed as a seeing person. Even when reading Braille, my posture indicates I'm reading the page. When I feel a strain on my back and neck and I try lifting my head, and I have trouble reading the Braille. It is just ingrained.

Mark's sense of humor emerges when he says, "Some people have commented that I act so natural, I must be faking some of the blindness. To those, I say, 'Thanks, let me borrow your car.'"

By 1990, Mark was married and knew he would have to quit driving. Using money he saved as a truck driver, he decided to return to college and pursue a degree in speech pathology. When he began his undergraduate program, he could still drive himself to campus and see well enough to keep up in class. By the time he started his masters program, he needed help from Disabled Student Services at SWT. His sight had deteriorated to the point he could not see overhead projections and writings on chalkboards.

So, what does one do when blindness occurs in adulthood? "I went to a training facility in Austin called Criss Cole, to learn how to be blind. I spent a couple weeks there 8 1/2 years ago. They provide counseling and mobility training to people like me. The last time I drove a car was in 1993 when my daughter was born. I drove her and my wife home from the hospital."

Mark's bachelor degree is in speech pathology, but after working temporarily in the field, he found he did not get to devote the time he wanted to with his students. He decided to teach. He found the Career Alternatives in Special Education (CASE) program at SWT. It seemed to offer just what he was searching for. After a little more than a year of intensive study, he earned a masters degree.

His first job interview was with the principal of Goodnight Junior High. A screening by the special ed committee followed and Mark was hired. Seven years later, he is still teaching there.

"I am responsible for 39 children with learning disabilities in language arts," Mark said. "I try to fill in all the gaps in their education because learning disabilities means one doesn't learn as easily or in the same way as other children. My job is to motivate them so that they are not disheartened when they have small setbacks. With my intensive training in the CASE program and follow-up training, I am well qualified and I think I make a difference."

The chaotic classroom returned to my imagination and I confronted Mark with my view of this group of kids who have been teased, rejected, ignored, berated, side-tracked and left for hopeless by others. "My approach to teaching my students is to keep them engaged; keep academic learning time as high as possible. Don't give them a lot of time off to be distracted. I get a lot of students who have what I call the 'resource syndrome.' Not much has been expected of them, so my approach is to try to put myself out of business. I push them as hard as possible. I am the last stop before high school where things will change drastically."

Mark pointed out that he has two years to work with the kids and his goal is to get every one of them into mainstream language arts. He uses every technique he knows to accomplish this and that goes for discipline as well. He says some of his students will often make the mistake of thinking that because his eyes don't work, his brain doesn't either.

"I can hear," he says, "and I have been around awhile, so sometimes the kids will accuse me of faking my blindness when I catch them sneaking a snack or acting out in some subtle way."

His job is to motivate kids to learn, but what motivated Mark to be a teacher? "While dating Debbie, she said one day, 'You want to go to work with me?' She teaches hearing impaired children and I saw the difference she was making and I was impressed. She started me on the road to becoming a teacher."

What's the hardest part of the job? Without hesitation, Mark responded, "The paperwork." He explained that his aid helps prepare a great deal of the administrative paper work and that he barters services with other teachers to get assistance.

At this point Mark began a demonstration of some of the technology he uses to do his job. First, he demonstrated a closed circuit television that enlarges the print of an ordinary document. In addition, he is working on a conversion to Braille for his own files and papers. He is looking forward to a computer program that will print text and Braille simultaneously.

At that point, he demonstrated his talking computer. As he began pulling up programs, his computer orally identified each one. Then as he began typing, the computer spelled each word aloud. He corrected his text as rapidly and accurately as I do as I look at my mistakes on the screen.

This article would not be complete without paying tribute to Demitri. Demitri is a beautiful blond with the personality of a saint. Demitri is patient, loving, obedient, responds instantly, and never wants to control the television clicker. Demitri is a Golden Lab who is Mark's guide dog. He and Mark got together this past summer in Morristown, New Jersey at Seeing Eye, a facility for matching guide dogs with people.

Mark explains that the Seeing Eye program was a positive experience. Not only did they treat all their clients with exceptional respect, they emphasize the need for the seeing-impaired to maintain their own dignity. He pointed out that they go to great lengths to match animal dispositions with human personalities. The training with Demitri took about one month.

OK, so Mark Burroughs is a great example to those who have suffered significant physical impairment. He is making his own way with minimal help. He, with wife, Debbie and daughter, Katy, have created a beautiful family. End of story? Not quite.

As Paul Harvey is wont to say, "Now for the rest of the story."

Mark is the lead guitar and singer with a country band known as Most Wanted. They play about once a month at some of the larger dance venues in this part of the country. The band took a year off recently and returned to performing about 3 months ago.

Mark writes songs and says, "I guess my dream would be to sell some songs on my CD—in production—and be able to stay home or go to Nashville occasionally and record music. My real goal is to be a song writer."

Don't be surprised if one day you hear Willie Nelson or Garth Brooks announce that he will do a number by a new songwriter named Mark Burroughs. Nothing has stopped him yet.

Allyn Gill

Gill's Fried Chicken store on Hopkins Street began as something of a challenge. It might also be used as an example of how not to go into business. But then, Allyn Gill, owner of that store and similar stores in Big Spring, Sweetwater, Snyder, Kyle, and New Braunfels has never followed the beaten path. He has often taken the road less traveled. And by his own admission, there were times when he had no idea where that road led.

Allyn was born on a ranch in Coleman County. The closest town was Whon which is now as extinct as the homing pigeon.

His great grandfather was a Confederate soldier in the Civil War and was twice a Union prisoner. He came to Texas with Allyn's grandfather almost immediately after the Civil War and eventually settled in Coleman County in 1899. They were pioneers in the development of polled (hornless) Hereford cattle.

As Allyn describes his early life: "I was born on the ranch and lived there until I was 11 years old when I moved to Brownwood to live with my grandparents to go to high school. From the ranch it was too long a bus ride and when it rained, which was rare, the roads were so muddy the bus couldn't make it. The high school was 19 miles from our house.

"My grandmother and my mother were school teachers and since I was the first grandchild on either side of the family, I can't remember when I wasn't being schooled by one or the other.

"They couldn't wait to get me in school. So, at five, I started the first grade. There were only six kids in my class and after one day in first grade, I was moved to second grade. I was terribly bored there and since I was sitting in the same room with the third graders, I found I knew more math than the third graders. All through school I was by far the youngest, the least mature and frailest kid in my class."

After graduating from Santa Anna High School at 15, Allyn went to the University of Texas where he encountered a whole new world. In 1943, there were 4,400 students at UT and 3,300 were girls. The first year, he studied and made his grades. The second year he pledged a fraternity. It was there he got on the fast track learning about girls and parties. His grades plummeted and the university invited him to take some time off.

Allyn's father rented about 1,000 cultivated acres of the ranch to local farmers who seemed to be making lots of money growing milo.

Allyn said, "I talked my dad into leasing me 300 acres on which I imagined I would get rich quickly. I went in debt to buy tractors and all the necessary equipment. When it came time to harvest the milo, I found I had more Johnson grass seed than milo. I was way pretty deeply in debt and in the meantime, I had married Besse.

"Two of my brothers-in-law worked for Phelps-Dodge Mining in Arizona," Allyn says. "They invited me to come out and assured me I could work for the big copper mining company.

"That's where I got my real education," he said. "It was tradition that the newest fellow hired would be Dr. Nat Aribiter's assistant until the next new guy came along. He was a researcher from New York who had been crippled by polio. I was told he had a terrible personality—cantankerous, over-bearing, impatient, and impossible.

"He was an absolute genius—no question about it. For some reason he and I got along perfectly. I worked with him for three years on a process to recover a greater percentage of the copper from the ore. I had a chance to leave, but we got along so well he wouldn't let me go and I really didn't want to leave. I have never seen such a brilliant man. We did all sorts of experiments involving hydraulics, pneumatics and physics. I learned electronics, surface chemistry, and extractive metallurgy as I worked for him."

Allyn and Besse moved back to Texas in 1951 to assist his father with the ranch. Registered cattle were popular with ranchers at that time, but marketing was crucial to a good sale and the telephone was a necessity for the business.

"We still had the old wooden telephone box hanging on the wall," Allyn said. "For a long distance call, the operator in Rockwood would tell me to come to Rockwood (10 miles) or go to Santa Anna (20 miles) and call the party back. I made two or three trips a day sometimes to talk on the phone.

"That's how I became involved with the Farm Bureau and the REA in developing a rural phone system. From 1952 to 1955, we managed to buy out eight small telephone companies and consolidate them and create a rural system. We were able to get our first dial equipment installed in 1957. So, I was in the phone business for 12 years."

As a small phone cooperative executive, Allyn became active in the General Independent Telephone Companies Association. As such, he became deeply involved in state legislative matters. It was through this work that he met and came to know intimately Mr. H.Y. Price, former long-time owner and operator of San Marcos Telephone Company.

"I developed a real affinity for the telephone business," Allyn said. "I wanted to buy a phone company, but could just never find the right situation. One day Mr. Price invited me to come to San Marcos and look at his company. He said he wanted me to develop a computer company to support the commercial aspects of his phone company.

"I didn't know what a computed looked like," Allyn related. "But Mr. Price told me I could learn. He told me to pick out a school, and take as much time as I needed to learn computers and he would put me on full salary immediately."

Texas A&M had the program he needed. It took a special provision to get Allyn into graduate school because he did not have an undergraduate degree. However, he not only got in grad school, he had an office next to the university's main computer. He would spend as much as 20 hours a day running programs.

"I took the heaviest load of classes that had ever been taken," Allen said, "but I still did not get a degree. Mr. Price asked me to come back to San Marcos early to take over the commercial operation of the company because one of his key employees was threatening to quit if he introduced computers."

Allyn has yet to get a college degree of any type, but he did return to San Marcos where he formed Teledata Corporation and San Marcos Telephone Company was the first client. Teledata was housed in a telephone company building, but did business with other clients.

His first computer used mark-sense data cards and Allyn says it was considered a giant computer. It was a giant only in physical dimensions. It had eight kilobytes of memory. His was the third computer in San Marcos. Texas State and Gary Job Corps computers preceded his.

Allyn operated his computer company for 30 years. One of his early accounts was a small building supply company from the Galveston area. When he got their account, they had five stores in Texas. That company was McCoy's Building and Supply Company, now with over 120 stores throughout the southwest.

Back to Gill's Fried Chicken. Allyn and Gil Rainosek, owner of Gil's Broiler, have been friends for years and it was habit for Allyn to eat frequently at one of the local chicken establishments. He often bragged to his friend, Gil, about the quality of the establishment's chicken.

Apparaently Gil took this as something of a challenge and invited Allyn to join him for some chicken he had prepared at the Broiler. Allyn was so impressed, he immediately suggested they open a store and go into the fried chicken business. They formed a partnership and after several missed opportunities to get a suitable location, finally settled on the current Hopkins Street location.

After several months, the business was not doing particularly well and with two people sharing its meager profits, neither was overly enthusiastic about the progress. They had a buyout arrangement and so Allyn told Gil (are you confused, yet?) to set a price for the business. When Gil presented Allyn with what he thought was a fair market value for the store, Allyn decided to buy it.

Allyn says, "I don't know what happened, but within two months the profits started going up and it has become quite a successful business. I continued to look around the state for other locations and found the West Texas area was sorely lacking in good fried chicken places."

Allyn Gill is well beyond the normal age of retirement, but he has opened two fried chicken stores in the past year—one in New Braunfels and one in Kyle. And he still has a sense of humor common to farm and ranch folks in dry west Texas. He laughed heartily when I suggested he had to get booted from the University of Texas and go broke farming to finally find success.

Betty Jack Rains

She knows as much about treating screw-worms and blow flies as she does about *pointe* and *pas de deux*. In the corner of her ornately decorated family room is a child's saddle. It seems oddly out of place until you start talking to her. Betty Jack Rains grew up in West Texas on a ranch and spent her early years weathering a seven year drought. She can talk about tough times, hard work, and making do. She can also talk about family, loyalty, sharing, praying, and giving.

Family is huge with Betty Jack. With a smile as big as Dallas and dark eyes glowing, she begins "Growing up on a ranch was wonderful for home life, family, and God. It was tough on Momma and Daddy's pocketbook. I was born in Fort Stockton in 1945 and in the early '50's we had the seven year drought. My parents went to Fort Stockton as newlyweds and leased a ranch 50 miles from town.

"My precious Pappy, my granddaddy, who was from Sonora, said to my daddy, 'Pat, what are you going to raise out there?' Well, it is great sheep country. But during that drought, I can remember my brother and me and my daddy loading up in the pick-up and going to burn prickly pear so the sheep would have something to eat. It was like this: God first, family second and then friends. We had no money, but I was so blessed. We did not know we were poor, because everyone was in the same boat.

"My folks were never able to buy the ranch. About the time they got a little bit ahead and thought they might be able to buy it, the drought hit. As a child, I didn't know there were any prayers that did not end with, 'God, please send us some rain.' "

When she started school, Betty Jack, her brother and mother lived on a small farm near Fort Stockton. Her mother made baked goods and sold them to the local grocery store in Fort Stockton to help make ends meet. Her daddy lived on the ranch and Friday afternoons her mother took her and her brother to the ranch where they worked all weekend. Sunday morning, they returned to Fort Stockton—fifty miles, one way—to attend church.

"We would get there before anyone else and help Dr. Brewster, our precious Presbyterian minister open up the church. It was just the greatest life in the world," says Betty Jack. "We ate every Sunday dinner with the minister and his wife. They had no family in the area, so we became their family."

Betty Jack began her dancing career at age four. She was taught by Mr. Bingham who drove from Midland, "because Fort Stockton wasn't quite that cultured yet." The dance studio was in an old community center which had hardwood floors—the very best, according to Betty Jack.

"I loved it, I loved it. From the very beginning, I loved it. That was my life. Growing up, I was on a horse or in the dance studio," says Betty Jack. With a halting voice and fighting back tears, she relates, "Momma told me that she and Daddy were looking over the finances one day and it was during the drought and she told Daddy, they were going to have to cut out music and dance lessons for me. My Daddy said, 'She loves it so and you know, I think she might have a knack. It just might prove to be an investment some day.' They found the money somehow for me to continue. Little did they know they were giving me the gift of my life."

The drought finally broke. The rains finally came. The grass turned green and the sheep no longer ate prickly pear. But then real tragedy struck the family. When Betty Jack was 12 years old, her father died. The cause of his death was aplastic anemia, a disease caused, ironically, from prolonged exposure to chemicals in livestock dip. The course of his disease ran approximately four years, but he became too weak to continue ranching so the family moved back to Sonora where her father took it on himself to begin the Presbyterian Church in Sonora.

"He did not live to see the building go up," says Betty Jack, "but he knew it was going to happen."

In the fashion of a person who overcame the drought, coyotes, long distances, broken windmills, all the challenges of ranching in West Texas, and the loss of a husband, Betty Jack's mother set about creating a new life for her family. She obtained a college degree and a teaching certificate through correspondence and was employed as a fourth grade teacher in Sonora until her retirement.

Betty Jack remembers, "I continued dancing through all of this. It could not have happened without our precious friends. When my daddy was so sick, neighbors drove me 36 miles to Ozona so I could take my dance lessons and appear in the recitals. That is West Texas."

After high school, Betty Jack chose to attend Texas Christian University because it was one of the few universities with a degree program in dance. There was one in Virginia, but "this old West Texas girl could *not* go to Virginia. That was too far from home.

"My Pappy and Mammy (grandparents) had a little ranch in Sonora and my precious Mammy had a small source of income and every semester, she sent me her money so that I could continue in school. I give all the credit to them for my going to TCU to major in dance, my dream come true."

Following graduation from TCU with a degree in Ballet Theater, Betty Jack returned to Sonora to teach…dance, of course. Mothers and fathers in Sonora, Ozona and Eldorado were waiting for her to come back and teach 'their little angels to dance.' Life couldn't have been better. One day a week she taught in Ozona and one day in Eldorado and three days in Sonora. On the weekends, she helped her precious Pappy in the stock pens.

"I taught dancing night and day," Betty Jack enthuses. "I would teach all morning to the little angels not yet in school. Then I would teach older school kids until dark, then came my ballroom dancing classes for the cute young couples who wanted to learn how to waltz, or schottische. I had 150 students. I loved it. I absolutely loooved it. Everyone in Eldorado, Ozona and Sonora knew me and my family—I had a gravy train. I was making $3,000.00 a month."

A trip to Hawaii eventually led to Betty Jack's coming to San Marcos. She met Don Rains, a US Marine at the time, while studying Hawaiian dances. After she returned home, she and Don had a whirlwind courtship and in less than a year, they were married. As do many SWT graduates, Don wanted to return to San Marcos. So, he and Betty Jack married in 1970, moved to San Marcos and have been here ever since.

The Betty Jack School of Dance opened that same year in a vacant garage, once the home of Allen Motor Company. It was located on I-35 between Hopkins Street and Wonder World Drive.

"I had about 10 or 12 students," she says. "Four of them were the Cooper girls, so that gave me a little boost. The two Crook girls, Missy Smith and Eleanor Owen were some of my first students. When we first came here, we couldn't find anything to rent. Everything was so expensive. Finally, that precious Mr. and Mrs. Allen told me that if I could make that garage into a dance studio to just have at it. It had concrete floors, galvanized walls, no air conditioning. It was a shell.

"Don and I got in high gear. We put down a particle board floor, paneled the walls and I put up a ballet bar and mirrors. It got hot in that building, hot, hot, hot. And it got cold, really cold. I eventually borrowed $500.00 and put in an air conditioner. Don put a stove in the place and we would dance in a circle around the stove in the winter time."

Eventually, she bought a paint warehouse at 1405 Bishop Street. It consisted of four walls and a floor when she got it. Again, she and Don, put their sweat and their talents to turning it into a dance studio. It has been enlarged three times since she bought it more than 20 years ago.

I asked about her aspirations as a performer. "Maybe when I was at TCU when all those girls from Washington and New York were there, I wanted to go on stage, but I have such a love for people and teaching, I just know this is where I am supposed to be."

As this article goes to press, Betty Jack is undergoing therapy for her right knee, destroyed in a car wreck last November. Following the car wreck, "...the bones in my knee resembled cornflakes..." she was back in the studio by February—not dancing, but teaching. She is irrepressible. She talks of ways in which she can bring joy to all those precious people in nursing homes by teaching them to dance in wheel chairs.

When Don was in politics, how did that affect you and the family? I asked. Without hesitation, she replied, "It was like the seven year drought."

What is next for Betty Jack Rains? "I can just hardly wait to see what God wants me to do with the next 100 years of my life."

Beth Ledoux

To say that she is modest is to say that the Texas Legislature is fractious on occasions. Her modesty is matched by an undaunted determination that comes into play whenever she sees an unmet need or an unanswered problem. Mix her modesty and determination with an unshakable spiritual faith and you have the quiet, persistent, irrepressible Beth Ledoux who makes the impossible happen.

A nurse by profession, a homemaker by choice and a problem solver by God, she finds herself making things happen for the benefit of like-minded people. She looks upon her achievements, and they are many, as answers to her prayers.

Coming to San Marcos was not an automatic choice for Beth and her physician husband, Lance. Describing their search for a place to settle as Lance completed his medical studies in the Dallas area, she says, "On weekends it seemed we visited every small town hospital in the state, especially in central and east Texas. I got to know hospital lobbies very well. We didn't want to remain in a large city like Dallas.

"Midland needed physicians and was interested in our coming there. We drove out there. I grew up in east Texas and I had never been west of Fort Worth. That was an eye-opening experience. On the way back we drove through San Marcos because Emmy Craddock was the aunt of one of Lance's best friends. We had visited her and Ann on holidays. As we drove to San Marcos, it just got greener and greener and when we got to the river, Lance said, 'This is it.'"

In 1980 the San Marcos hospital was small, overcrowded and did not have room for another physician, but Lance and Beth chose to come anyway. "We found San Marcos to be a wonderful place," says Beth. "Everyone was helpful and friendly. They just welcomed us with open arms. It was a very good move for us."

Beth's modesty surfaces as she dismisses the next few years with the declaration that she spent her time having children. She also became involved with the Christian Women's Club. As a newcomer, Beth says this was wonderful because through their Friendship Bible Coffees she met a widely diversified group of people which allowed her to feel at home in San Marcos.

A few years later, the medical wives formed an auxiliary. The group took on the challenge of insuring that every newborn that left the hospital had a car seat. "I'm not a very good joiner," Beth says, as she explains her role in the project. "The auxiliary asked me to take on the job. I agreed to get it started, but I was six months pregnant with our third child—I'm not very good with new babies—I'm just not very efficient. And so I agreed to acquire the seats and organize the initial operation, but then the hospital auxiliary was to take over. That was the first thing I had to organize.

"I learned from a lot of different people. One year I helped with the Heritage Tour of Homes. Kathy Morris was the chair. You could take notes on how to run a meeting from her. Bruce Harper helped me approach the civic clubs to help us raise money to purchase the seats. It was surprising to me how well everything came together."

Beth has always been an eager student of the Bible. She explains that the Christian Women's Club was seeking a Bible study program that would provide continuity and would last more than a few weeks. She and four or five of her fellow Bible students formed a prayer group in 1980 which met every Saturday morning at 7:00 to pray that they would find a Bible study program to answer their needs. This group prayed for 10 years before Community Bible Study was introduced to San Marcos in 1990.

"I became the children's director of that program," Beth says. "By that time my youngest child was four and I thought I had the time to devote to it. After one year, I became Teaching Director. I have had that job ever since. I just thoroughly love it. It is one of those jobs where you get to do everything you enjoy doing. This past year we had about 135 ladies attend the program.

"School is the other big thing I felt prompted to do," she says in an off-hand manner. "When our oldest, Spencer, was in about the sixth or seventh grade, we became concerned about the lack of content in what he was getting in school. Bottom line is that there was a difference in philosophy of education. We and the school just did not identify the same things as problems. So, we had a choice—Go along or get out."

Beth goes on, "About the same time we learned that Sarah, our fifth grader could not read."

As Beth explains, they were told not to worry about Sarah's progress. She was on grade level and was doing fine. By the end of fourth grade, she could not read a paragraph. Sarah was a compliant, quiet, and easily overlooked child. It took testing at the insistence of Beth to discover Sarah had major learning problems. Somehow, her grades masked the true failures Sarah experienced in school. She reached the point where she was convinced she could not learn.

The recognition of Sarah's problem, coupled with the philosophy differences in Spencer's education, resulted in both going to San Marcos Baptist Academy.

"The small class at the Academy allowed me to coordinate with her teacher and make Sarah accountable for her work.

"The education of our two younger children then grabbed our attention. Some of the same problems began to arise with them. I began to pray for guidance. What to do about their education became a real concern."

In typical fashion, Beth coupled action with her prayers. She surveyed surrounding communities, but found nothing that met the standards she envisioned. A survey of churches in the community revealed a lack of capability or interest in initiating a program of the type she imagined.

"At that time, the Lord said to me, 'If you will pray, I will do.' I said OK! I thought my job was to find this person who was going to start this school I had not heard of yet."

Beth went to the Baptist Academy to explore the possibility of a day program for elementary students. For a year she held meetings and conducted surveys to determine the feasibility of such an endeavor. Eventually, the Academy decided they would not attempt the project.

"I felt the Lord was really pressing me to do something. During all this research I discovered the Providence Christian School in Dallas. They have a spectacular curriculum. I visited them. I asked professional educators to look them over. The school impressed us. I found the school I was looking for. I came home and told Lance, the easy thing to do is move. That will take care of our education problems."

Lance, a bit more pragmatic, and a little less nomadic, suggested Beth start a similar school here. Once again, she applied action to her vision. She entered into a three year contract with the Dallas school, wherein, the Masters School in San Marcos would be much like a franchise. Curriculum, supervision, special resources, training of teachers and almost daily guidance came from Providence.

"They just held our hand that first year," Beth explains. "This is how you use this part of the curriculum. This is how you conduct tests. For three years, we had their close supervision.

"We began the Masters School with two teachers and nine students in this house," says Beth, referring to her private home. When I registered my astonishment, she reiterated, "In this house. We lived in a public building for five months. Parents worked at my dining room table. There were no offices. We were teaching first to fourth grade. We had wonderful parental support."

An element of the Masters School philosophy is that a large part of early learning is developing habits which dictate success in later years.

From humble beginnings of nine students in a private home, teaching 1st and 2d grade only, Masters School has grown to an institution with projection of 110 students next year, 11 teachers and expanding facilities. The curriculum now goes through 6th grade. Beth, who is president of the board of directors of the school, has visions for further expansion and inclusion.

She admits, however, that, though they have carefully selected their teachers, the curriculum is specially designed, and classes are small by public school standards, the Masters School is not necessarily appropriate for all students.

Following a suggestion, I asked about her health. "Very poor," she said. "I was diagnosed with breast cancer about two and a half years ago. Went through chemo and radiation and a stem cell transplant. It returned and we found it had metastasized to the bone. In January it had metastasized to the liver and has since gone into my lungs."

All of this she says with a calm resignation that reflects the depth of her faith. She is unshaken in her quest for answers to problems most of us would deem much too difficult to tackle.

Author's note: Beth Ledoux passed away June 8, 2002.

Johnnie Armstead

It would be easy to underestimate Johnnie Armstead. She is a wisp of a woman who greets one with a wide smile and an air of friendliness. She seemed a bit shy as she welcomed me to the Calaboose African American History Museum at 200 Martin Luther King, Jr. Drive. I would soon learn she is not a bit shy and when she fixes you with her determined gaze, it becomes apparent that she is '...one tough great-grandmother.'

To get this interview underway, I reminded her that she is known as a volunteer's volunteer, a civic minded citizen and is, I believe, involved in politics.

"Let me speak to the subject of politics first," Johnnie said. "Politics is change. Jesus Christ was the first politician. He was a politician because he changed things. Some changes are good and some are bad. But it is all politics. Politics is involved in everything we touch. The cost of bread and milk depends on political actions—subsidies, that sort of thing."

Johnnie was born in Prairie Lee, but came to San Marcos when she was seven years old. Though she would not reveal when she was born—39 and holding, she said—she informed me that the town was segregated.

"My mother went to San Marcos Colored School, but by the time I entered school, political correctness changed the name to San Marcos *Negro* High School," Johnnie related with a note of sarcasm. "As a matter of fact, my daughter, Shelley, at the age of six, was one of five little girls who integrated the San Marcos Elementary School in 1968.

"It took 12 years to integrate the schools in San Marcos. It was a frightening time. Imagine taking your six year-old to a place where she was not wanted. There were only five black children who entered school because there were only five teachers at Bowie who would take those kids. Oh, how I love those teachers!

"Mrs. Milligan, my daughter's teacher, requested Shelley because she was fascinated with her name, Adrianne La'Shell. She walked Shelley everywhere—the restroom, the lunch room and outside to the playground. She had other teachers watch her class while she made sure nothing happened to Shelley.

"Being the first is frightening—but being the first in the face of threats, animosity and ignorance is really frightening," Johnnie related. "So, I want those teachers and the principal of Bowie at the time to know how much I appreciate them."

Johnnie relates that she married in 1949 before she graduated from high school, but that she never gave up on education. She went back to school and got her high school diploma in 1952. Though she was the mother of three, she continued to go to school at every opportunity. She learned typing skills, took shorthand, psychology and English courses as time allowed. In addition, she took a Great Books Leadership Course and earned a salesman's certificate at the Austin Academy of Real Estate.

She began college full-time at SWT in 1988, but when her daughter wanted to go back to graduate school, she put grandmothering ahead of education. At present, she is classified a junior in elementary education.

"I want you to know why I have this museum," Johnnie said, abruptly in the midst of our discussion about education. "I heard stories from my grandmother, and older black folks about these wonderful contributions of black Americans. I was so confused because my text books did not reinforce their stories. My teachers confirmed the stories, but none of these exploits were recorded in the books.

"I spent a lot of time in Austin doing research. For instance, in 1893, Dr. Daniel Hale Williams opened a man's chest and repaired his heart and the patient lived. American history tells us that Dr. Cooley was the first man to operate on the heart.

"I thought, if these Black people have done all these things, I'm going to have to do something about it—so other folks can see it. I felt half-educated because I wasn't getting the full story. And, in a sense, we haven't progressed all that much. Whoever writes the history books gets to tell the story their way."

Jumping back to education, Johnnie pointed out, "SWT has not always been integrated. Dr. Flowers, bless his heart, said publicly, a black kid would never walk the halls of Old Main. However, my youngest sister, Gloria, was one of four young women who integrated the college in 1963. By the way, those four will be honored on February 3d this year. We have made progress, but being first was nerve-wracking."

Johnnie spent her early married years having children and being a 'home executive' (once known as a housewife). Later, she worked for the San Marcos school district for eight years as a teacher's aide. She worked with Vy Carswell Hammond in the math department and later she taught English as a second language to children of Mexican Nationals.

She laughed as she related, "I didn't speak Spanish all that well. But I was able to help those kids communicate with other students.

"For 20 years, I worked for the Democratic Headquarters here in San Marcos. In the beginning, it was a volunteer position. Only in the last few years was it a paid position. I was office manager and executive assistant."

For the past three years Johnnie has directed almost all her attention to grandmothering and to the Calaboose Museum. Sixteen-year old grandson, John, lives full-time with her. In addition, she helps daughter Shelley who lives in San Antonio. Shelley is a full-time school teacher and a single parent with two children. Frequently Johnnie is on I-35 to San Antonio to make sure the kids meet dental appointments, attend extra-curricular activities, or have transportation to special events.

"For two years when the kids were smaller, I went to San Antonio every single school day at 3:00 PM and picked up the children because my daughter was working two jobs."

Johnnie's mind is never far from politics. "I would really like to get involved enough in politics to get teachers a decent salary," she said. "Teachers spend more time with our kids during waking hours than do the parents."

I asked Johnnie how she viewed the rise of conservatism in the country in recent years and how it is affecting progress in racial understanding and equality.

"Well," she said, "it has become more fashionable to be a conservative Republican these days, but I'm liberal and proud of it. As for our progress in race relations, we are not going to let them take us back to the back of the bus. We are NOT going to go back to the back of the bus. But don't be complacent. Racism is alive and well. It is more covert, but it is there in education, finance, and just about any area of our life."

I asked her opinion of the future. She quickly offered that she thought Bush is destined to be a four-year president. "When you and I hurt badly enough, we will quit doing crazy things. The Enrons and other horrors that have hurt the little people will be remembered when we go to the polls again."

With no hint of self-pity or apologia, Johnnie said, "Affirmative action is under attack and is losing ground rapidly. I believe it is still essential to help us get on an equal footing," she said. "We were denied for so many years, that I don't know if we will ever catch up."

Closer to home, I asked what's life been like in San Marcos for a Black woman.

"You mean a loud-mouth Black woman," Johnnie answered. "My mother instilled in me my importance, my worth. She said when you look in the mirror, the image looking back at you is as good and important as anyone else. But, young woman, don't you ever, ever think you are better than anyone else. You may have a bigger house, you may have more education, and your circumstances may be superior, but God created us all equal. That has been ingrained in me all my life. And so I have always expected to be treated equal and that has allowed me to do things in this town that many Black women would never dream of."

A sampling of Johnnie Armstead's list of volunteer activities is convincing evidence of the foregoing. She is a 12 year member of the Hays County Historical Commission; has been secretary of the Preservation Associates; member of the Heritage Association, serving three years as secretary; Chair of the Calaboose Committee; member of the Blue Ribbon Committee on Tourism; President of Church Women United; Chair, Fine Arts Committee; Chair of the Committee for Renaming Comal Street to Martin Luther King, Jr. Drive; speaker/lecturer on women's issues and Black history; deeply involved in Girl Scouts for 22 years; and published a chapter, Black Women and Texas History in Dr. David Williams <u>Bricks without Straw,</u> a comprehensive study of African Americans in Texas.

These 1500 words represent the bare essence of Johnnie Armstead. If you are interested in sampling the full strength, unabridged version, set aside two hours and visit her at the Calaboose African American History Museum. It will be time well spent.

Jim Wacker

Jim Wacker is retiring, however, he is anything but retiring. His legendary enthusiasm is communicated by the glint in his eyes and the perpetual grin on his face. He expresses the same eagerness about the future with wife, Lil, that he did on game day for 37 years as a football coach.

In the first few words of this interview he revealed the source of his persistence, moral character, and ethical standards.

"I grew up in Detroit, Michigan where my father was a Lutheran minister for 42 years. He began by ringing doorbells as part of a mission in the inner city. There were four kids in the family. I was the baby. Spoiled rotten.

"I struggled academically while my siblings were good students. But in high school, I got involved in athletics. My coach, Don Tuomi, who was just out of college, had played football at Valparaiso University. I was a senior in high school and we became very close. He got me a half scholarship to play football at Valpo. No one else offered me anything. You take what you can get.

"He is the reason I went into coaching. It looked as if he was having so much fun, I thought, 'Why don't I try to do that.'"

Jim graduated in five years—he was hurt and did not play one year—with a double major, physical education and geography. Before taking a coaching/teaching job in a Portland, Oregon high school, Jim got his masters degree in geography from Wayne State University in Detroit while substitute teaching three days a week.

At Portland, he was head football coach, junior varsity basketball coach, head track coach, started a wrestling team, taught PE, geography, health and was resident director of the dormitory.

Jim says, "That was the hardest job I ever had. I made $3,600.00 a year at this small Lutheran High School. This was 1960. Lil and I got married the following summer and until we went to Portland, we had never been across the Mississippi River. She cried all the way across Iowa, at the thought of going that far away from home."

Ron Harms, a familiar name to those who remember the SWT rivalry with, then Texas A&I, was Jim's high school classmate, college teammate and roommate at Valparaiso. In the early 60's he became the head coach at Concordia College in Seward, Nebraska and hired Jim to be his defensive coordinator.

Jim coached with Ron for five years, during which, he put his spare time to good use and obtained a doctorate in education from the University of Nebraska.

As Jim puts it, "The only reason I got a doctorate is that I saw another guy get his doctorate and get a head football coaching job. It worked. It helped me get the Texas Lutheran job. But before that, I went to Augustana College where I was defensive coordinator for two years.

"I applied for every little college in America and I never got a sniff. Finally, I got a call from Texas Lutheran and I was set to interview with them. They called me back and said, not to bother. Another guy who had been there had agreed to come back. While taking a couple of kids to a national wrestling tournament—I was also the wrestling coach at Augustana—I heard from Texas Lutheran. As it turned out, the first fellow turned the job down for family reasons. There was a another fellow ahead of me, but he died and I was the only one left."

Jim credits luck and Mike Washington, a quarterback out of Austin, with his success at Texas Lutheran. With Washington at quarterback, the team did not lose a game and Texas Lutheran won two NAIA national championships. In typical fashion, Jim says, "Mike had a lot more to do with that than I did."

From Texas Lutheran, Jim went to North Dakota State where he took his team to the national semifinals twice in three years. In 1979, Jim and Lil returned to central Texas when he was hired to coach the Bobcats of SWT. Recounting that first year, he points out they started 6-0 and then lost four of the next five games.

"Mike Miller took over at quarterback the second year and we won the conference. Then '81 and '82 were our national championship years."

In his shorthand fashion of speaking, Jim says, "Got a call from TCU. Never thought I would ever coach at Division I level. Was at TCU nine years. Left there and went to Minnesota for five years. Thirty-seven years of coaching, tried retirement, wasn't ready for it. Got a call from SWT asking me who I could recommend as Athletic Director."

Like Dick Cheney, Jim recommended himself. "They hired me. Glad I coached 37 years and was not an AD for 37 years."

What was the best year in coaching for Jim Wacker? "There were so many. My last year in high school was really fun because they had not won more than two games for years and we ended up in a battle for the conference championship.

"Obviously, I enjoyed the successes we had at Texas Lutheran and Southwest Texas. I enjoyed the Division II level so much more because it is so much more hands on. I only had four assistants here and at Texas Lutheran.

"At Division I, the head coach is so much more of an administrator. At TCU, I had nine coaches, five graduate assistants, eight trainers, two strength coaches. One is removed from the hands-on coaching."

What was the worst year for Jim Wacker. "Oh, definitely the TCU thing in 1985 when we found seven of our kids taking illegal payments. When I went there, I announced that we were not going to buy athletes. I don't care what everyone else is doing.

"At the end of my first season at TCU, I got two letters. One was from a former swimmer at SMU. It was a great letter that asked, 'Why don't you coaches get together and clean up your act? You are buying athletes and destroying young people's value systems and it's not healthy for them or the universities.'

"The other was written by a student and published in the University of Texas student newspaper. My son, Mike, who was playing basketball there, sent me a copy. It took just the opposite stance. The student's position was that if Texas was going to try to compete, it should get the boosters involved and buy the players needed to win.

"These letters presented both sides of the issue. I wrote a cover letter to all the other coaches which suggested we ought to have the guts to talk about these issues at our upcoming league meeting.

"The next morning, I opened the sports page and there was *the Wacker letter*. The media then called the other coaches to get their response and they really ripped me. Many were seriously threatened by it."

Jim points out that he had a most unlikely ally. Arkansas coach, Lou Holtz, wrote a letter supporting Jim's position. The meeting of coaches was held and the only coach who did not show up was Lou Holtz. However, he was represented by his AD, Frank Broyles. The meeting turned into a shouting match with coaches denying that any of the illegal activities were happening. Nothing was accomplished.

A disgruntled athlete broke the story of SMU's wholesale cheating the week before they were scheduled to play TCU. Jim held a team meeting and congratulated his players on the clean program at TCU. Kenneth Davis, the TCU All-American running back spoke to his position coach and asked, 'doesn't Coach Wacker know there are several of us who are still being paid?' The position coach immediately told Jim. He informed the NCAA and the rest is history.

Jim left TCU for Minnesota where he coached for five years. But he admits the TCU experience probably took a toll from which he never quite recovered.

Jim Wacker's football coaching career has taken him to the heights of glory and to the depths of despair. Even he would describe it with a word with which he has become inseparably associated. It has been **UNBELIEVABLE.** He relates that he did not realize how frequently he used the word until it was pointed out to him. While he was at TCU, a *TCUnbelieeeeevable* bumper sticker was created.

But the biggest **W** in Jim Wacker's win column has nothing to do with first downs, completed passes or touchdowns. It has to do with surgery, radiation, and chemotherapy.

"A year ago, the week before Thanksgiving, I had a slight pain in my chest. Unusual for me. Never had that before. My daughter-in-law, who is a physician, told me to get to the emergency room. I laughed at her until she told Lil and they got me in the car and we went to the emergency room.

"They found a lump and my family doctor thought it might be heart related, and sent me to a heart specialist. I went to Austin Heart Specialists. One look and they told me it was surgery. After the surgery, the doctor told me, the tumor, which was about the size of an orange, was no longer encapsulated. Next would be radiation.

"Six weeks of radiation, five days a week followed. Then Dr. Supple strongly suggested M.D. Anderson in Houston. There, they suggested I do three months of chemo. That is baaaad stuff. But I'm happy to announce my last examination showed I am cancer free and I'm feeling great. I'm walking about three miles every morning with Vernon McDonald. I'm a lucky man."

Jim Wacker is as transparent as glass. But there isn't enough space in this paper to capture the whole man. Suffice to say, he is an iconoclast whose lasting reputation will have nothing to do with won-lost records.

Author's Note: Jim Wacker passed away August 26, 2003

Pat Price

The neurosurgeon, with a handful of CAT scan films, approached the hospital bed where Pat Price lay. As if he were chatting with a friend about the weather, the doctor began, "Mr. Price, you have an intercranial aneurysm and it has ruptured. About half of the people who have these aneurysms die. The half who live may have difficulty with walking, talking, or other day to day functions following surgery…Do you have a will?"

Pat answered in the affirmative and the doctor's next remark was, "I suggest you get it up to date because you may very well die on the operating table."

That was the scene in March 1981. It followed two days of Pat's enduring excruciating headaches, a trip to the doctor who gave him headache medicine and sent him home, and a spinal tap.

In October, Pat Price, with Moe Johnson, will journey to Ireland to participate in a marathon sponsored by the Arthritis Foundation. Yes, it is the same Pat Price who 20 years earlier had, at best, a 50 percent chance of survival and a less than 50 percent chance of recovering to a normal life.

Following the operation, Price relates, he lost his senses of taste and smell. He began overeating and ballooned up to 190 pounds. Doctors had him taking blood pressure medicine, anti-seizure medicine, and many other prescriptions for the possible maladies that might strike someone with his medical history.

Some of the medicines that he was given in the hospital contributed to a severe deterioration of his hip, leading eventually to a hip replacement in 1993. As a result of the hip operation, Pat was put on even more medicines.

By 1997, Price had become sick and tired of feeling sick and tired and he determined he might feel better if he began some sort of routine physical conditioning. After consulting his doctor and all the specialists under whose care he had been, he was cleared to begin a fitness program.

Because his children were in public school with Moe Johnson's children, he was familiar with Moe as a fitness expert and lifestyle consultant. Johnson agreed to take him on as a client. They met on a Friday in August of 1997 and Price suggested they start a program on Monday. Johnson said, "What's wrong with starting today?" From that day to this, except for a few short interruptions, the two have worked together.

To illustrate the physical condition at which Price began his journey to health, it must be reported that after three light exercises during the first workout, he was hyperventilating, experiencing dizziness, and almost lost consciousness. Johnson drove him back to his office for fear Price might lose control of his car.

"I began documenting my blood pressure before and after each workout," says Price. "I kept my doctor informed of the results and in six months of exercising three days a week with Moe, I was off *all* medication. I had been on about four or five different medicines. I credit Moe Johnson with getting me off the meds.

"All this happens in March. In April, I go back to my insurance company to see about getting a lower premium. A few years earlier, I could not get insurance—three companies turned me down. They tend to steer clear of people who have had hip replacement and brain surgery—and have been treated for seizures. After undergoing a thorough evaluation by the insurance company's doctors, I received the highest health rating given by the insurance industry."

As Johnson continued to encourage Price in his workout program, people began suggesting he enter a few contests to gauge his own progress. The program has now changed from recovering a bloated, over-medicated, gimpy couch potato to training one to compete with life-long fitness addicts.

"At first, it seemed a totally foreign notion. *Me, a power-lifter?,*" says Price. "But the idea was planted. I conferred with Moe. Naturally, he encouraged it.

"I'm thinking, I started all this just to get fit, now I'm power-lifting. What's going on here? My first meet was at Brooks Air Force Base and, to my surprise and delight, I won first place in my age and weight group. I had never even been to a power-lifting contest, much less, competed in one."

A few months later, Price entered the Longhorn 2000 Power-lifting contest where he won two gold medals. In competition he was able to do a squat with 225 pounds, bench press 165 pounds and dead-lift 280. After his dead-lift, several of his contemporaries commented that he 'left at least 20 pounds on the bar.' After Pat inquired about the meaning of that remark, he was told it meant that he could have lifted 300 pounds.

Price's interest became more intense as months went by and he began to study nutrition and fitness on his own. He bought books, studied physiology, read up on nutrition and began going to classes to obtain his certification as a personal trainer. He is now certified through Aerobics and Fitness Association of America (AFAA).

Price says he often makes presentations to university psychology and physical fitness classes. He explains as he points to his aging canine companion, Annie (for Orphan Annie), "My topic is Surviving and Coping with Trauma. Annie helps me with my presentations because she was rescued from near death, just as I was."

As Price gets ready to walk his marathon in Dublin Ireland—his artificial hip precludes his running—he describes a routine where he works out six days a week. I suggested his compulsion had perhaps been a plus in his pursuit of health and fitness. He corrected me. "The word I use," he said, "is passion. Have a passion for life. Have a passion for collecting butterflies, or have a passion for raising flowers. But most importantly, have a passion for your own health. Take it seriously!"

For those who arrived in San Marcos since 1980, it is worthwhile to mention that at the time of his aneurysm in 1981, Price was president of the San Marcos Telephone Company. In 1976, when his father suffered a stroke, he took over as CEO of the business which had been in the family since 1949. During his tenure with the phone company, he achieved national recognition as President of the National Association of Independent Telephone Companies, a position which frequently required him to travel Washington, DC At the time of his aneurysm, he had just returned from China, Hong Kong and Thailand where he met with the Ministers of Communication of those countries.

Pat did not assume he would automatically go into the business. After graduating from Southwest Texas, he began a promising career in teaching at Lamar Middle School in 1968. The pride Pat takes in his teaching career is illustrated by the following story. He was always known as 'Hy Price's son.' One day his father came home and told Mrs. Price he had met the parents of one of Pat's student's who asked him if he was 'Pat Price's father.'

Pat Price is a man of many parts. He is also a man of many passions. But as he puts it so succinctly, his real passion is 'for life at its fullest.'

"Physical fitness is a major contributor to that. Exercise stimulates your endorphins and you feel better. You become more fit and you gain confidence. You become spiritually and mentally more enlightened. It produces optimism, greater belief in self; you do not quit. You begin to re-label yourself in positive terms.

"Above all things, I want this story to emphasize that my accomplishments are directly attributable to the patience, experience, knowledge, and human understanding of Moe Johnson. He has literally given me a life worth living." *Author's note: Pat completed the walking marathon in Ireland, did another in Hawaii, and remains dedicated to fitness and nutrition.*

Karl Brown

The seemingly shy, almost reticent, individual who displays surprise with his selection as a profile subject is a complex man. To understand Karl Brown, it is important to know his roots.

"I was born in Mercedes, Texas," says Karl, "the son of a Methodist minister and my mother was a Methodist deaconess. A deaconess was as close as a woman could come to being a minister in those days. I got a double dose of Methodism in my home.

"I grew up in the church and it became my extended family wherever we went. We moved around a lot—on average about every three to five years. However, I went through high school at Lockhart. I'm a graduate of Lockhart High."

His appreciation for the ecumenical view of religion began as a high school student. He and his classmates habitually attended services together and rotated among the several churches in Lockhart. Karl explains that one week they attended the Methodist Church, next week, Episcopalian, while the following week, they would be at First Christian.

At this point, Karl draws a parallel. "Here I am working for Campus Christian Community, an ecumenical center with support from Presbyterian, Methodist, Disciples of Christ, and United Church of Christ. I have a feeling my success and my comfort level in this ministry began in my high school days."

Karl's parents were a team and worked as co-ministers wherever they went. His father was the pastor who built the Methodist Church in Lockhart. Karl credits his strong attraction to the ministry with what he saw in his family.

"My dad did a lot of things," Karl relates. "He was probably best known for bringing children from Germany for adoption. From the mid-50's to the late 60's, he brought 168 children to this country. I traveled with him all over the world. What he did to help people and their families made a major impression on me.

"He was a student of history and was concerned with world affairs. My travels with him stimulated my interest in other religions and their practices. I recall waking up in Turkey one morning and hearing the Muslim call to prayer and I thought, 'Toto, we are not in Lockhart anymore.'"

Karl's father was engaged in politics, though he never held public office. He gained access to Senator Lyndon Johnson and subsequently,

President Eisenhower, when he sought assistance with immigration problems.

Karl continues to relate stories about his father to illustrate how he came to his deep interest in civic affairs. (I am tempted to remind Karl that this interview features him, not his father.)

"I was taking my dad to the hospital on election day last year (2000). He wanted to stop and vote. I insisted he needed to get to the hospital as soon as possible. We got to the hospital and the medical staff put him on a respirator. He still insisted he wanted to vote. I went out and got a ballot. He voted. Next morning, he asked how it turned out (the Bush-Gore election). I told him, 'We don't know.' He died exactly a week later, not knowing the results of the election."

Karl came to San Marcos in1973 to his present job. After 29 years, he describes it as a long and enjoyable career. It could also be described as varied. In addition to directing the Campus Christian Community, he has served on the SWT faculty. He has taught in the Social Work Department with wife, Karen; taught group relationships in the psychology department; taught religion in the philosophy department; taught religion in the English department; and at present, Karl is teaching in general studies, part-time.

Campus Christian Community also has a varied history. Among programs it has fostered are the Crisis Hot Line, which grew from a two or three person volunteer program to a 24/7 volunteer operation with a paid part-time staff. That program now resides at the Hays/Caldwell Alcohol and Drug Abuse Council.

Karl elaborates, "One of the things I am most grateful for is that the little Hot Line operation provided a major impetus for the Hays/Caldwell Women's Shelter. One of the early coordinators began to see, from the calls we got, the need for such a facility. She got the movement started. So, while we were not directly involved, I think we uncovered a community need that was unmet. It has become one of the models in the state for this service.

"Incidentally, I became the first male president of their board of directors, and I just recently completed my term.

"Another community project in which we have had a hand is the Habitat for Humanity. We encourage our students to take on projects of this sort as part of their community activities."

This is the third Easter this column has appeared. I asked Karl to explain the meaning of the celebration. "It relates to one of the central beliefs of the Christian Church," he began. "Life can come out of death. It is a season for reflection on the Resurrection of Christ. For some Christians, it is a literal truth. Others see it as a paradigm for life as we live it. I have always thought Easter has more significance for me in the life I'm leading now than in a future existence of some sort. It is the many deaths and many conversions that happen in our life day by day that Easter addresses for me.

"We continue to find growth in the spirit, growth in compassion and love and Easter is a reminder that there is always the possibility of new life. I think it was Martin Luther who said that every Sunday is a small Easter. I see that with students who are rather quick to despair and rather quick to rise from the depths.

"It is one of the more difficult aspects of belief for Christians to discuss because it deals so heavily with faith. Some say that the Easter story encompasses and defines the faith of the church.

"For me, Easter talks about a journey that is opposite of the physical life. The physical life goes from birth to death. The Easter Story goes from death to birth, and these roads are somewhat parallel. We can move along them simultaneously."

In discussing Karl's career choice, I suggested he, unlike many, did not have a sudden awakening to his calling—that his background inexorably led him to the ministry.

"I had a slight detour," he admits. "I majored in chemistry and pre-med at UT-Austin, but my last semester, I took a philosophy course and that sort of hooked me. I found a scholarship to Perkins Seminary where one could go for one year without commitment…just to see if there was a fit. I went for a year. Then I went for another year and the next thing I knew, I was ordained. After Perkins, I went one year to the University of Edinburgh in Scotland."

Prior to coming to the Campus Christian Community, Karl had experience in church ministry. In addition to a stint in Abilene as a youth minister, he served churches in the small towns of Mertzon and Barnhart, west of San Angelo, from 1966 to 1968. In addition to ministering two churches, he taught religion at Angelo State and chemistry at Mertzon High School.

In 1968, he went to Texas A&I as a campus minister where he stayed until coming to San Marcos in his present job in 1973.

Karl has deep roots in San Marcos and he has honored those roots by serving his community in one of the most delicate, stressful, demanding, thankless tasks at any level of government. He served the city for three terms—nine years—as a councilman.

"I had always lived in a parsonage until I came here and owned my home. I became active in my neighborhood association and the discussions there were aimed at getting the council to be more responsive to our needs.

"Someone suggested we ought to have our own candidate and much to my surprise, that turned out to be me. It was a wonderful learning experience and I deeply appreciate the city giving me the opportunity to participate in the process."

Asked about the accomplishments of those nine years, Karl pointed out that the community became more involved in the planning process and neighborhood associations became a significant voice at city hall. In addition, the city purchased the electric utility. It was a time when the council enacted a number of ordinances which helped define the quality of life the community desired.

"Reading about Kyle's concern with growth makes me think that maybe we did some things that helped us get a little bit ahead of the game. I think we have some balance between growth and environment. It isn't perfect. But that is always a struggle.

"Religion and politics are sort of like oil and water, but I tried to bring to my politics that part of my religion that helped me understand the concerns and needs of the community. I wouldn't want the city to be run by clergy, but occasionally, it is not bad to have that voice in the mix."

A student of comparative religion, psychology, chemistry and relationships; a practitioner of spiritual ministry, counseling, and politics; a father, husband, and teacher; Karl Brown is indeed a complex figure whose complexity lies deep beneath his taciturn personality and self-effacing demeanor.

Jeff Kester

Jeff Kester lives in a church. And why not? He is an evangelist. And a missionary.

His life is a seamless melding of religion and vocation to form a whole so smoothly constructed as to remove all wonder at the inspiration of the artist. His life is a story of searching and finding; of doubt and answered prayers; of sacrifice and reward; of faith and fulfillment. Jeff Kester is an artist whose best work is not on canvas or poster board. His best work is Jeff Kester, the man.

He introduces his odyssey with, "This journey begins in English class in the ninth grade at Adams High School in Dallas, Texas. I was assigned to write two papers on careers that I might pursue. One of the papers I wrote was on aeronautical engineering because my dad was in the Air Force, and I liked the idea of flying airplanes. The other paper was inspired by my grandfather who lived in Moline, Illinois. He drew the plans for Moline High School. His drawing equipment, the 'T'square, the drawing table, and all those pencils fascinated me.

"I discovered that engineering required way too much math and science for me. Since I was always pretty good at drawing, I was attracted to architecture. It seemed to afford the opportunity for the creativity I was seeking."

The soul of the artist combines with the intellect of the pragmatist, when Jeff says, "Architecture is an expression of art which lends itself to practical use. A building is a piece of sculpture that can be inhabited."

With life's vocation already in mind, he took three years of architectural drafting in high school. His junior year his home design won first place in competition among more than 100 contestants in the annual Home Show awards in Dallas. This was his springboard to enrolling in the University of Texas School of Architecture.

At this point Jeff begins to discuss a parallel journey, a spiritual journey, which as he says, "is an integral part of my life. I could not talk about myself without including my faith, the spiritual side of my life."

Jeff calls his first four years of college his 'shadowy past.' It was a time when this young adult, raised a loyal Presbyterian, was passing through the chrysalis of spiritual identity. It was a time of seeking, questioning, doubting, and neglecting.

"During this time, I had a lot of inner turmoil," says Jeff. "I was dealing with being a shy kid whose parents moved every few years—my dad was in the military—and at the same time, I was looking for something that had meaning in my life. I knew enough about conventional religion to know I was not attracted to all form and no substance. I branched out to try things like Transcendental Meditation. In 1970 I rode my motorcycle from Dallas to Maine to study under Maharishi Mahesh Yogi.

"One night while there, I had a profound spiritual experience that wiped out my agnostic point of view. I was alone, under a Maine sky so clear I could see every star in the galaxy. I was enveloped by loneliness—I was still quite shy—when all of a sudden, I felt this incredible spirit. I realized it was a connection to my Creator. Tears came to my eyes as it became clear I was getting an answer that would propel me into my spiritual journey. At that point, I decided to look into what religion is about."

Jeff returned to Texas and began to cultivate his spirituality. He tried several forums, in search of an answer. At one point he considered becoming a missionary, but he realized something was still missing. He opened himself up to all possibilities. He was studying eastern and western philosophers, Swami Satchinanda, C.S. Lewis, Erich Fromm and others. He had also resumed prayer. In his prayers he was beseeching his Creator to guide him to his life mate. The response to Jeff's quests for spiritual fulfillment and a life-mate came to him in one package, his wife, Rhea.

As Jeff describes it, "There were these two boys, about four and eight, who lived nearby and they enjoyed hanging out at my place and doing little projects with me. One day, their mother came looking for them. I was on my hands and knees in my front yard looking for a contact lens. After a short introduction, we began discussing prayer. She told me she was a Bah'ai'. Later she gave me a couple of books and I became very excited because I began to read what I already believed. I found what I had been seeking.

"Rhea and I were married March 19, 1972 and about a year later we decided to come to San Marcos to help promote the efforts of the few Bah'ai' who were struggling to get established."

Questioned about coming to San Marcos as a missionary, rather than seeking a career, Jeff responded, "It's the last place I would go looking for a career.

"A professor friend at UT told me to go see Frances Stovall. He was working with her on the Bicentennial Commission. I knocked on her door and said Professor Copeland told me you might have some ideas about employment for an architecture student. She said, 'I don't have a clue about jobs for architects, but I sure would like you to draw the Vola Thompson house on Belvin Street.' And that is how I came to do my first drawing for the Heritage Association—then the Bicentennial Commission. That led to the series of drawings that are now displayed in the Cock House.

"I did not get a job through Frances, but she sure gave me a lot of work. I ended up working for J.B. Roberts, the only architect in San Marcos. He was about as hard-headed as they come. But I just loved him. However, he retired about six months after I started working for him."

Jeff relates he then went to work for A&W Construction where he hoped to learn the practical skills of a carpenter. Mr. Adcock, the owner, put him to work as a helper—at about $1.80 an hour. The first day was spent moving a giant mound of dirt by wheelbarrow. The second day he moved a pallet of plywood from the ground floor to the second floor of a building under construction. Disappointed that he was not driving nails, putting up studs or mitering a corner, Jeff arranged to casually drop the information that he had skills in architectural drawing. Mr. Adcock reassigned him immediately to drawing plans and models for his construction company.

When the construction business softened in the mid-80's, Jeff left A&W and went to work for Jim Byrn's engineering firm. "He assigned me to draw a master map of San Marcos for the tax department," says Jeff. "I drew a master at 1:500,000 scale and then we produced about 120 sheets of maps at 1:100,000 scale. The city is still using these maps we created. The map project required an incredible amount of research on the history of San Marcos.

"A stint with Rod Baughn, interior decorator, also gave me an interesting perspective on San Marcos. He was a most flamboyant character. Eventually, however, I was able to open my own business with Ron Balderach and we embarked on a rather successful venture. Had anyone suggested in 1973 I would have my own architecture business in San Marcos, I would have said, 'You're crazy.'"

Here again the spiritual side of Jeff surfaces, as he explains, "When you do something or go somewhere for the right reasons, doors open for you. The community has been wonderful to me and my family in that it has supported us in this career."

Pressed to elaborate on his part in the San Marcos Heritage Association, Jeff responded, "I have to go back to that first meeting with Frances Stovall. By the way she is like an aunt to me. Every year she would ask me to do another drawing. Then she asked me to do some work for the Bicentennial Commission which I gladly did.

"One of my projects was the design of the River Walk. I also designed the Bicentennial Medallion that has been incorporated into a lot of the Heritage Association art work. When the Bicentennial Commission became the Heritage Association, I continued to serve on several committees.

Through the late 70's and early 80's I was doing a lot of illustrations for the Heritage Association. In 1990, I was invited to serve as president."

He was also involved in the establishment of the Main Street Project and working with them and the Heritage Association he has been deeply involved with the renovation and restoration of many of the buildings around the square. In addition to creating and donating to the people of San Marcos a unique pictorial representation of the city, Jeff continues to advise and consult on matters in his area of expertise. At present he is deeply involved with the plans for restoration of the old Hays County Jail, located between MLK and San Antonio Streets and the Baptist Church on MLK.

Jeff contributes a ton of time to researching his restoration projects. He says, "It is so much fun. It is like being a detective. It's like Sherlock Holmes, with a magnifying glass, deerstalker hat and a cloak. Why was a wall removed? What was the buildings original function? What did it become? The building starts telling a story as it evolves—like this building," as he takes in his surroundings. "It is a home, but it is also a place of worship."

Jeff Kester is no mystery, but he tells a beautiful story, and most assuredly, he is still evolving.

Tiffany Snyder

This profile has been lingering in the back of my mind since I met her on her first day of work at the Daily Record. It may have a somewhat different angle than you have come to expect from me.

As I entered the bullpen where the reporters and section editors create the words, phrases, sentences and punctuation that make up the stories that convert blank newsprint into a *newspaper,* I was preparing to meet my new boss. My old boss, Tess Mallory, told me her name was Tiffany. That fact alone set up a sort of suspicion about what kind of person would be handling my stuff. Then, when Tess told me she was under 30, I began to think a human resources manager right out of the Dilbert cartoon had taken over the hiring for the Record.

After almost two years of working with Linda Keese and Tess Mallory, two tough ladies who have been around the block a couple of times, I had some real doubts about this young dilettante. She was on the phone when I ambled up to her desk—it's a wide open work area, not even cubicle dividers—and the conversation went something like this.

Tiffany: Well, I'm terribly sorry. We will get it in today's paper, but I really must have your copy at least a day ahead of time. I just can't get your announcement in Tuesday's edition when you bring it in at 11:30 on Tuesday.

Pause.

Tiffany: Because my deadline is 10:30 and I have to proof it, retype it and make sure it fits the layout.

Pause.

Tiffany: If you would like to speak to the Mr. Ray, I will put him on the line. OK, well, thanks for calling.

She put the phone down, gave me a cursory glance and returned to some business on her computer. She was as cool as October in Colorado.

I introduced myself and made small talk while thinking, "I better not miss any deadlines. I'm not dealing with Tiffany Airhead, here."

This lady spoke softly but with an edge of steel in her voice. She was also not impressed with me or my credentials. Respectful, but not impressed.

As I left the Record, I pondered how I might melt this little iceberg of efficiency. Flattery and an offer to buy lunch usually works wonders.

A few days later, I went by her *office* and complimented her on what she was wearing (Tiffany has a great sense of style. She dresses with a

157

flair, not copied from the magazines, but perfectly coordinated in a quirky sort of way.) and invited her to lunch. She promptly found an excuse not to go. Probably did not want to mix social life with business.

Time passed. The iceberg began to melt. A few weeks later she took me up on my offer to buy lunch. I discovered she grew up in Houston. When My Big Fat Greek Wedding came out, I discovered she has Greek ancestry from both sides of the family.

In spite of her tender years, Tiffany is anything but tender. She fearlessly took on New York just out of high school. She has backpacked Europe, she has lived in Paris, she has managed a bar/nightclub in Austin and she is the mother of a four year old and is expecting her second child in October. Did I mention that she has also worked on a fishing boat in Alaska?

When Tiffany graduated from high school, she went to New York where, with a small scholarship, a job at a bookstore and help from her father, she enrolled at Long Island University (LIU).

Why, New York, I asked.

"It wasn't Texas—more specifically, it wasn't Houston," she said. "It was far, far away from home."

After a year at LIU, she took off a semester and returned to Texas where she landed in Austin, managing La Zona Rosa, a well-known live music venue. It was there she met Brian Hofeldt, vocalist and guitarist for the popular Derailers band. More about that later.

She had other jobs in Austin before returning to New York. She was, for a time, a mechanic at a QuickLube store and somehow found time to work for the Austin American Statesman in graphic design and layout.

When she returned to New York, she enrolled at Hunter College and graduated with a double major in political science and English literature. During the summer before her junior year at Hunter College, she took off for Paris where she studied literature in translation at the famed Sorbonne University. To pay for that sojourn, she worked at the Shakespeare Book Company, hang out of Hemingway, Stein, and Fitzgerald in the 20's and 30's. She also wrote and published small books while she worked as a photographer on the side.

After graduating from Hunter, she enrolled in graduate school at Columbia University. The Derailers had a gig in New York and Tiffany went to see her old Austin buddies perform. She and Brian re-connected.

"I wasn't very happy at Columbia," she said. "One day in December, 1999, Brian drove up in a moving van and said, 'Let's go back to Texas.'"

Harlan Hofeldt was born in November of 2000 and before Tiffany came to work at the Daily Record, she was a mom, a grad student at Texas

State University, a professional photographer and taught country/western dancing as continuing education at the University.

Since she has been at the Record, she has delighted us with a number of funny, enlightening, poignant, informative and ironical essays. She has managed the unmanageable calendar of events, and she has given us an attractive, readable and interesting Neighbors Section. Her headlines on my profiles have been creative, humorous and appropriate.

So, now you know Tiffany Snyder Hofeldt, the personality behind the byline and the layout.

Not yet.

That energetic, efficient, bright professional person on public display disguises the real Tiffany.

There are some other parts of Tiffany. She is a miserable driver, at best. Aside from knocking the mirror off the side of her car while backing out of the garage, there have been a couple of other occasions when her car has made trips to the garage to have dings repaired and scrapes healed.

She is a great storyteller and a wonderful listener. It would be difficult to find a more entertaining and interesting luncheon partner. Life has not been easy for her, but she tends to make lemonade out of the lemons life has dropped in her lap. Her difficulties tend to become funny stories or pieces of irony that she openly shares with those she trusts. Aside from her physical attractiveness, her humor and understanding lighten and brighten the atmosphere wherever she may be.

The real Tiffany is Harlan's mom who can never find enough time to be with her son. The real Tiffany is leaving the Record to cement her motherhood role with the birth of her second son in October. The real Tiffany would trade a Pulitzer for the opportunity to dry Harlan's tears or feel his little arms around her neck or gaze upon his face in the peaceful repose of sleep.

Tiffany, the steel-nerved, efficient, dedicated, organized, innovator will be missed at the newspaper. But that will allow us to have more of the other Tiffany. And that is a *good thing.* **Author's note: October 11, 2004, Tiffany gave birth to a healthy, happy, beautiful child, Van Hofeldt.**

Virginia Witte

With just a bit of exaggeration, Virginia Witte said, "I have done everything at this high school except coach football."

She continues with no exaggeration at all, "I am a walking, talking miracle. They gave me a zero chance to live."

That introduction piqued my interest in this bright-eyed, attractive lady who was sitting in for a teacher colleague at San Marcos High School on this particular day. She had a pet name for every student who entered the room. First, there was "Precious Girl," then "Sweet Thing," then "Dear Baby."

Who are you, really, I asked. "I am a BISM, Born In San Marcos," Virginia stated. "Spent most of my life in San Marcos and I always wanted to be a teacher. When my children were old enough, I went back to school and got my degree so that I could go to school with them. I was 28 or 30 when I returned to school.

"I met my husband, Chester, the first year of college and we married. However, to get permission from my daddy, I had to promise to go back and finish school. He made me follow through on that promise."

Chester and Virginia moved to the Corpus Christi area after marriage and they lived in several places: Ingleside, Gregory, Portland, as Virginia looked for a place she could like after growing up in San Marcos. Chester was a supervisor for Reynolds Metals.

In 1970, Virginia graduated from Texas A&I after racing through the program, taking 19 hours a semester and getting special permission to take extra summer courses. Her first teaching job was in Alice, Texas. As she described her experience there, she revealed what was then, and continued to be, her first priority as a teacher.

"It was a heartbreaking experience," she said. "We were in the midst of a drug epidemic and so many of my students were ruined by it. Many of them did not make it to their 20's. After two years in Alice, we decided to come back to San Marcos where I imagined I would save the world by teaching at Gary Job Corps."

She was there for a year. But, as she explained, she felt she couldn't make a real difference. And, as was typical of her entire teaching career, she couldn't leave the problems at the Job Corps at the end of the day.

"I went to San Marcos High School in 1973 and John Faseler and Roddy Bagley hired me to teach English. I later taught history which was my real love. In 2001 I had to retire.

"I only taught nine weeks the year I was diagnosed—August 1999," she said. "The diagnosis was lung cancer, but the wonderful, generous, magnificent people at this school donated enough days to cover me to the end of the year. Yes, I was a smoker, but the type cancer I had was not smoking related."

She describes her cancer experience as a series of miracles.

"Every summer we take our four children, the grandchildren and all the spouses to South Padre for a week of family time. The second day at the beach, while playing in a small boat, I was upended by a huge wave. I had some sprains and bruises and the medical people in South Padre told me to go to my doctor as soon as I got home.

"Dr. Rogers ordered x-rays of my neck and the upper portion of my lungs showed up on the photo. That's how he detected the cancer. I had no symptoms, not a clue."

Further tests showed possible cancer in the liver, spine and one lymph node. When the surgeon operated, he told the family there was nothing to be done. Take her home, make her comfortable and wait for the inevitable he told the family. She was given six to 18 months to live. Another doctor, an oncologist, reinforced the surgeon's prognosis. Dr. Rogers, along with her family, refused to accept the prognosis.

"Randy [Rogers] insisted I see Dr. Tweedy. He (Tweedy) prepared an experimental chemo cocktail for me, put me in radiation therapy and told me I was the only patient he ever had under that treatment regimen to gain weight. I did get very bald. Actually, I became really ill after the treatment because I abruptly quit taking my pain medication and experienced narcotic withdrawal."

As her eyes glistened with the effort to hold back the tears, she emphasized the influence of a prayer group who supported her through her illness. "I am just totally blessed," she insisted.

In 2001, she returned to school with the notion of teaching forever. Shortly, she developed a crippling, disfiguring, form of paralysis in her hands, arms and lower leg. It was thought to be rheumatoid arthritis. However, it proved to be the after effects of her cancer and its treatment. Miraculously, the paralysis is clearing up as her recovery progresses

She continues to talk about miracles when she explains that husband, Chester, had a heart attack. During his treatment…"they found a humongous aneurysm. It would have surely killed him soon."

I recalled her miraculous success with the academic decathlon team a few years ago. "As mentioned, I have done everything here except coach football," she said. "I have had the cheerleaders, the dance team, the spirit group, and the gifted and talented, all while still teaching a full load. Two years after I began with the gifted and talented program, the superintendent informed my principal that I was to have an academic decathlon team ready for competition in November. This was October of 1994."

She rounded up a group of her 'sweet things, precious darlings, and dear babies' and after just more than a month of preparation, her team's first competition resulted in eight medals. They were walking on water because her team had surpassed most of the schools in the Austin district.

That was to be mere prelude to the next year's achievements. Her academic decathlon team finished third in statewide competition. She gives most of the credit to others. "We had absolutely marvelous kids, but we had the support of all the teachers on campus. And many college professors spent hours tutoring the kids. Dr. Warshauer, with Dr. Passty did the math, Howard Yeargan tutored them in economics—people came out of the woodwork to assist us.

"I did that for four years and it made a huge difference for many of my students. It gave them a way to compete and be recognized on a much larger stage than they imagined. It instilled confidence in kids who never saw themselves as the special people they were. It changed lives."

Then I asked why a local citizen would email me about retired schoolteacher, Virginia Witte, who is still changing lives through some sort of program that she has made a huge success.

"I began receiving calls last August from the gifted and talented teacher. She wanted me to put together a mentor program for first generation Americans who are potential college students.

"My first reaction was, I don't do discretionary programs. It has to be open to all, if I am involved. So, they gave me free rein. We put out the word that any student who would like to have a mentor should sign up. Our initial response resulted in 135 students who requested mentors."

She explained the details of the program. Every student who signed up for a mentor will have an adult who is to help them understand the process of applying for college, how to fill out the application, how to get financial aid, how to gain access to local scholarships. If college is not an immediate goal, the adult will assist the student with locating tech schools, and the attendant scholarships for that avenue of continued education.

Students who wish to go into the trades are matched with an adult who can provide advice, training, and perhaps, a work experience, in that particular trade.

"The greatest thing about the program is that, come next June, none of these kids will, without the security of mandatory school, look around and say to him/herself, 'Now what?' Imagine, we have one senior counselor for over 300 students.

"I started calling friends, strangers, people on the street, and the response was wonderful. My goal is to have an adult mentor for every student who wants one, but I haven't quite made that goal. I'm still working on it."

In the spring, Virginia plans to have a reception to get feedback from all the mentors and her hopes are that their experience will convince them to sign up for future mentoring. She feels the program will then be established so that it will perpetuate itself.

But, typically, her vision goes beyond the success with which most of us would be happy. "My dream of dreams," she says is that every incoming high school freshman will have a mentor who will be with them for four years. I have never seen it happen anywhere, but that doesn't mean it can't."

Miracles and success are Virginia Witte's trademarks. When she sets out to do something, she gets it done. Even if it means she has to coach football.

Richard Cruz

If I were to write that Richard Cruz is a product of the 60's, many might visualize a long-haired, unwashed, dope-smoking hippy, waving a peace sign and living in a commune. Wrong.

Richard Cruz is the other side of that coin. He graduated from San Marcos High School in 1965 and in spite of the disdain in which the military was held, had plans to make the army a career. Since the draft was in operation at the time, Richard allowed as how he would wait for his number to come up.

"It didn't take long," he said. "By June of 1966, I was drafted and in basic training at Fort Polk, LA. Advanced individual training was at Tigerland, North Fort Polk. By the end of November, I was in Viet Nam.

"I was with A Company, 35th Infantry of the 25th Division. We were a part of a combat team that operated all over South Viet Nam, but largely in the Central Highlands and in relief of the marines, north of Anh Khe."

Richard was a Grunt, an enlisted infantryman, who spent endless days in the jungle, dodging booby traps, searching tunnels, setting ambushes, avoiding ambushes, and praying that his DEROS (Date estimated return overseas) would arrive before he stepped on a land mine or appeared in a sniper's sights. There is more to this part of the story.

By the time his discharge date arrived in 1968, Richard had abandoned the idea of a military career. He returned home and found a job with WideLite. It took about a month for him to decide he wasn't crazy about the work there.

"I started looking at schools," Richard said. "In 1968, data processing was a big thing and it seemed an interesting field. A successful friend gave me advice that matched my desires. The Veteran's Administration helped me find Durham's Business School in Austin where I could get the training I wanted.

"Using my Veteran's benefits, I enrolled for their course. It was 30 months and proved to be exactly what I wanted. I worked part time for IRS where they were already integrating on-line operations. It fit right in with my school. In fact, I was still learning punch-card operations at school, so the IRS was more advanced than the school."

In 1969, before he finished his training at Durham, Richard was hired to work in the computer room at SWT. He worked nights and attended classes during the day. Today, he is in charge of computer operations for the administrative side of the University.

You have seen lots of changes in the computer industry, I noted.

"When I started, there were about 6,500 students and each record required eight punch cards. We had an IBM 360 and often projects ran all night. We had no online capability and the machines occupied a huge room. Now we have one little unit about three feet by six feet that does it all."

Author's Note: Richard has worked for five university presidents.

I mentioned that he was referred to me as the person in San Marcos with whom to discuss Cinco de Mayo.

"Well, Frank Arredondo and I were friends from about the second grade," Richard began. "He was working for Dolph Briscoe, governor of Texas in the 70's. He asked me if I were familiar with LULAC—League of United Latin American Citizens. After he explained the organization, their principles and goals, I was convinced San Marcos could benefit from such an organization.

"Our first meeting was attended by 16 people. We only needed 10 members to be chartered. All 16 signed up and, with Frank's help, we got our state charter for LULAC Council # 654. Like all organizations, we needed to raise funds for our civic projects. Washing cars and a little barbecue once in awhile didn't produce much money or publicity.

"We kicked around ideas to improve our image and our treasure. September 16, or Dies y Sies, was more or less the property of the Cuauhtemoc Association and the Hispanic community in Kyle. No one was interested, it seemed in Cinco de Mayo. So, we settled on that date to put on a celebration.

"The original 16 LULAC members put on a three day affair just about as large as we have now. Of course, 16 people couldn't possibly do it. We enlisted wives, girl friends, kids, everybody who would help."

Somehow, word got out through the media and the first event in 1974 was well attended, according to Richard. The success of San Marcos's first celebration spawned competition in the area. The next year Seguin had a Cinco de Mayo celebration. Then Lockhart and New Braunfels followed suit. However, the San Marcos celebration is the only one to survive.

May 5th is not Mexican Independence Day, as many might think. It marks the anniversary of Texas-born General Zaragoza's 1862 victory over an 8,000 man force of French and disloyal Mexicans. Zaragoza's victory rid Mexico of the last foreign invaders and had major implications for the outcome of the U.S. Civil War, especially the little known French involvement.

Richard went on to explain, "We also received a state charter to hold the official state menudo cook-off. We got patents on the title *Viva, Cinco de Mayo,* and on our logo. So, we have certain exclusive rights to our name and competition.

"This is our 29th year and we have never missed one. It is interesting to note that Frank Arredondo's, son, Frankie is the chair of this year's celebration."

How many people does the event pull into San Marcos?

"It is hard to know," Richard said. "Over the three day period, we have 23,000 to 25, 000 attendance and probably 6,000 to 7,000 are out of town tourists. We have people come from as far away as Idaho.

"We have a web site at www.vivacincodemayo.org. It includes the significance of May 5th, a schedule of events, a list of sponsors, photos, and links to other online sites of interest. I think it is important for people to know that *Viva Cinco de Mayo* is a family affair that celebrates our culture."

Cinco de Mayo is just one of Richard Cruz's contributions to San Marcos. Notice the construction underway at Hopkins and Riverside

"I went to Cotulla, a small town south of here, to a community event and as I walked into the park, I noticed they had a memorial honoring their veterans. I later looked up the state registry of veteran's memorials and of 254 counties in Texas, 49 had nothing honoring veterans. Sad to say, Hays County was among the 49.

"I started talking to people around town and asking questions about why we did not have a memorial for our veterans when I got a call from Kathy Morris, the mayor at the time. She heard about the small noise I was making and suggested I take it on and get something done."

Once again, Richard waded through the red tape of getting an organization charter from the state of Texas so that he could legally raise money. After several unsuccessful attempts, he got his charter through the Disabled Veterans of America (DAV).

"I tried the VFW and the American Legion and both turned me down. As a last resort, I called the DAV. They asked if I were a disabled veteran. When I said yes, they said, 'Cruz, you will have your letter in 24 hours."

To emphasize Richard's tenacity, it is important to note that The Veteran's Memorial project has taken about 35 years to go from the germ of an idea to a shovel in the ground. What's behind that kind of determination?

"It didn't take long in Viet Nam to become the most seasoned veteran in your outfit," Richard said. "It seemed I had been there about a month when I was made a team leader and a little while after, I was the squad leader. I was 19 years old, but I grew up real fast.

"Right after Christmas, 1966, we took off on an operation and I didn't see base camp until seven months later. Our mission was to interdict infiltration through Cambodia from the north.

"I had just returned from my R&R in Hong Kong about two days earlier when on August 23d, our ambush was ambushed. A couple of people went to sleep and the enemy got inside our position and I took two hand grenades right close by. Shrapnel from one grenade ripped my right eyelid and the second one tore up my knee and leg.

"Next thing I knew I was on a helicopter to Quinh Nhon. Later I was evacuated to Camp Drake, Japan."

Richard's sense of humor emerges as he relates an example of military Catch 22. "They would not send me home from Camp Drake because I couldn't focus my eye. But the reason I couldn't focus is that the doctors kept dilating it."

Richard was awarded the Purple Heart for his wounds, and as he retrieved his mortally wounded platoon leader from outside the defensive perimeter, the officer assured Richard he would recommend him for a Bronze Star. The officer died before he could be evacuated The recommendation was never completed.

Richard holds no anger toward anyone. He has no regrets, only pride in the service he performed. He is as determined today as he was on that hill in Viet Nam 36 years ago. Cinco de Mayo and The Hays County Veterans Memorial represent Richard's efforts to retrieve and keep alive precious elements of our culture and heritage.

Gwen Smith

There are roughly two and a half columns of Smiths in the San Marcos telephone directory. Nationwide, Smith is no less ubiquitous. With the name, Smith, it is difficult to establish one's persona so that the mere mention of the name brings a look of recognition from the most naive listener…unless it is prefaced with *Gwen*. Only the most recent arrival or the most reclusive hermit in San Marcos doesn't know Gwen Smith.

"I'm part of a vanishing breed," she says. "That is, I am a BISM (Born In San Marcos). Oh, I suppose there are a number of them born every day, but I am one who is approaching her exit."

Gwen Smith made her entry to San Marcos September 8, 1915 when, "San Marcos probably had a population of 5,000. I was born at what is now 736 Smith Avenue. My father built the original house on that property in 1906. In 1936, he built the house that stands there now. It was on the edge of town—well, we felt like we were out in the country."

Gwen went to elementary school at West End School, then located at about the 900 block of Hopkins Street. She graduated from San Marcos High in 1933 and since her class has never had a reunion, ("It just wasn't the thing to do at the depth of the depression…") she suggests she may be the only remaining member of the Class of '33.

"I went to Southwest Texas, and graduated in 1937," she says. "I majored in history and immediately after graduating, I went back and got my masters degree. I wanted to major in physical education, but I was told it was not an acceptable major. It was not a major discipline at the time. Nevertheless, I took all the hours I could in the field and had more hours in PE than in history. After my masters degree, I began teaching in the San Marcos public school. The only time I ever taught history was when I did my practice teaching. I guess I did all right. I got an A."

She taught dance and physical education to fourth grade through high school with no facilities. She found herself getting a little burned out with trying to teach dance to young women on a rocky, unimproved field. Gwen resolved to find a place where her talents might be better appreciated. That led her to Hockaday Girls School, a junior college in Dallas. Once again, facilities were sorely lacking and she was motivated to go to graduate school.

At this point in her career, 1941-42, WW II occupied the nation's attention and Gwen says, "I really wanted to join the Marines, but my mother did not think that was appropriate for her only daughter. I did not want to violate the wishes of my mother, so I decided to go to the University of Iowa, at that time, the prime place to go for advanced work in Physical Education. The other major influence affecting my decision was Oscar 'Oskie' Strahan, a native Iowan, who came to SWT about 1919.

"He was a wonderful coach and PE teacher—the coliseum is named for him. I took all the courses I could from him and he encouraged me to pursue advanced education at his alma mater. I obtained a fellowship in 1944 and finished my doctorate in 1946."

Illinois State Normal University in Bloomington, IL offered her the best teaching opportunity at the handsome annual salary of $3,000.00. Pay notwithstanding, she describes the program at IS(N)U as ambitious, demanding, and creative. Her department chair had a doctorate from the University of Iowa as well and was determined to have a PE department in the top rank. In keeping with the demands of the program, Gwen taught just about every course offered for the professional preparation of PE majors. This runs the gamut from social dance to swimming and includes coaching tennis, softball and basketball teams.

"Dance was my real love," Gwen says. "In our program at Illinois State we had dance performance majors and dance education majors. I taught PE majors to go out and teach dance. I was particularly interested in what we call the social forms of dance: ball room dance, the fox-trot, the waltz, the samba, the tango, and American square dance. Today, dance has more or less lost its way, unfortunately."

In 1979 after 34 years teaching teachers to teach, Gwen retired from Illinois State and returned to San Marcos. It must be noted the only things she retired from was her official job and the institution where she pursued it. She most assuredly did not retire from civic involvement, volunteer activities, and creativity.

Following a pattern set by her family, especially her father and her brother, Max, she immersed herself in the affairs of her community. While her father and brother were involved in politics for many years, Gwen has studiously avoided that means of public service. Her father served San Marcos as a city councilman, mayor, and fire commissioner. Max served several terms in the Texas legislature and seventeen years as Judge of the Hays County Commissioner's Court. As a legislator, he chaired the appropriations committee which is the most powerful committee in the legislature.

Asked to talk about her broad and deep involvement in the affairs of San Marcos, she begins: "Well, 1986 marked the 150th birthday of the state of Texas. I had a long involvement with the Heritage Association, having served on the board and, at the time, I was serving as president of the Association. I was asked to co-chair the Sesquicentennial Committee with Gordon Hyatt. San Marcos became deeply involved in the Texas Sesquicentennial because Emmy Craddock, our former mayor, was the chairman of the State Sesquicentennial Committee. The goal of our commission was to establish the San Marcos River Foundation. We agreed that any money realized from any events or activities would go to seed the funding of the River Foundation.

"As a part of the celebration, we held a one day event called FestaFair at Strahan Coliseum. That is important because it was the impetus for us to resurrect the city fire bell. Dr. Habengreither and his crew at SWT restored the bell for us. We had it in the parade and then we set it in front of the coliseum and people rang it all day." More about the bell later.

It takes a lot of prodding to get Gwen to talk about herself. She deflects questions about herself with stories about her brothers or her parents. There is not room in this piece to list all her activities and the recognition she has received. A partial list includes her aforementioned two years as president of the Heritage Association; co-chair of the Texas Sesquicentennial celebration; selected in 1985 to the San Marcos Women's Hall of Fame; co-chair of the Heritage Neighborhood Association; member of the city Planning Commission; member of the Historic Preservation Commission; Summerfest Committee; and the San Marcos Zoning Board of Adjustments and Appeals. Her academic achievements are equally impressive. Among those she is most proud of is her inclusion in the President's Commission for Women in Higher Education, Southwest Texas State University Women: First 100 years.

Among her latest accomplishments is finding a home for San Marcos's original fire bell. As a part of the 150th birthday of San Marcos, she, with the help of Robert Cotner and the Heritage Association, convinced the city council it would be an appropriate time to venerate an artifact of the town's history. The council agreed with her (most are familiar with her tenacity) and erected in front of city hall two Texas limestone columns, joined by a steel rafter from which hangs the 1000 pound bell.

When queried about the growth of San Marcos, she said, "We can't prevent it. The people are coming." With a wry grin, she added a pungent, "But I would like to tell them to bring their own water." Then she continued, "I would like to know we are doing everything possible to get them immersed in the San Marcos we have strived so hard to retain—the San Marcos we know and love."

So, how do we do that? "We must pay attention to the people we elect to public office. We must lobby the city to keep us better informed. We must get people involved in neighborhood associations, volunteer activities, and be willing to stand up and tell our leaders what we want. We must learn to care. We must care about our neighborhoods; we must care about our neighbors; we must care about our downtown. We must decide what kind of San Marcos we want and care enough about it to work toward achieving that goal."

Ollie Giles

When I see Ollie Giles in the grocery store, she always has a report about her new project. At our most recent encounter, she urged me to go to the library to see her display honoring February as Black History month. Ollie is a San Marcos icon. Her involvement in activities, city, county, and state-wide, is longer than my monthly grocery list. Suffice to say, she was selected to the San Marcos Women's Hall of Fame in 1988-89.

"To start with," she says, "I was born in San Marcos in 1933." Then, like the genealogist that she is, she says, "My father was Lawrence Hargis and my mother was Enola Hollins. And I'm an only child."

Her sense of humor emerges as she continues, "When I was born, God just threw the pattern away. He said, there were none before her, there will be none after her. She's perfect. My parents never had any more children. Both my parents remarried, but neither of them had any more children."

Recounting her early childhood, Ollie says she started to the Colored School at the age of five. Her uncle, Edward Hollins, was a teacher at the school and he kept her supplied with books and taught her to read. "I was five at home, but I was six at school," Ollie says. "I went to school here until I was about eight years old. My mother married again and we moved to California.

"We went to the Bay Area—Oakland and Berkley. I had been used to the all-Colored schools of Texas, the students, the teachers—all Colored. When I got to California, I was the only little Colored girl in the whole Franklin Elementary School. I thought, 'Oh, my goodness, what are all these white folks going to do to me?' I was scared to death.

"Then I began to realize they were not looking at the color of my skin. It's what's inside they care about. It came to me, 'We're not any different!'"

Ollie finished school in California where, she says, there were few people of color in her classes. Following high school, she married and began to have children. Five of her seven children were born in California.

Her unwavering independence and her outspoken manner are revealed as she says, "My husband seemed to keep me barefoot and pregnant, and I decided, if this is it, I don't want to be married anymore. Meantime, my mother went back to Texas, so I decided to join her. I came back with five children and I have been here ever since. But when I needed him, my first husband was always there for me. We are still good friends. I am even friends with his second wife. We are like sisters."

Following a divorce from her second marriage which produced twins, Linda and Brenda Bell, Ollie found herself a single mom again. It was necessary for her to work. She began cleaning houses.

Always the historian, she interrupts herself to talk about her grandmother's restaurant on Center Street. It was born of necessity because… "When the visiting minstrel shows would come to town, the Negroes had no place to eat.

"My grandmother finished school and she was not born during slavery, so when she found she could not use the bathroom in the houses she was cleaning, she decided she didn't need that. She started a laundry. Jack Gary, one-time sheriff of Hays County, was one of her customers. He loved her hoe cakes and when he came to pick up his laundry, he headed straight for the kitchen to get his hoe cakes and molasses."

Ollie cleaned houses until she got a call from Sammy Hardeman who was a food service manager at Gary Air Base. He offered her a job as a cook She knew nothing about cooking, but she accepted because the pay was much better and she had benefits. One of her employees resented her leaving and let it be known that the military was disrupting the whole community by 'taking all our colored help.'

According to Ollie, Mr. Hardeman taught his employees all aspects of food preparation and after the military closed Gary, she went to Austin and cooked in several restaurants. Mr. Carson of the once popular Carson's Restaurant of San Marcos hired Ollie and she worked there for a number of years.

Ollie took the opportunity to give me a history lesson when I asked for some details of her life. "I returned from California just as the schools were beginning to integrate," she replied. "My daughter was still in school and she never went to the Colored School. I remember that some of the African-American teachers held students back in the Colored School. Integration was accomplished one grade at a time and they were afraid of losing their job. When integration was complete, not one Negro teacher had a job here. Not one! Not a single one!"

After integration, the building which housed the Colored School, later named Dunbar for Lawrence Dunbar, a famous African-American poet, was purchased by Mr. Marshall and given to the city's Parks and Recreation.

"The city was using it to store a lot of junk," says Ollie, as a trace of anger wipes away her perpetual smile. "I went down there and told the city to get that junk out of there. Then there was a fire which burned the back of the building. The insurance paid for the building to be torn down completely and Jeff Kester designed a new building which conformed to the old building as nearly as possible and it has become a great meeting and recreation facility."

I directed Ollie back to her own story. "I went to Durham Business College after I had to quit cooking and I specialized in data processing. I couldn't find a job in San Marcos because I had no experience, but the college got me a job in San Antonio with no trouble. I worked in a CPA office and that is how I became interested in accounting."

After a year in San Antonio, Ollie again sought work in San Marcos. "Now I had experience, but I still could not find work in this town.

"Finally, I interviewed with the San Marcos Baptist Academy and the president informed me I would be 'the first…er, ah…Negro to hold this type position at the Academy.' He said, what if somebody were to call you a name, what would you do? I said, 'Sir, I ignore ignorant people because they just don't know any better.' He said, OK. I worked for the Academy for 23 years."

Ollie became sick from an intestinal infection and was in a coma for 41 days. The doctors called in her family and her minister and told them she was not expected to make it through the night. She reports she had a vision and was told that her job on earth was not finished.

She came out of the coma, but it was thought she would probably be brain-damaged. As she continued to improve, she was told she would never be able to go anywhere without her oxygen tank. Ollie punctuates this portion of her story with, "That tank is at home in the back of my closet. I'm celebrating 12 years and I have never used oxygen. One of my doctors said to me, 'You see these gray hairs on my head. Everyone of them has Ollie Giles written on it.'"

Finally discharged from the hospital, Ollie found the Academy no longer had a job for her. She did what Ollie has always done. She found other jobs. One was at Tuttle Lumber where her off the wall sense of humor got her fired.

When she turned 62, God told her it was time to step out on faith and start her own business. She started ACTORS, Ancestors Chart Tracer, Ollie's Research Service. Ollie worked three years exclusively for the Austin American Statesman researching court records for one of their departments.

"Other customers heard about me, and I have clients from California to South Carolina," she informed. "I can trace your family tree, but I do almost any court house research you want me to do. The biggest share of my work is deed and title search, criminal search, and foreclosures. I sell foreclosure lists to various companies. I started this company six years ago and it keeps me real busy. When I go home this evening, I will have faxes to go to Lockhart, Bastrop or wherever."

So, at 68, Ollie has a business that provides well, keeps her busy, and sort of gives her a last laugh on some of the people and institutions who might have doubted her in years past. She is content with her lot and ready to relax.

Are you kidding?! One of the projects of which she is proudest— worthy of a grocery store aisle conversation—is her status as a student at SWT. With the enthusiasm of a co-ed, she will tell you she is a junior, majoring in history with emphasis on African-American history.

Ollie Giles has stories to tell. Humorous, historical, sad, candid, cruel, delightful, frightening, and revealing. She is a woman with an enduring faith in the goodness of mankind and a great love for all people, but don't engage her in conversation if you are not in the mood for the unvarnished truth.

Raul Contreras

There are fathers in San Marcos who are more visible than Raul Contreras. There are fathers who have, perhaps sacrificed more for their children. But there are no fathers who are more patient and more thoughtful of their children. Raul is a quiet man, who, like so many of his generation, has gone about doing what is required of him, asking no special favors, expecting no special treatment. Standing straight as a post, at 79 he wears his years with dignity and aplomb.

His father was a sharecropper on the Jackson farm, located between Hunter Road and Highway 123. One of nine children, Raul's education ended in the ninth grade when he went to work to help support the family. His school was the Springtown School on Hunter Road.

Citing the presence of Dunbar School and the segregation that existed in those days, I asked if it was a segregated school. He laughed as he replied, "There were nothing but Latins there when I went to school. But I didn't know any difference. I think it was called the Mexican School."

Raul relates that his family moved off the farm into town in 1939. "Times were hard," he says, "and I had a chance to join the Civilian Conservation Corps (CCC). I signed up for one year. They sent me to Yuma, Arizona to work on the irrigation project for the Imperial Valley. We built the irrigation gates to regulate the flow of the water. I was paid $20.00 a month and they sent $20.00 home."

At the end of that year, times were still hard in San Marcos, so Raul gave the CCC another try. This time, he went to Laramie, Wyoming. He was at Laramie six months when WWII started.

"They put us to work building concentration camps for Japanese citizens," Raul relates. "However, it wasn't long before the government began inactivating the CCC. I came home and almost immediately got orders to report for the draft."

Basic training was at Fort Belvoir, Virginia. Raul took advantage of his training location by visiting Washington, DC almost every week. "After basic, we got orders to go overseas. From Ft. Belvoir, we went to Ft. Banks, NY where we boarded the Queen Mary. They crammed 26,000 of us on this huge ship. There was a whole flotilla guarding us. I was young at the time and I wanted to see action. I thought, why don't they bomb us. It took us seven days to cross the Atlantic."

After landing in Scotland, Raul's unit was in the vicinity of Salsbury, Southampton, and Stratford on Avon. "We were in Shakespeare country,

176

but I didn't know it at the time. It is only since I have read later that I realized it," he explains.

As a member of the 347th Combat Engineers, Raul was engaged in building airstrips for B-17's prior to the invasion of Europe. His unit was scheduled to be a part of the D-Day invasion, but because of bad weather, the 347th was delayed six days to June 12. In France, they were charged with repairing the railroads which Germans destroyed as they retreated. Upon reaching the Rhine River, they were given the mission of getting a pontoon bridge across the river to accommodate Patton's Third Army. It took two divisions to guard them as they put the bridge in place.

Raul recounts his experience during the Battle of the Bulge. "We had to go back all the way to Bastogne to open the roads. Along the way, we would see GIs sitting under trees, with their head down as if they were napping. They were dead and frozen in that position. There was an outfit following us, just picking up bodies."

For three and a half years Raul was in Europe. He returned to the United States only after the war was over. In fact, when Germany surrendered, he was informed he would be sent to the Pacific Theater. But before his unit could be withdrawn from Europe, the war in the Pacific also ended.

Raul returned home, and as did so many, he simply wanted to get on with his life. One of the first things he did was return to school and get his high school GED. He began work at Gary Army Air Base as a mechanic in the early 50's.

It was about this time he married Oralia, his wife of 51 years. As he talked about Oralia, he could not resist showing wedding pictures of their second marriage on their 40th anniversary.

In 1956, he was transferred to Randolph AFB where he spent 30 years as a mechanic and instructor, prior to his retirement in 1981. Meanwhile, he and Oralia had three children. Gloria is the eldest, Minerva is the second child and George is the youngest. Gloria and George are graduates of SWT. Gloria teaches school in San Antonio while George, in Raul's words, "is some sort of a big shot with the Internal Revenue Service in Austin."

Minerva, Minnie, as she is affectionately known to everyone, is the second child. Raul says, "When Minnie was born, we didn't know what was wrong with her. About a month after she was born, we knew there was something different. She could not see. It was about three years before she could see. She did not walk until she was about two years old. And she did not talk. We did not know what to do."

Raul took Minnie to several doctors in an effort to find answers to his little girl's problems. No one seemed to have any. So, he and Oralia nurtured her, and did what they knew how, to help her survive. When

177

Minnie was about seven years old, two important things happened. First, Mr. Thomas, a school administrator with the public schools had a meeting in the old State Bank Building for parents with handicapped children. Twelve parents showed up. He told the parents the schools would start a program for their children. Second, Minnie became seriously ill with pneumonia. Her family physician was unavailable, so Dr. Scheib was called to answer the emergency. Her temperature was so high, the doctor put her in a bathtub full of ice water. Dr. Scheib said he had never seen a person survive such a high temperature. Following that visit, he took a special interest in Minnie.

Raul reports that up to that time, Minnie hardly spoke at all. "Following her recovery," he says, "something happened because she began to talk all the time. It was hard to get her to stop talking. Minnie also still has the manners of a blind person. When I drop something, I look for it. Minnie feels for it with her fingertips."

Oralia says, "Sometime between her second and third birthday, I believe she spontaneously began to see. One day, she began to move her head as if she were looking at things and she began to laugh. She seemed so excited, she just could not stop laughing."

What is a parent's reaction when they discover their child is not going to be a normal child. Raul pointed to Oralia and said, "She was crying every day." What about you, I asked? "I was too," he reluctantly admitted. "It was rough."

Raul turns serious as he says, "Not once did we ever consider putting Minnie in a home or a state school or an institution. As a result of Mr. Thomas's efforts, she was allowed to go to public school until she was twenty. She then was eligible for services at the Scheib Opportunity Center where she has gone for about 25 years."

He has lived a life of sacrifice. The burden seems unfair. Three and a half prime years of life given to one's country, only to be rewarded with the fear and confusion that accompanied the realization that one of your children would never live a normal life seems almost more than a person should be asked to bear.

Raul Contreras has never flinched; never backed away from any challenge. He has asked for no special favors. He has seen his duty as a citizen and a father and gone about doing it in a quiet, conscientious, deliberate manner. His reward is the knowledge that he gave what was asked without reservation. He is the epitome of the Greatest Generation.

Laura Pratt

Laura Pratt said, "Sometimes I pass a mirror and catch a glimpse of my body and I do a slight double take. I don't look like everyone else. That is about the only time I am aware that I have only one arm."

Laura's missing right arm is the price she paid to be a cancer survivor. As Chairperson of the Survivors' Celebration, she is deeply involved with the Relay for Life program of the American Cancer Society. The Relay for Life will be held April 12 and 13, 2002. at Tanger Outlet Mall.

She was born in Waco in 1969 while her dad was a student at Baylor University. After graduating from Baylor, her father, Marty Gray, took a teaching job in Bynum, and lived in Hillsboro. Laura started school and went through the sixth grade in Bynum where her dad was the principal, head football coach, coached the track team, taught several classes and was coach of the girl's teams. She adds, there were only four students in her grade.

Laura says, "When I was in first grade, we noticed that my right arm would not straighten completely. My mom started taking me to doctors. We went to one after another. We saw doctors in Waco and all over the place and, actually, my best friend's orthodontist referred us to the doctor who did the surgery. My friend's mom was discussing my situation with the orthodontist and he said, let me see her. I have this surgeon friend at Fort Worth Children's Hospital.

"The orthodontist made the referral and the surgeon at Fort Worth Children's Hospital found a tumor. It was identified as *synovial sarcoma*, a soft tumor in the ligament of the elbow joint. It was a unique case because this type cancer is normally found in the elderly and I was only nine years old."

It usually spreads rapidly and it was known she had the tumor at least two years by the time she was diagnosed. When it was identified, she and her family went immediately to M.D. Anderson Hospital in Houston. Radiation treatment was considered, but the family was told the possibility of recurrence was near 80 per cent. Doctors found it had not spread at all, but, nevertheless, recommended radical treatment. With those odds, the family chose amputation.

Given the mixture of good news/bad news, Laura can speak only of how wonderfully blessed she has been. During this interview, there was not one word of bitterness, regret, blame, or recrimination. She expressed deep sympathy for her parents and their ordeal, but never a hint of self-pity.

Asked her reaction to learning she would lose her right arm, Laura said, "Nine year olds are bullet proof. Everything is still possible. If you jump off the roof, your umbrella will work just like Mary Poppins'. And it was so fast, it was unreal. I didn't really believe they were going to take off my arm until I woke up from the surgery. It wasn't all that traumatic for me.

"But I don't know how my parents went through it. As a parent now, I have a lot better appreciation of their situation. They assured me everything would come out OK and I believed them. I don't remember it being scary. There was pain and I hated being in the hospital, but there were kids four or five years old who had never been out of the hospital more than six months. They played soccer in the halls of the hospital as if they were in the middle of the school ground."

Shortly after discharge, Laura began a two year program of chemotherapy. The treatments were given every three months. With each treatment she lost her hair, so for two years she never had more than a couple inches of hair. She describes this phase of her illness as probably the ugliest. Her dad had to forcibly restrain her during a portion of these treatments.

Once again, Laura's feelings are for her parents. "I'm horrified that I made him do that. My parents were just incredible. They were fabulous.

"And because I went to a small school, and my dad was so much a part of the school, everyone knew me and my situation. First grade through 12th were all in the same building. No one ever laughed at me because I had no hair. No one teased me about my arm. I was in such a safe place, I grew comfortable with myself.

"By the time I had to venture out into the larger environment, I was so comfortable with myself, it was never an issue. That was another incredible blessing."

Laura recounts that she started wearing an arm, but she was an active, athletic young girl and the prostheses was in the shop more than it was on her. It was a bigger pain re-learning to use the arm each time she got it back than it was to be without it. Eventually, she stopped wearing it.

Laura describes her teen years, "My parents always convinced me that I could do anything I wanted to do. In the seventh grade, I transferred to Hillsboro schools where I played basketball and ran track, cross-country, and became a cheerleader. I had my group of friends. I did well academically. I don't ever remember my arm being an issue."

Perhaps the major concession she has made to the loss of her arm (one simply can not use the word handicapped with Laura Pratt) is learning to write with her non-dominant hand. She was a natural right-hander when the amputation occurred. But she impishly turned that to her advantage.

Laura confesses, "I was allowed to do a lot of my school work at home because I wrote slower than other students. My parents were allowed to write for me. As time went by, I found myself intentionally slowing my writing so that my parents would write for me. They caught on rather quickly, however."

Laura continued her education with a degree in social work from Stephen F. Austin University in 1991 and a masters degree from the University of Houston in 1993. She and her husband, Adam Pratt, her high school sweetheart, traveled around the country for a year while he completed his optometry internship. The internship process took them from New Mexico to Virginia with a stop in Houston before they settled initially in Copperas Cove, Texas. San Marcos beckoned when he was asked to establish optometry in the newly constructed Walmart store in 1996.

With two daughters, Allison, 6, and Brianna, 3, Laura explains, "They have been an adventure. I think I was always destined to be a mom, even though it was uncertain whether I would ever be able to have children. The chemo I took and the age at which I took it, made my getting pregnant uncertain. Everyone told me to just try. Incredibly, I had no trouble at all. It has been a miraculous blessing."

Laura explains that she has done things a bit differently as a mother. Changing diapers, is an example. She put the baby on the floor and used her foot to raise the baby's bottom so she could slide the diaper under the baby. She never paid attention to it until Brianna came along and Laura observed Allison using the same technique with her dolls.

In addition she relates that Allison was oblivious to her missing arm, but Brianna uses the 'little arm' as a security blanket. Her pet name for it is "Arnie." During this interview Brianna frequently rubbed her face against the remaining portion of the arm.

"I am deeply involved with my daughters," says Laura. "I work with PTO and Girl Scouts. Allison readily explains to her friends what happened to me and why I have only one arm. There seems to be no embarrassment whatever."

What about Relay for Life, I asked. "It is an incredible experience. That first year I was invited to be on a friend's team. I was amazed that I made it through the night. Last year, I had my own team. This year, we are going to have so much fun at the Survivors' Celebration. The dinner will be April 10th at the Activity Center. It will be a great opportunity for the survivors to get to know each other. There are things about survivorship that people ought to know. Yes, I am a cancer survivor, but it's way down the list of things I am. I am a mom, a wife, a volunteer, a friend, and a daughter—all those things are way ahead of my being a cancer survivor.

"Actually, my parents are the survivors more than I. They are the ones who convinced me that I could be whatever I wanted to be. I don't even think about being different. Whether people don't notice because I don't notice or whether I just don't notice that they are noticing, I don't know. Whatever. It works for me."

Ron and Marie Jager

How did the path of a fellow from Chicago intersect in Eldorado, Texas with the path of a girl from Iowa? That was my question of Ron and Marie Jager when they informed me of their origins. Ron Jager was born in Chicago December 31, 1927—20 minutes before midnight—and his father was overjoyed. He had a tax exemption.

Marie was born in Brooks County, Iowa in 1929, but her family returned to Denton, Texas, her mother's birthplace, when Marie was two and a half years old.

As Ron explains this unlikely happenstance: "I had just graduated from the University of Miami with a degree in geology and chemistry and a friend and I were on our way to California to work in the bauxite mine fields. By the time we got to Texas, we were out of money.

"We knew of an oilfield engineering firm in San Antonio that hired one of our colleagues. We applied for a job there and were hired on the spot. They sent me to San Angelo to open a field office. My San Angelo roommate was engaged to an Eldorado school teacher. Her roommate had just graduated from North Texas State and was in Eldorado for her first teaching job. They got us together and needless to say I didn't make it to California."

They were married December 23, 1952. The first year of that long-running production saw the Jagers move 13 times and after the first year of marriage, both took teaching jobs at Webster, Texas, the home of NASA.

Ron taught high school chemistry while Marie taught sixth grade. While teaching, Ron went to law school at night at the University of Houston. Upon graduating from law school, Ron went to work for Sinclair Oil and Gas, this time as a geologist/lawyer, negotiating joint operating agreements with other oil companies.

"We stayed there for nine years," said Ron, "and Marie went to work in the field of her primary interest, which was drama."

Marie explains, "When Ron graduated from law school, I resigned my position as a sixth grade teacher at Webster, thinking we might move on. But he stayed in Houston and I applied to teach drama at the newly opened Clear Creek High School.

"I had children of John Glenn and Scott Carpenter in my classes. We established the Clear Creek Country Theater and Buzz Aldrin's wife, Joan, played the lead in Look Homeward Angel."

Ron interjected. "Marie was recognized as one of the five most outstanding drama teachers in the state. She had, at the time, a state record of taking a one-act play to UIL state competition seven times. She won first place four of the seven times. I sort of uprooted her when I decided to come to UT."

Marie interrupted Ron. "He wrote three of the plays that I did at state. They have been published and we still get royalties from his work. I wish he had time to write more."

I pressed Ron to explain how they left this seemingly ideal situation in the Houston area and found their way to San Marcos. There have been some rather sharp turns in Ron Jager's career path.

"I met a friend in law school who taught history at Rice University. He got me interested in history by explaining interpretive history as opposed to my experience of knowing dates, places and names. I drove right by the University of Houston on my way home, so I enrolled in the history program. First thing I know, I have a masters degree in history."

Meanwhile, the oil business changed drastically. The Suez Crisis changed what had been a free-flowing, fun business into a bureaucratic maze of frustration. And that did not appeal to this man of many interests.

"I thought I could be a reasonably good teacher, based on my year of teaching chemistry. I was encouraged by my professors at the University of Houston to continue with history and pursue a PhD. I polled 20 people at Sinclair about a career choice and 19 said, 'forget history.'"

With that sort of encouragement, Ron and Marie left the Houston area to come to the University of Texas at Austin to finish his PhD. A position came open in 1966 in the history department at SWT.

"I turned down a fellowship at UT to come to SWT with the idea that we would probably be here about five years," said Ron. "We lived in Austin seven years before we finally moved here in 1972."

Meanwhile, Marie gave up teaching and spent the seven years they were in Austin raising their adopted daughter and helping Ron re-do their "honeymoon cottage" on Lake Austin.

Upon moving to San Marcos, their first priority was to re-do the house at 626 West San Antonio Street. Built in 1914, it had been converted to apartments during WWII. A stairway was removed and another re-routed to accommodate the apartments. Ron and Marie spent a couple of years, working a lot at night, restoring the house to near its original structure.

I discovered one could fill an afternoon discussing early American and Revolutionary history with Ron, but my purpose is to chronicle more recent events such as the Jagers' contribution to the Heritage Association,

San Marcos Performing Arts Association, (SMPAA) and Greater San Marcos Area Seniors Association (GSMASA).

The Jagers have belonged to the Heritage Association since its inception. They have served as docent, van driver and have used their front porch as a bake sale vending locale.

The Performing Arts Association has been their first love. As mentioned earlier, Ron is a playwright. He wrote four one act plays for Marie's high school drama classes and after coming to San Marcos, he wrote Falderal, a full length play, which he and Harry Wayne turned into a musical. He is also a set designer and builder of no small talent. Angus McLeod, recently choir director of San Marcos High, credits Ron with making possible many of his 19 productions of Broadway shows.

In 1979 Ron and Marie created Summer Musicale. Marie says, "There had never been a community musical produced in San Marcos and it was said it could not be done. Bob Kercheville was the only person who really encouraged us. Ruben Meeks tapped a lot of business people for underwriting funds. The Lions Club gave us $100.00. We promised every underwriter we would repay them.

"That play was "The Boyfriend," and we repaid every cent to our underwriters and had money left to do our show the next year. We eventually did six community musical theater productions in the years that followed."

They were invited in 1985 to develop an appropriate extravaganza for the local celebration of the Texas Sesquicentennial. In March of 1986, after a year's preparation, they put on Fest-A-Fair, visited by approximately 9,000 people.

The Jagers then organized the San Marcos Performing Arts Association through which the Summer in the Park concert series was born. They directed the production of the concerts for the next six years. In addition, in 1985 they were instrumental in establishing the San Antonio Street of Lights during the Christmas Season. This event, in conjunction with Central Texas Medical Center's Santa Claus Christmas on the Square, was the seed that grew into the three day presentation of the Sights and Sounds of Christmas.

The current project which occupies 60 hours per week of Marie's *and* Ron's time (that's 120 hours per week) is the H.Y.Price, Jr. Senior Center and the GSMASA. The building once occupied by the First Christian Church is home to this project. In 1993, the building was purchased by its namesake, Mr. Price, and deeded to the city expressly for the purpose of youth or seniors programs.

A disenchanted city council, through a comedy of errors, came very close to: a) selling the building for $1,000.00 and b) demolishing it. The Jagers, once again, stepped forward and because of their long and close association with Mr. Price in the SMPAA, took necessary action to rescue the structure so that it might be used for the purpose Price intended. Their actions resulted in the organization of the GSMASA, and acquisition of a 30 year lease on the building.

As noted, Ron, as president of GSMASA, and Marie, as special events director, spend about 60 hours per week overseeing the operation of the Senior Center and the ongoing renovation of the building. At this point there has been roughly $152 thousand in renovation work accomplished since 1999. One of the community outreach programs of the center includes a Price Center Dining Room as a funding source for ongoing preservation and renovation.

For those who who find the Jagers' civic and volunteer involvement almost beyond belief, let me add that both are cancer survivors. Marie is a two-time survivor. Her first bout was with breast cancer in 1976. Her second round was cancer of the uterus in 1982. She also wears a pacemaker. Ron had prostate cancer in 1991. This followed heart problems in 1990 severe enough to require angioplasty.

If you would like to show your appreciation to the Jagers, they will be honored with an open house, celebrating their 50th Wedding Anniversary December 21, 2002 at—where else—the H.Y.Price, Jr. Senior Center at 222 West San Antonio Street. *Author's note: The Jagers continue their 60 hours a week at the Senior Center.*

Robert Cotner

Robert Cotner is a man of passion. It takes about five minutes to understand his foremost passion is lights. Here, it seems, is a man whose career as an electrician is based much more on his need to follow his passion than to earn a living. Robert is a major player in San Marcos's annual light festival, the Sights and Sounds of Christmas. He is the head technician, the chief electrician, and the main reason those lights you are enjoying during this season come on...and stay on when the switch is thrown.

He is also the spark (pun intended) for the Scott Street light display, one of the highlights of residential decorating in this town. It is the Aurora Borealis of Christmas lighting. It is a San Marcos Extravaganza. It is an expression of exuberance that erases our cynicism and takes all of us back to the age of wonder and amazement.

All this began at an early age. As Robert explains, "I've always been interested in electricity and while my dad, a history professor at the University of Texas, was not mechanically inclined, we would go to the hardware store together because that is where I wanted to go. I was always taking things apart to see how they worked and my dad had to call the repairman to get them back together."

Robert enjoys relating that, as a kid growing up, he found great satisfaction in wiring his parents' house for sound. "I had microphones all through the house so I could listen to people. I just generally enjoyed doing things with wires and electricity."

In 1968 Robert came to Southwest Texas State where he majored in business and continued his avocation of stringing wires as he worked part-time for his uncle, Ted Breihan owner of Ted Breihan, Electric.

When I expressed amazement at the familial connection, Robert admitted he is surprised at how few people are aware of this relationship. "I always assumed everyone knew," he said.

"Ted Breihan taught me the correct way of doing electricity. I worked for him until 1980 when I began my own business. That was a little touchy for awhile, but today we are very close friends. His children, my cousins, are like brothers and sisters to me."

While the Scott Street display at Christmas is familiar to almost all San Marcos people, what is not so familiar is another of Robert's passions—Christmas trees and decorations. Walking into his house is like walking into an enchanted forest where every tree is decorated using a theme evoking the familiar, the whimsical, the spiritual, the artistic, or the technological cutting edge.

Robert goes evangelical when discussing the lights and decorations displayed by the *more than sixty*—yes, SIXTY PLUS—Christmas trees located throughout his house. When asked what inspires such effort, he responded, "I think it is the Christmas lights; the fantasy of electricity and what electricity can do; the lights at Christmas lend themselves to such an opportunity for expression."

Describing the trees in detail is beyond the scope of this article, but to provide a flavor of the display: A ten foot neon outline of a Christmas tree filled with green garland and what must be thousands of miniature lights, guards the front entrance to the house. A huge 15 foot traditional tree full of nutcracker replicas greets you as you enter the vaulted-ceiling living room. Among the trees one passes on the way to the center of the house, is the Texas tree, festooned with the Lone Star flag and other Texana; the Coca Cola tree with miniature bottles which spin and rise and fall; the Teddy Bear tree with over 500 teddy bears of all sizes and lighted with teddy bear light fixtures; the Angel tree located in the Angel room, decorated with beautifully dressed porcelain angels of varying sizes; the Technology tree, a silver-metallic creation, decorated with many faceted silver balls of varying sizes. It rotates and is lighted indirectly and fills the room with light as it reflects the red and green spot lights aimed in its direction. The fiber optic tree is placed high on the wall of the bedroom and exudes red and green light as if the light were coming through pores in the leaves.

With the belief that Christmas should be celebrated year-round, Robert hopes to eventually establish a permanent display of Christmas trees. Under present conditions, he must dismantle his trees, store them and the ornaments in a warehouse until the season rolls around. For him the season begins in early October. He removes virtually all the furniture from his home and replaces it with Christmas trees. It then requires two months to erect and decorate all the trees.

"I was fortunate to go to Market in Dallas about seven years ago with Barry Breed, who was then with Breed Hardware. She introduced me to a whole new world of Christmas. At the market you see what will be on the shelves in three years. For instance, fiber optics were at market three years ago and this year is the first year they have been available to the general public. Light rope, halite lamps in all shades of colors, all sorts of technology make working with lights an ever-changing challenge and provides great opportunity. For instance, this year using the halite lamps, we did Scott Street in green.

"When you go to market in January, you buy for December so you can be assured it will be made and be shipped on time. Then I go back to market in July and that is when I fill in the gaps that I may have. I buy wholesale."

Wholesale what, he was asked. "Wholesale Christmas," he replied. "And this is everything from Christmas lights to Christmas trees, to ornaments, and whatever else I might need."

"You go to Dallas market twice a year?" I asked.

"I go to Dallas, San Francisco and Atlanta to market every year. Then, if I see something in my travels, vacations, conventions, etc., I buy it. The Mardi Gras room in the bar, (That tree is decorated with porcelain masks, beads, and other Mardi Gras trappings.) for instance, is the result of more than 10 years of going to New Orleans."

Robert modestly refuses to call himself an artist. He prefers a more mundane term such as experimenter. But he reluctantly admits that, "anyone who plays with lights and electricity in this way is dabbling in art."

Always looking for new experiments, he pointed out that neon is regaining popularity as an art form. As Robert talks, the accidental artist begins to dominate his conversation. "You can do so many things with it. It can be used safely in water for instance. There are no grounding problems. It makes a wonderful addition to aquariums. It can be mixed and matched and lends itself to all sorts of creativity. A lot of the neon here is left over pieces I have picked up from job sites—scraps, junk, actually which would have otherwise been thrown away."

Finally, steered to discussing his voluntary contributions to the community, he began, "My parents are the king and queen of volunteerism. They taught me you must give something back to your community if you can. I became involved with the Heritage Association in 1990 and I thought it was just fantastic. The things they were doing to preserve our history and to look toward and prepare for the future impressed me. The Heritage Association is not just Belvin and San Antonio Streets. It is all of San Marcos.

"The most important historical aspect of San Marcos is the river and all of us claim that as ours. And it is. So, when I was asked two years ago to become president, I had to turn them down because I was so busy, but I also promised I would do it the next year. I was president last year and we saw the association grow and accomplish lots of good things for San Marcos. I sponsor the Pi Kappa Alpha fraternity and I work with the Aquatic Club of San Marcos. In addition, I am on the SWT Alumni Board of Directors."

Those are the official volunteer roles with which Robert is identified, but it is fairly well known around town that if a group of people is trying to put together something that will benefit the town, promote a worthy cause, or raise consciousness by shining a light on a thing—tangible or otherwise—Robert Cotner will answer the call.

Joanne Bunker

Joanne Bunker (she is much better known as 'Ms B') is retired. Well, not exactly. She is out of the business, but she still shows up three days a week to work with pre-school kids. After 33 years in the business, 18 of which have been in San Marcos, she is no longer an owner/coach of Tumbling Tots. 'Ms B' is still a surrogate mother, grandmother, leaning post, strong shoulder, and always a friend to about 1,000 alumni of the program.

In 1982, she and her husband moved to San Marcos from Saginaw, Michigan to retire and take it easy in the mild climate and laid back ambiance of the Hill Country. She was not here long when, following a pattern established in Saginaw, she opened a gymnastics program in a tiny room in Jim's Gym. She had about 10 students at the beginning. In a short while, the program required a bigger room, and then a bigger room.

In Ms B's words, " We built the front addition to Jim's Gym of which I had half, and then I said, 'we need more room.' Jim moved a lot of stuff and gave me the entire front part of the gym. Jim Neuhaus is one of our biggest supporters. He would come in and encourage those kids and every time something new happened, we would run out to get Jim to cheer those kids on."

The program continued to grow so she decided to move to Center Point Road some five years ago. But that was not to be the end of her connection with Jim Neuhaus. In 1999, Jim suggested building a place for Tumbling Tots next to his location on McCarty Road. In the early stages of the planning for the new facility, Ms B discovered she had lymphoma.

"I went to Jim and told him he might want to reconsider his plans in light of my condition, she said. He asked me what my feelings were, and I said 'I'm going to beat this and I'm going to go on. This isn't going to stop me.' He showed a lot of faith in me and continued with his plans and we moved into this building in November of 1999.

"I was still on chemo when we made the move. I had parents, kids, my husband, everybody, truck loads of people, came over to the Center Point gym, and told me to just watch while they packed it all and brought it over here to McCarty Lane. Parents whose kids were no longer in my program showed up to help when they found we were moving."

It is difficult to understand the magnitude of that task unless you have seen the size of the building and the staggering amount of equipment that fills it. A short list of the equipment—acres of floor mats, enough balance beams to fence New Jersey, enough parallel bars to outfit a primate zoo, high bars too numerous to count, a trampoline half the length of the building—will give you some idea of the infinite inventory.

"Without the encouragement of all those people, I just couldn't have done it," she says.

Ms B describes her business, "Our program is a physical fitness program. It is not just a gymnastics program for kids who want to be on a team. If they do not want to compete, there is still a place for them here. It has grown from its humble beginning with about 10 students to about 250. In the 18 years I have had the program, I have begun to see children finish the program and come back with me to teach. I am now seeing children I taught bring their own children to the program.

"On Wednesday morning, we have a play group of up to 100 children, crawlers through five-year olds, and their parents. That part of the program was started for Homespun, an early intervention program for developmentally delayed children. The Homespun people were looking for a place to mainstream a group of kids, so I asked parents of toddlers if they would bring their kids in to play with them. That was about 10 years ago."

Ms B is especially qualified to work with special populations. She has extensive experience working in special education in schools. With the help of Connie Falleur, a long time supporter and assistant, she developed a program that provides the children a safe environment for unstructured self-expression through physical activity, exploration, experimentation, and interaction. Since parents are expected to just come and watch, it provides them an opportunity to talk with each other, discuss mutual concerns, and get to know a wider slice of the community. In short, it has become a huge support group.

Her expertise with children is no accident. She is the mother of eight of her own. One might ask, with eight children of her own, how did she find the time to teach special education and develop a gymnastics program? She explains, "When my oldest started college, I started going with her. At about that time, the federal government mandated that all children would receive education in the least restrictive environment. Most of the schools had no idea how to teach these kids, so a friend of mine who had seven children and I, with eight, were asked by the principal of the school to come in and give them a hand. I started as a teacher's aide and we were given kids at the lowest level of functioning. Our students were from five to 16 years old. I eventually got burned out with that job."

By the time she was ready to quit her work in special education, her daughters had developed an interest in gymnastics and she began working with them and decided she could open her own gym in Saginaw. For 15 years she taught/coached gymnastics until her husband retired from General Motors. They were looking for a warm place to live, and the Central Texas area was appealing. Since three of her children lived in the area, San Marcos became their destination.

"I had no intention of starting another gym, but I got really bored," says Ms B. "At this point, I am probably the oldest gymnastics coach in the area," she says as she unabashedly admits to being 68. "Up until I had the chemo treatments, I was spotting kids, lifting them to the bars, and working full time. The chemo made me slow down."

Asked what her program accomplishes, she began, "We work on developmental skills, reading readiness skills, adaptation to environment, spatial awareness, coordination, and self discipline. Walking a balance beam aids reading readiness. We teach them to use all their body—for instance in running, we teach them to use their arms effectively. Children develop self-confidence in our program. We help prepare the young ones for kindergarten by teaching them to listen, to follow instructions and to interact with others. We do all this in a positive atmosphere. There are no negatives here.

"There are consequences for their behavior. We give short time-outs, but we do not let the kids sit out any length of time. I am known as the Gummy Bear Lady because we reward them with gummy bears at the end of a session. We inform them when their behavior has cost them a gummy bear and we give them an opportunity to earn it back."

Ms B informed me she has had several girls pursue their gymnastics to the state level. None have made it to the national level, but Since it is not a recognized sport in the school system, there is a lack of real support for her 'team girls,' those who compete. At present there are a couple of girls who are competing at the state level.

Asked to talk about herself, she said she was not an athlete, "In fact, I was always the last one chosen for the baseball team, but when my girls started to parochial school, the nuns asked me to come in and start a phys ed program. They handed me a book and said, 'You can do it.' So, I did."

What do you want this article to say about you?, I asked. "The love I have for these children. I love it when these kids that are now taller than I am come up to me and give me a hug. I run into my kids when I'm shopping and it is such a joy to see them grow so much, physically and otherwise. Kids that are long out of the program are not at all bashful about coming up to me and giving me a big hug. That is what it is all about for me." *Authors note: Ms B passed away since this article was published.*

Hossein "Hagi" Hagigholan

Hossein Hagigholan or "Hagi," (Ha-jee) as he is affectionately known by almost everyone, began by telling a self-deprecating story on himself.

"When I came to America from Iran, I was 18 years old and my English consisted of 'yes, no, and thank you.' When I arrived in New York, I went to the Braniff Airlines desk and said I had a ticket to Houston—except my pronunciation at the time made it sound like 'Hos-ton.' I knew it was about a four hour trip to Houston, so when the plane started to land after about 45 minutes, I knew something was not right. Braniff had sent me to Boston."

Twenty-four years later the owner of Mamacita's restaurant chain has improved his English significantly, but he still retains the wide-eyed enthusiasm, the belief in himself, and the faith in America that the 18 year-old had when he stepped off that plane in 1976. He could rightly be labeled a cheerleader for hard work, self-reliance, and the land of opportunity. He is a member of the Anything is Possible School and with genuine modesty is quick to use himself as an example.

Hagi says, with a wry smile and a deep sense of irony, "I came to America to learn to be an engineer so I could return to Iran and make my parents proud." That it didn't happen that way can be attributed to a number of factors, not the least of which was the Iranian revolution of the late 70's and the taking of American hostages by the revolutionary government.

Upon arriving in Houston by way of Boston, Hagi found himself studying English as a second language. His class consisted of 20 or so students, 80 per cent of whom were Iranian. The teacher, after repeated exposure to the language of the students, had learned Farsi. So he and a few friends decided if they were to ever learn English, they must go to a school where there were no Iranians. Efforts were made to locate such a school. Colleges in San Antonio, Dallas, and Austin all had enrollments of Iranians in the hundreds. They finally found Schreiner College in Kerrville which had *zero* Iranians. That is how he came to be in Kerrville, home of the first Mamacita's.

"As the revolution consolidated, my money quit coming. So I had to work to stay here and stay in school." Hagi continued, "It was easy to get a job in a restaurant and I have worked in every kind of restaurant— pizza, burger joint, Mexican, any kind you can think of. During this time,

I learned a lot about the public and about how to persevere and how to survive."

In a straight, matter of fact way with no bitterness Hagi relates how during the height of the hostage situation he was working in the Acapulco Restaurant in Kerrville and customers went to his boss and demanded he be fired. Others, when they discovered he was Iranian, threw a quarter on the floor and instructed him to 'pick it up.' "I did," he said. "I understood the emotions of the people even though they were not right." It was also during the hostage crisis that tensions became so grave between the United States and Iran that all Iranians without visas were required to leave.

He laughs at himself at this point as he admits he married his wife to get a green card. "Oh, we were dating for a long time, but she broke up with me because she was afraid I would have to go back to Iran. I told her we should get married—I was only 20 years old, she was about 18—and I could stay. Finally, she agreed and in April of 1980 we got married in the courthouse. Six months later we were married in the church." Hagi proudly points out he has now been married twenty years and has been blessed by two beautiful adopted children, Roya, a six year old girl, and Nick, a boy, one year old.

The green card incident prompts a thought. "I am an American now— **proudly** an American citizen," Hagi says as he leans into the tape recorder for emphasis.

In 1984 Hagi was running Burger Island, his small place in Kerrville when three businessmen approached him to open a Mexican Restaurant. They had the land and were willing to put up $2,000,000.00 and make him an equal partner. "I couldn't pass that," he says, still somewhat astonished at such good fortune. "We opened Mamacita's in Kerrville in 1985. In 1988 we opened in Fredericksburg and four years ago, here in San Marcos. New Braunfels is the latest venture."

Hagi explains his success in business, "There is only one secret to a successful restaurant—the number one secret, 'Treat people the way you want to be treated.' Let people know you are interested in them. For example our managers are required to visit every table, every meal."

At this point Hagi surprisingly introduces religion into the interview. "If we just do what God tells us to do we will be all right. God made people and he sent all the many prophets to tell us how to treat everyone. And we try to treat everyone the way we are told. In the restaurant business there are two things most people worry about—labor and food costs. We don't worry about that at all. At Mamacita's we want everyone to leave with a smile on his/her face. If we do that, food costs and labor will take care of themselves.

"By the way, I am a Muslim," he informed. But to illustrate the extent to which Hagi has adapted to circumstances, he adds, "Well, I am half Christian because my wife is a Christian. We are raising our children in the Catholic Church and I am happy with that. When my father came to Texas and visited our restaurants, as a Muslim he admonished me about serving liquor. He reminded me that God would give me much greater rewards if I refused to serve liquor. I said, 'Dad, have you thought about drinking it and finding out how much more God has to give you.' After all, we have to be realistic.

"Without the bar we couldn't survive. But we do not have a happy hour at Mamacita's. We do not want people to get drunk. Liquor is necessary for a restaurant's survival, but we serve liquor only to enhance the dining experience."

It becomes clear that Hagi's business decisions are driven more by his religious, social, and ethical philosophy than by the bottom line. When asked the reason for Mamacita's location away from IH 35, Hagi explained, "We considered a location near Chili's and Red Lobster (on IH 35), but we are a local restaurant. We go into a city to be the best restaurant in that town. We consider ourselves a permanent resident of that city. Though with four locations it looks like we are a chain, we do not consider our company a chain. We are a company with local restaurants in different towns. We are there to serve the people of that town and if people are passing through and ask where is the best restaurant, the local people are going to direct them to us."

To discover more about Hagi's remarkable success we asked him to comment on Mamacita's extensive menu, Hagi explained that thirty per cent of the menu would never appear in most Mexican restaurants. "For example," he said, looking at the menu, "item number 37, Guisada Monterrey, is really an Iranian dish, disguised by its name. We also have an extensive selection of steaks and seafood. Of course, we have what you would expect to find in a Mexican restaurant." Here he digressed to say, there are five things he emphasizes in his restaurants. "Location, atmosphere, quality, service, and a reasonable price." He was emphatic about the reasonable price. "Our prices average between $5.00 and $7.00. We want to be accessible to everybody. Of course, we have more expensive foods, but we sell most of them at cost and figure we will make a few dollars off the drinks at those tables."

Given the transient nature of cooks, waiters, even managers Hagi was asked to explain the intricacies of keeping an efficient, friendly, professional staff. "First, we hire more staff than we need so we are never short-handed. We expect more from our people than most. We hire almost exclusively students as wait staff. We tell them, 'You will spend $30,000.00 in four years to learn to be a teacher, an engineer, an accountant. In four years with us, you will earn $60,000.00 and we will teach you how to get along in the world; how to discipline yourself; how to treat people; and the importance of work.' For example, we require people who call in sick to bring a doctor's note to justify their absence. Some people think this is petty, but other people are depending on them and we want them to understand *they* are important and this job is important." When discussing his managers, he pointed out that they get 130 days off each year— "unheard of in the restaurant business. We make sure they have time to spend with their family. This is a very tough business. We have 34 managers for four restaurants and we divide the responsibility. We have kitchen managers and floor managers. This allows us to get people who are more qualified in their field. We pay more money than any other kitchen. We want to have very little turn-over in our kitchen."

Hagi's contagious enthusiasm evoked a question about the most satisfying aspect of the business. "The pursuit of excellence. Every quarter we want to do better than the last quarter. When we can do that we know we are improving. It shows that we are doing our job and we are achieving our number one goal—customer satisfaction. We are making a lot of people happy."

Asked what made him believe he could run a restaurant, he unabashedly responded, "Tips. When I was a waiter, I took great pride in having people ask for my table. In fact, the men who offered me a partnership would always ask for me when I was a waiter. One year I took home ninety grand in tips. So, I thought, if I can do this as a waiter, how much more can I do if I own the business. I was 26 years old when I opened the first Mamacita's."

At 42, Hagi has achieved a remarkable success, so when asked what he would do differently, he took a long pause before responding, "Nobody has ever asked me that before and I have never given it any thought. I grew up in the restaurant business and maybe it is all I know, but I never thought of doing anything different. I have been very lucky to have such success. I am not smart enough to be this successful so God has been with me and has blessed me very generously."

His reference to God must have stirred some memory of his Muslim beginnings. He pointed out that "Hagi" means a Muslim who has made a journey to Mecca, the holy city of Islam. When questioned by friends in Iran or America as to how he became a Hagi, he relates that his trip to America is his Hagi. America represents his Mecca.

He is not bashful about revealing his passion for his adopted country. When asked what he wants this profile to convey to San Marcos about him, he responded, "I want not only San Marcos, but all of America to appreciate what they have because truly, God has blessed America. Americans do not always appreciate their country. Too many take it for granted. I return to Iran for three reasons: 1) To be with my family; 2) to help the poor because [by Iranian standards], there are no poor in America; 3) *to appreciate America.*"

Questioned about the future of his company, Hagi readily explained that his five year plan calls for a new restaurant in College Station, Austin and Georgetown. "We believe in going slowly. We do not open a restaurant until our newest is firmly entrenched and doing the kind of business we projected. We have not planned beyond that point. We have been pestered by a number of corporations who want to buy us out and expand our concept and of course, they want me to work for them. Why should I work for someone else when I'm having so much fun."

When asked what he would like to do that he has not done, Hagi did not hesitate. "I would like to make Texas more prosperous than ever. The lottery! For example, the jackpot becomes ten million, fifteen million and one person gets the money. Not a lot of people benefit from it. If I had the power I would change the prize. I would give the winner two million dollars. Every week when there is a winner, there are 300 or so people who have five numbers. I would divide the remaining eight, ten, twenty million among those people. They would receive twenty, thirty, thirty-five thousand each. That would allow each of those people to buy a house, a car, or do something worthwhile for a family. Can you imagine what would happen if we had 300 or 400 people who could invest that kind of money every few weeks. Most of the people who play the lottery are poor. It would change their life."

Why was I not surprised with Hagi's response. His creativity is always aimed at improving the lot of those around him. That seems to be *his* bottom line.

Stephanie Langenkamp

Stephanie Langenkamp describes her first thoughts of living in San Marcos.

"I can vividly recall sitting at the icehouse area, near that beautiful waterfall and thinking, 'I could enjoy living in San Marcos. It would be a great place to get a job.'

Today, the icehouse area is Joe's Crab Shack and there is a fence around the falls, but Stephanie is here and directs, perhaps, the most visited public facility in San Marcos, the library.

Several events had to come to a confluence to bring her to the place she now fills. First, while at the University of Texas, she majored in geography…well, sort of…"I really didn't major in anything," she says. "I was a complete dabbler and it offered such a variety—physical geography, climatology, economics and cultural geography—but I kept looking at the catalogue of courses and library science attracted me. The University also had a masters program in library science."

Second, she began dating this 'great guy' who later became her husband. They loved swimming. After Barton Springs and Lake Travis, he introduced her to San Marcos and the river.

Third, she did get a job in San Marcos in 1977. After getting her masters in library science, she went to work for the library when it was at 310 West Hutchison Street. She accepted a CETA position. "It was a grant funded position," says Stephanie. "And it was designed to revamp the focus of the library from a self-serve facility to a facility which could provide more individual attention to customers."

When reminded that CETA positions did not pay all that much, she said, "I found one of my receipts the other day while cleaning out some files and it reflected that I made $4.36 and hour.

"I worked for Eden Mosely, a wonderful person, who really wanted to make something of the library. She had high standards and really expected me to make a mark on the library, and I really think I did. I was the first reference librarian, had lots of public contact and did all the inter-library loan work. Then we began to get more programs. There really had not been any programming prior to that time. We did story-time for children, puppet shows, reading programs for kids, and conversational Spanish for adults, gardening seminars and things of that sort."

After just more than two years with the San Marcos library, Stephanie decided to return to the library at her alma mater where she said she learned a lot and made a lot of contacts, but discovered her heart was in public library work. She returned to San Marcos to become the librarian in 1982.

According to her, "I would have never expected in 1977 to have still been in San Marcos in 2001, but I have enjoyed it. It has been just a great experience.

"Working for the city exposes you to so many professions. Our meetings include all the department heads, so I know the fire chief, the police chief, head of the water department, etc. and we share our problems, so I get an insight on many aspects of the city. I have such an interesting job," she says with emphasis.

When one talks with Stephanie, it is readily apparent that she still brings the enthusiasm of that young CETA worker to her job. Asked to talk about what the library is doing now, she began with a description of the adult learning center.

"That is something we got started back in the late 80's with a federal grant. Its aim is to bring services to a disadvantaged population. We began working with the Ten County Adult Education Co Op. It includes classes in literacy, GED, English as a second language and other adult education areas. We have about 1,000 contact hours a month."

While discussing the adult education program, Stephanie pointed out the dichotomy of the San Marcos community. At one end, there is the highly educated population at Southwest Texas State and at the other end, we have a large population, up to 40 per cent, that has not completed high school. She takes seriously her responsibility to serve the needs of both.

Out of the adult education classes, other programs have developed. For example, she pointed out, "In coordination with the Chamber of Commerce, we developed San Marcos Literacy Action which has broadened to become Hays County Literacy Action. They provide a voucher program for people who want to take the GED, but can't afford the testing and they put on a cap and gown ceremony for GED graduates. The speakers at these ceremonies are always students and they will bring you to tears with their stories of finally realizing, with the help of the library, their educational dream. Many of these people have been struggling with so many other aspects of their lives, education could not be a priority."

Those of you whose view of the librarian is the prim and proper, subdued, keep the lid on, do not ruffle the status quo, little lady with her lips permanently pursed in a shhhhh, have not met Stephanie Langenkamp. She is an aggressive, grant-writing, innovative, networking, how-can-we-serve-you-better librarian. For instance, she tells about the state program known as the Telecommunications Infrastructure Fund. She has tapped into the fund twice and with the second grant, she will be able to add 29 computers which will be available to the public. That will bring the total available in the library to 35.

"Fourteen of them," she explains, "will be used to offer computer classes. Ten or twenty times a week people call our reference desk and want to know where they can get a computer class. So, we will teach basic computer classes, introduce them to Microsoft Word and show them some basics about navigating the Internet. The demand in this town is incredible for computer classes."

Where are all these teachers coming from? Again, Stephanie is an aggressive recruiter of volunteers. She calls it luck, but behind her broad smile, pleasant personality, and self-effacing manner is a persuasive force that communicates her deep belief in what she is doing. Her enthusiasm for the library, its mission, and the people it serves is infectious.

"The tax aid program is all volunteer," she says. "So is the music program, and I have already had two people volunteer to teach computers. I will go out and try to get people. Also, my librarians are very good at helping people on the Internet, plus there are education agencies from which I can get help. We will cobble it together and make it work.

"This town is a volunteer town. We have been offering a class in sign language this month and as soon as it was posted, it was filled. The person teaching that is a volunteer. So, a great number of my programs are initiatives of volunteers."

The library has a great working relationship with the university. Many of the book discussion programs, guest speakers, and visiting scholars are joint efforts between the library and the university. Often a university grant will be designed to benefit the community of San Marcos rather than just the students.

To satisfy one of my curiosities, I asked how she managed all the children who showed up on her doorstep after school when the library was located on Hutchison Street.

"I'm not sure we managed all that well," she responded. "We just coped. Fortunately, they were pretty good kids. There was just such a quantity of them. We had our moments. I remember putting a row of five chairs in front of the reference desk and when they got too bad, I would just say, 'You sit in this chair, you sit in this one, and you sit here.' It wasn't really resolved until we moved the library."

I asked Stephanie to talk about the new library. "This is one of those situations where the city was so good to me in letting me run with the project. The library board and some city staff members and I selected an architect and thereafter, it was largely the architect and I working on the project. It was so rewarding. I really got into it. I got into every detail. What fun!

"Then there was the closing of the old library. I can still remember that last book checked out at 310 West Hutchison. It was an emotional thing for me. We closed the doors at 9:00 PM December 31, 1993. We opened the doors of this library January 9, 1994. In nine days we had everything moved, all books in place and our grand opening was to be on Sunday. It was to be a fun opening, high school kids dressed as story book characters, the city council was to arrive by carriage, not a lot of speechifying. It was a party kind of event. Amazingly, everything was ready. It was perfect. How could this have happened? That was the highlight of my professional life."

There are 126,000 volumes in the San Marcos Public Library, but the most interesting read in the building is the librarian.

Vernon McDonald

"I was looking at the gallery of past presidents of Southwest Texas—excuse me, Texas State—the other day and reflecting on the institution's 100th anniversary. I have personally known every president except the first one."

That is Vernon McDonald illustrating his long association with Texas State University. (At this point, I should add he was strongly opposed to the name change, so as he reads this, I expect he will cringe slightly when I use Texas State to identify his alma mater and life-long employer.)

Vernon, better known as "Coach Mac," has not strayed very far from his birth place over the 74 years of his life. He was born in Dale, near Lockhart in 1929. When he was in the fifth grade, his family moved to Moran, west of Waco where they stayed for about a year. From there, they moved to Bartlett, but shortly after, moved to Taylor (his dad was with the Katy Railroad) where he graduated from high school in 1947.

"I didn't play football in high school," Vernon said. "I was the drum major of the band all four years. I played all sorts of instruments, the clarinet, the French horn, the cornet. I sort of had a scholarship to the A&M band.

"My brother returned from the service in 1946 and enrolled at Texas Lutheran College (TLC), and when I graduated, my mother wanted me to go to college at TLC. I went without a scholarship, but I made the basketball team and played for two years. It was a junior college at the time."

After two years at TLC, Coach Milton Jowers offered Vernon a basketball scholarship to Southwest Texas. He came to SWT in the fall of 1949.

"I came to Southwest Texas to play basketball with a bunch of 'nobodies.' We had guys like Bob Baty, Bookie Brammer, and Slim Berry, who was on a half-basketball, half-football scholarship. We had Spider Mays who could only make the B team at Livingston High School. The reason I'm telling you this is to show you that we were a bunch of nobodies. Lewis Gilcrease was a freshman when I came here.

"My senior year, 1952, we were 30-1. At the end of the year, we had six players who were first or second team All Conference. We beat A&M two games in College Station, we beat Texas Tech in Lubbock and we beat Baylor in Waco."

The real reason Vernon dwelt on the no-name basketball team, which came within one victory of a national championship in 1952, was to reflect the coaching genius that was Milton Jowers. On more than one occasion during this interview, I reminded Vernon, I was after his story, not Jowers'.

Vernon's athletic career was not the only aspect of his life that was germinated and nurtured in the shadow of Old Main.

"I met Dolores here and we were married in April of 1951. I was scared to death to tell Coach Jowers. I was afraid he was going to run me off. But he didn't. After I graduated, he got me a job coaching at Eagle Pass. We were there nine months. It was 110 degrees for five consecutive days and Dolores said, 'We have to leave here.'

"One Sunday afternoon I got a phone call and Coach Jowers said, 'Do you want to come up here?' That was all he said.

"I asked, 'For what?'

"To coach with me," he said.

"We moved up here the summer of 1953 and I have been here ever since. He told me I would be the assistant basketball coach and the defensive secondary football coach. I had no knowledge of football, but Jowers told me it was a lot like playing defense in basketball.

"I also filmed all the games. The camera had three lens options. One year we were playing Trinity University and I inadvertently set the lens halfway between two settings. For the entire game the only pictures I took were of the skyline of San Antonio. Coach Jowers was not very happy about that. But he wouldn't fire me. I still had to film the games."

In 1961, SWT's football program was desperately in need of revival. They were 1-9 the previous year and the university president asked Coach Jowers to coach football. Jowers agreed on the condition that Coach Mac take over the basketball program.

"I knew nothing about any of this," said Vernon. "Jowers walked into my office and said, 'McDonald, do you want to be the basketball coach of Southwest Texas?'

"I hope to be someday, I responded. He threw the keys on my desk and said, 'You're the coach.'"

Vernon pointed out that in three years, Jowers had the Bobcat football team at 10-0 and number one in the nation at the NAIA level. He goes on to say that, aside from his family, Coach Jowers is the best thing that ever happened to him.

"There is no doubt in my mind that he was the best coach ever. He never had star players to work with. He worked with good people, but his recruiting budget was limited. Pence Dacus, probably the best all-around athlete ever at SWT, was recruited with a penny postcard."

(Note: Lewis Gilcrease, another outstanding SWT athlete, hitchhiked home after his recruiting interview with Coach Jowers.)

Coach Mac coached the SWT basketball team from 1961 to 1977.

He describes his retirement from coaching. "In January we were getting ready to play our first conference game with Sam Houston. Suddenly, my chest felt like someone was standing on it. Dolores called the doctor and after he examined me, he told me he was sending me to the hospital in Austin. I told him, I couldn't go, I had a ball game. I went to the hospital."

"I did not have a heart attack, but I had a blockage which they decided to treat with medication. I still take seven pills every morning and seven every night."

While surgery was not required, Vernon was ordered to give up basketball. Bill Miller, Athletic Director at the time, made Coach Mac the assistant AD. He continued to contribute by teaching classes until 1988.

He and Dolores, who taught in San Marcos Public Schools, retired the same year, 1988. Retirement was not a problem for the McDonalds.

"You are probably looking at the two happiest people in San Marcos. I bought a motor home the year we retired and for five years, we traveled all over the country. We have been to every state in the lwer forty-eight."

Their travel habits have evolved from more to less. From the RV they went to a tag-along with a pick-up. That proved a bit big for Dolores and so they went to a fifth wheel and a pick-up. Following a recent trip to Knoxville, Tennessee with the fifth wheel, they concluded that for the price of their rig, they could stay in lots of motel rooms.

I must add that their love of travel has not diminished. As I began this interview, Vernon informed me that he and Dolores had just returned from an Alaskan cruise.

Returning to his long association with SWT, Coach Mac recounted that there were about 1200 students here when he came as a student.

"My first salary as a coach was $3,600.00 a year. To make enough to live on, I took any job I could get. I ran the swimming pool, and I was a dorm director—at the same time. We were just trying to survive. When we played out of town, I would take my car and a college car. Dolores was left here with three children and no car.

"I will never make it up to her. If we played two games, she was here from Friday to Tuesday with no car."

I asked about the difference between college athletics today and when he was coaching. He proudly remarked, "My players all graduated."

"We went to Washington, D.C. for a game when Lyndon Johnson was president. I thought nothing of it, but I got a message while there that I was to bring the team to the White House. That morning, the president walked in and greeted the team with 'Hi, Bobcats'. My boys were thrilled to see the president."

On integration, Vernon says: "I brought the first black athlete to SWT. A boy by the name of Johnny Brown and he wasn't that good a basketball player. I don't know where he is now, but I know he has a PhD."

The apple doesn't fall far from the tree. Vernon and Dolores have two boys and one girl. Lynn McDonald played for his dad at SWT and is the boys head basketball coach at Clear Lake, Texas. Donnie McDonald is the girls basketball coach at Hays High school and their daughter, Lola is an elementary school principal in San Antonio.

"One more thing you have to put in the article," Vernon said with enthusiasm. "Lola, went to Russia and adopted a little boy who is three now. We get to keep him every other weekend. He is a great joy."

Coach Mac has a bottomless bag of interesting stories about family, former players, teammates, SWT, San Marcos, and Milton Jowers. Forgoing his great stories, I have tried to capture his personal optimism, enthusiasm, and intense loyalty to SWT— er, ah, ...Texas State University.

Eric Slocombe

Under the form-fitting brown shirt and the trademark shorts of this energetic UPS delivery-man there is a passionate, talented artist. As a child Eric Slocombe liked to play in the dirt (actually, it was clay) and make things with his hands. And the things he liked to make were likenesses of the wildlife he saw all around him in Alamosa, Colorado where he grew up and went to high school and college.

Eric is 38 years old and says, "I have been with UPS about 12 years and I have been doing professional sculpting for about 10 years. When I say professional, I mean I have been systematically producing and actively showing and selling my work."

When asked how he developed an interest in wildlife sculpture, Eric replied, "We lived in the last house on the block in Alamosa and right behind our house was the Rio Grande River. I spent all the time I could at the river, camping, fishing, hunting, anything for the opportunity to observe animals in their natural form. When I enrolled in Adams State College in Alamosa, my professor required me to carve stone, weld abstract pieces, do wood carvings and would not let me do anything I really wanted to do." Eric continues, "He really knew what he was doing because the principles and techniques I learned from him have had a significant influence on my work."

Eric confesses to finishing only three years of college before coming to San Marcos in 1983. When asked why he came to Texas, he responded, "There was no reason not to." His first job in San Marcos was a continuation of part-time work he did in Colorado—he went to work for HEB. And continued in the grocery business with HEB and Kroger until 1988 when he joined UPS.

Shortly after coming to Texas, Eric exhibited at a couple of small shows, hunting and fishing expos, actually. One of these shows was held in McAllen. He took four bronzes and exhibited them in a small 10x10 booth. As Eric tells it, "I sold one of my bronzes at that show for about $1500.00 and I thought, 'Man this is easy.' The next two shows I did not sell a thing."

But that did not dampen his enthusiasm. After those two shows, he went to work and produced about twenty pieces. He felt he needed a body of work and though he was unable to have them all cast, he had a broader representation of his skill. He says, "People saw my work. I got some exposure and years down the road it all started coming together. People who saw my work then and see my work now can see my growth as an artist. It is all a building process. For example, I exhibited at the Fiesta at Laguna Gloria Museum in Austin and won best three-dimensional sculptor. It was a big boost for me, personally, but more important, collectors like to see that sort of thing on an artists resume."

When it comes to the business of being an artist, Eric shows an awareness of the intricacies involved, but readily admits a general distaste for a great deal of it. However, he points out, there must be, "a balance between 'playing with the clay' and producing a sculpture that is a fine piece of art that has real value so that when someone buys it, he or she will be moved…hopefully they will be moved spiritually."

How do you know when a piece has captured your spirit, I asked. Eric replied, "It starts in the thought process. I will be driving down the road in my UPS truck and a deer will run across the road and hop over the fence. It is like my mind takes a picture of that. It may be days, or a month or just hours before it starts growing in my mind and I start putting it together and I can't stop it. I may get up at two o'clock in the morning and feel it is time to sculpt. I go in and rough out my idea and right then the passion starts building. I may work on it for days to the exclusion of everything else, but then I may step back for a few days and let it set. It is all part of a learning process."

When asked if the passion for a piece ever grows cold, Eric responded, "Absolutely! A lot of my early pieces ended up back in the clay bin because at that time I didn't have the discipline to just set them aside. Many of them weren't really that bad. But then some of them were. I worked on an elephant for three years and it was great. It was perfect. I studied video tapes. I read books. I had it exactly right. Then one day I took a long look at it and I said, '…that's wrong. That's all wrong.' I took it completely apart—except for the head. The basic forms, the muscles, the shape was there, but the sculpture was not doing what I needed it to do."

In explaining how he learned anatomy, Eric recounted how he took dead squirrels off the road when he was a kid and his dad, who has a degree in agriculture, would encourage him to study them as if he were in an anatomy lab. "With respect to the elephant, I watched a PBS special on elephants where they showed their movements from the hide all the way down to the skeleton through computerized images. I saw how the shoulders moved, how hindquarters had to shift and move, how they actually walk on their tip-toes and they are so graceful. I learned that elephants have a dominant tusk—like being right-handed or left-handed—which, because of more use, is normally broken. I broke one of the tusks of my elephant. After watching the show, I had my elephant done in two hours."

Eric enjoys discussing the learning and growth process of becoming an artist, but is also aware of the importance of innocence in art. He readily admits that some people like his early work better than what he does now. It has an appealing spontaneity, he says, "Early on, when I did an elk, I just did an elk. One of the hardest things now is knowing when to stop; knowing when I have completed the piece."

'How do you know you have completed a piece?' I asked. He responded, "Most of my pieces are action pieces, movement pieces. Even when it appears they are still, there is movement, a look in the eye, the tilt of the head. There is something going on in the piece. (I later saw an illustration of this in his studio with a sculpture of a moose lying down, but the head pose announced that it had just heard a limb snap and there was the questioning alertness of a wild animal searching his environment with all his senses.) And so when I see the piece moving, I know it is finished."

So, what about the myth that all UPS guys are hunks? "To tell you the truth, I think that is really just a myth, however, I do find myself in the grocery store occasionally talking to some housewife to whom I have delivered several packages and her husband will walk up and give me a dirty look. Meanwhile, I'm happily married with a wonderful bunch of kids.

"But I enjoy working for UPS. It gets me out in the country with the wild life, I have time between deliveries to think of my art work and I can't think of a better day job. It provides me a certain security, but it also keeps me hungry to get back to my sculpting. I can use ten minutes and get something done. It may only be re-looking at something I'm working on and seeing it differently. "

The next time that chocolate colored van pulls up to your house and the man/woman in the brown shirt and shorts drops off a package at your door, you might ask yourself, 'What dreams are being formed into a beautiful reality in that mundane vehicle?'

Don Cradit

Time's up for Don's Time Shop. After more than 50 years in San Marcos—that's a lot of time—Don's Time Shop closed February 1, 2003. Another skilled craftsman has become as obsolete as a wheelwright and a mule-skinner. The closing is partially due to the disappearance of jewelry stores, a closely related business. "Actually," Don explains, "I can't find a place to work the way I would like. At my age I would like to work about three days a week and I need a place that will support that schedule."

"I'm the last of the Mohicans," Don said as he explained that a fellow from San Antonio bought his equipment and he was just waiting for the fellow to pick it up.

When I asked him to tell me about himself, he began, "I was born in the Valley and grew up and finished high school in San Benito. In 1939, I joined the navy and planned to make it a career. We had not yet come out of the Great Depression and $21.00 a month looked awful good. When I was a kid about 12, I got a job on a milk truck. I got on the truck at 4:00 AM and worked until 8:00 AM. Made $1.00 a week.

"In the navy, I found out I had to buy my own clothes and also pay for my $3,000.00 insurance policy. So I wasn't making real big money."

After boot camp, Don was assigned to the light cruiser, Phoenix. His desire for travel was partially satisfied when the Phoenix sailed to Chile and Peru. It was billed as a goodwill mission, but the primary reason for the trip was to counter the Germans' incursion into South America. While in South America, Don had the opportunity to volunteer for what was then called the Asiatic Fleet.

As he put it, "I put my name in the pot and I won the pot. I always wanted to see China and I got my chance. I was assigned to a supply ship that took supplies to the marine garrison and the embassy in Peking. Though we thought of it as peacetime, Japan was at war with China and as a teen-age country boy, I couldn't believe some of the atrocities of the Japanese.

"From Peking, we sailed down to Shanghai and took supplies to the Yangtze River patrol and then on to Hong Kong and eventually back to the Philippines."

I asked Don where he was December 7, 1941. "We had sailed to Pearl Harbor in late November to pick up a load of new torpedoes for the fleet submarines. In addition to the torpedoes, we picked up a large number of civilians, officers' wives and kids, who had been vacationing in Hawaii. They were going back to Manila.

"The Japanese attacked occurred about a week after we left Pearl Harbor. There we were in the middle of the Pacific, with no protection and a boatload of women and children. We sailed into Darwin, Australia and joined a task force of Australian, British and American ships. Then we sailed on down to Brisbane where we unloaded the women and kids."

Don relates that they then sailed down to Antarctica to avoid submarines. They refueled at the Fiji Islands before returning to Pearl Harbor. "As we came into Pearl, I didn't recognize it. Before leaving, we had been tied up next to the Ogallala and all we could see of that ship was the bottom."

Don's ship was ordered to Bremerton, Washington for a short period before sailing for Alaska. The Japanese attacked the islands of Adak and Attu and his ship was sent into Dutch Harbor, Alaska shortly after the Japanese bombed it.

After sailing all over the Pacific in a supply ship, he was sent back to Bremerton where he boarded a new destroyer. On a new ship, he was destined for new scenery. They sailed through the Panama Canal and joined the Atlantic Fleet, escorting convoys to Europe.

The mission of the destroyer was to protect the convoys from submarines and without elaborating on the extent of his combat, Don says, "We got rid of quite a few submarines. The depth charges were pretty effective."

His destroyer squadron returned to the states where it was assigned to escort a convoy of troop ships and the battleship, Texas to Belfast, Ireland. Upon arriving in Belfast, Don had an exciting experience for a country boy. He met General Eisenhower when he came aboard the Texas to give the crews a pep talk about the impending invasion of Europe.

About two weeks before the invasion, a German aircraft bombed Don's ship and destroyed the radar and range finder, rendering the guns useless. It appeared they would miss the invasion. However, another destroyer in the squadron was hit by a cargo ship and split almost in half. With GI ingenuity and around the clock effort, the radar and range finder equipment were removed from the disabled ship, installed on Don's ship and they were in the thick of D-Day operations off Omaha Beach.

Following the invasion across the English Channel, Don's ship participated in the invasion of the South of France before returning to the states.

It was during a short sojourn in the states that Don and Laura, a 17 year-old girl from Baltimore, decided to marry. Following a short courtship, he and Laura took the advice of a shipmate and tied the knot.

But the war was not over for Don. He boarded a new destroyer and sailed back through the Panama Canal to join the Pacific Fleet, in time for the assault on Iwo Jima.

"We had been briefed for the invasion of Japan," Don relates. "Then in August, we heard about the atomic bomb. So, instead of escorting troop ships and aircraft carriers into Japan, we escorted the battleship Missouri into Tokyo Bay and from a distance observed the signing of the peace agreements."

Don came home in December of 1945 and joined the active naval reserve in Harlingen, Texas where he spent another five years as an instructor.

His years in the navy convinced him he wanted a career that would keep him out of the weather. He loved to build things and fix things and thought he might like to be a watchmaker. Through the Veterans Administration, he found a watchmaker's school in San Antonio. After two years he was a certified horologist (watchmaker).

"When I finished school, I went back to San Benito to open a business. Well, there was the drought of the late 40's and two freezes which killed all the citrus. There wasn't much money in the Valley," according to Don.

"In 1952, Laura and I came to San Marcos to visit friends. She liked this area—she never liked the Valley with its flat fields and no trees.

"Allen Woods had opened a first class jewelry store the year before. He invited me to take over the repair department. I sold my business in the Valley and I came here—51 years ago. We were on Hopkins Street opposite the court house."

The jewelry store changed hands and eventually went out of business. Don then went into business for himself and has occupied several locations over the past 51 years. [For the past 25 years Don has repaired my watches and, to me, the most notable aspect of his business is that he still charges 1950 prices.]

In spite of the traveling he did in the navy, Don and Laura have seen a good part of the world together.

"When my wife retired from her job as a bookkeeper for a cattle company, she decided she wanted to travel," Don said. "After our first trip to Alaska, she decided she wanted to go to China. We went into Beijing and toured the country down to Canton. From there we took a train to Hong Kong. A great trip.

"These are all about three week trips. We then went to Egypt and took an extra week to visit Israel."

While the Red Sea did not part for their crossing, Don related that he and Laura did go swimming in the Dead Sea.

They have visited Turkey and seen the numerous archeological sites which are so crucial to so much of recorded history.

One trip took them to Finland and Estonia and then into Russia at St. Petersburg. From St. Petersburg, they took a river boat to Moscow. "As we went up the river, we took detours up the tributaries to visit historic sites," Don said. "We got to Moscow and saw Red Square and the Kremlin. The museums are remarkable for the artifacts—gold and jewelry of the czars."

Other trips on Don and Laura's itinerary include Rome where they visited the catacombs of the Vatican. Greece, Denmark, Sweden and Norway have enjoyed their company. While in Norway, they went to the Arctic Circle where they observed the midnight sun.

They have sailed around Cape Horn, visited almost all the countries of South America, and a good part of the rest of the world. Don can remember details of each trip and loves to relate the highlights.

Though the quartz watch has put him out of business, it has by no means taken him out of circulation. He says he is only 81 and he planned to work until 90. But there just isn't any place for him and he doesn't want to move again.

Don't fret for Don Cradit. He is visiting or dreaming of visiting a far off place full of history, wonder and excitement.

Bob Shelton

There have been football coaches who have spent long and distinguished careers at one location—Joe Paterno at Penn State; Gordon Wood at Brownwood High come to mind. There have been coaches who have won many more games than they lost—any number of coaching legends such as Bear Bryant and Eddie Robinson come to mind. But how many football coaches can you name who have coached a game in a stadium named for the coach? That's what I thought. Only one. Bob Shelton of Hays High School.

I was mildly surprised when I walked into Coach Shelton's office at 8:00 AM Tuesday morning. (That was the only time available this past week for an hour interview.) I was expecting to encounter a man with the somewhat aging build of a former college linebacker or running back. Instead, I was met by a rather bald, slightly built, soft-spoken man with piercing blue eyes, who was enjoying his coffee during a rare free moment.

"I grew up in Dripping Springs and have lived most of my life in Hays County," Coach Shelton began. "We lived on a ranch in Dripping Springs. My dad came as the high school principal and later became superintendent of the Dripping Springs school district.

"After graduating from Dripping Springs High School, I went to the University of Texas for a couple of years where I played basketball. I transferred to Southwest Texas so that I could continue working with the county surveyors, a job I had since high school. I received my bachelors and masters degree from SWT."

Bob Shelton graduated in the fall of 1964 and was looking for a job. A friend told him there was an opening at Buda and he eagerly accepted the position. As the only coach, he coached all the girls and boys sports which included boys football, basketball and track and girls basketball and track. At the end of his first year, he got one assistant. He also taught government, Texas history, American history and world history. In addition, he taught drivers ed. His princely stipend of $200.00 a month to coach was exceeded by his $400.00 a month to drive the bus.

He belatedly mentioned that he also served as high school principal at Buda for one year.

After four years at Buda where he modestly says he had "some success" (A regional championship—the limit of competition in those days), Buda, Kyle and Wiimberley school districts consolidated to form the Hays district. Coach Shelton was selected to be the athletic director and football coach of the new high school.

The consolidation was effective in 1968, but the new high school was under construction so the football team played at the Buda football field while the kids went to high school at Kyle. The actual move to the present campus occurred in 1969.

"When we started here," Shelton says, "our high school coaching staff consisted of four men and one woman. I would have to look it up to tell you how many coaches we now have. In addition there are three junior highs and I don't know how many elementary schools in the district."

Bob Shelton's competitiveness, intensity and work ethic was partially revealed when I asked why he chose to coach football when he could have been the head basketball coach or simply the athletic director.

"Football has always been my first love. I was too small to play in college, but I always enjoyed it. In Texas, football is the sport. When you talk sports in Texas, whether it be high school, college or professional, you start with football. As football coach, I was allowed to be the athletic director and I wanted to organize the program and run it my way."

Even at the larger high school his coaching duties were not limited to football. He mentioned that he coached boys and girls golf for several years. I thought he might play lots of golf.

"Well, I used to," he said, "but now I have a country music band and we play at various places. Terry Arenz and I started fooling around with it and we have added people along the way. Seven of us make up the Onion Creek Ramblers. We have three CD's out now. We do a lot of gospel music, so we are often invited to sing at churches."

I wondered where he found the time for a band. He explained that during football season his normal week requires 80 to 90 hours at work. The weekday begins at 6:45 AM and the weekend days begin at 6:00 AM. A short day during football season is about 12 hours. There are meetings, practices, film studies, junior varsity and junior high games to attend, and weekend critiques, not to mention the big game on Friday nights.

When I asked what has changed about coaching, he replied, "Everything. It has all gotten better. Training methods and technological innovations are most noticeable. When I started coaching, we didn't even have film. My first year, we had to raise money to buy a 16 mm camera to film the games. We used that for about 15 years. Now we have video and are moving to digital with CD's. Weight training is a major change in conditioning. "Specialization in one sport also represents a change. Unlike earlier days when a kid played whatever sport was in season, now they are almost forced to focus on one sport. There are exceptions but they are rare."

Forgetting for a moment his contributions to coaching, I asked what he has taken from coaching. "The number one thing in coaching," he said, "is the relationships, not only with your players and coaches, but with those coaches with whom you compete. It is a unique fraternity. We compete hard on Friday night, but then the rest of the year we are often good friends.

"With players there is a bond one gets nowhere else. We see these kids every day. In many cases, we spend more time with them than their parents. We work with them year-round. Many come back and tell us the most memorable times of their lives were here playing football."

Reflecting on the progression of his career, Coach Shelton said. "I have coached teams from class B to class 5A, although I did skip one class when we consolidated in 1968. When we started, it was tough because we didn't have many kids. We were at the bottom of the totem pole. We had about 28 kids out for football that first year. Now, we have about 200 to 250.

"We don't cut kids. It is difficult not to do so, but if they make it through our off-season program, I hate to cut a kid. We are up front with our players. We tell them if we don't think they will ever play and so it is up to the player to stay or to cut himself."

Is there too much emphasis on athletics today? "No, I don't think so at the high school level. The kids get things from football they will never get anywhere else. They learn to give extra effort, to pay the price, to understand teamwork. They learn to get up after being knocked down. And they come to understand there is always a winner and a loser on Friday night; there aren't any degrees of success; you win or you lose."

Coach Shelton emphasized that athletics is a motivation for many kids to work harder in the classroom. If they don't pass they don't play, and as a general rule, kids who are involved in extra curricular activities do better in their studies than other students.

I asked what message he wanted to send to the community. "I want people to know we try to have a quality program, follow the rules, work hard and put a good product on the field on Friday night. We have always wanted our teams to play to the best of their ability whatever that was.

"We also look beyond our time with the kids. We want them to be successful once they leave us. We hope that things they learn and accomplish here will help them achieve that success."

Coach Shelton coached his three sons and apparently instilled the drive for success in all three. The oldest son, Robert III, is in advertising in Austin. Ryan, the second son, is an attorney in Austin, and Clay, the youngest, works in a fitness center in Dripping Springs. Robert and Clay are Texas A&M graduates while Ryan graduated from the University of Texas law school. Daughter, Megan, will graduate from Texas State University this year.

At the time of this interview, Coach Shelton's won-lost record was 262-157-7. He has had 13 playoff teams, including two quarter-finalists and one state finalist. The stadium was named for him in 1996; in 1997, he received the Tom Landry Award and was also chosen 4-A Coach of the Year by the Texas Sports Writer's Association. More recently, he was named a Distinguished Alumnus of [Southwest] Texas State University. In 2002, he was inducted into the Texas High School Coaches Hall of Honor.

Since Coach Shelton is beginning his 40th year of this all-consuming career, I wondered if retirement might be in his thoughts.

"I'll tell you this, I'm not going to be in it as long as Joe Paterno. I'm 63 and I won't be doing this when I'm 77. But right now I enjoy good health and I'm enjoying life, I'm enjoying my work, I'm enjoying the kids, and I still enjoy coaching and the competition of football. I enjoy everything about what I do."

By the time you read this, you will know if Bob Shelton is preparing for another 90 hour week or if he might be tuning his guitar for a set with the Onion Creek Ramblers. The Hays Rebels will have played San Antonio Roosevelt in yet another playoff. *Author's note: Bob Shelton continues his successful coaching career at Hays High School.*

Sylvester Perez

Dr. Sylvester Perez is about to complete his first year as San Marcos Superintendent of Schools. It seems to have been a relatively quiet year. But after spending an hour with him, I left with the impression that Syl Perez is like a duck on a pond. It all seems so serene on top, but underneath, he is paddling like mad.

He is almost a home town boy. He grew up in San Antonio and went to a private Catholic school for six years before transferring to public school and graduating from Harlandale High in 1967. Syl quickly adds that John Connally and Cliff Gustafson are also alums of Harlandale.

A pretty fair athlete, he says, "I played a little football, a little baseball—one semester at Wharton Junior College, then I played three years at New Mexico Highlands in Las Vegas, New Mexico. Graduated from there in 1972.

"That led to a 13 year coaching and teaching career after college. I began in Lubbock and I finished my coaching career at Judson High, just down the road from San Marcos. Two baseball players I coached have World Series Championship rings. One is Norm Charlton, formerly of the Cincinnati Reds and the other is John Givens of the New York Mets."

What Syl doesn't say—I had to find this out by reading plaques on his wall—is that he was an NAIA All-American baseball player in his college days. And as a baseball coach, he won district titles with three different high schools. In 1985 he won the 5A state baseball championship with Judson High.

"I am one of those kids who wouldn't be sitting here if it weren't for athletics. I learned discipline and a strong work ethic from athletics. I have a great respect for coaches and all they do. But after 13 years and four knee operations—coaching is very physical—I decided it was time to go in a different direction.

"I wanted to stay in education. I love learning. I am an excited learner and I thought, perhaps I could make a bigger impact on more kids in another area."

After obtaining his mid-management certification from Texas A&I in 1986, he had assignments at various locations. He has moved up the ranks from assistant principal at a middle school and a high school to Harlandale Athletic Director. He was there for seven years. He became principal at McCollom High School from 1995 to 1997.

"I am very proud of some of the programs we developed at Harlandale and McCollom. Both schools had been doormats athletically for a long time. We hired some new coaches and began some good programs for kids. We started the Little Dribbler program for girls and installed the no-cut policy at the junior high."

Dr. Perez's first experience as superintendent was at Mathis, Texas from 1997 through 1999. In late December of 1999, he went to the Clint school district, in El Paso County. There are approximately 8,000 students in the district with two 4A high schools.

During his tenure, the district was, for the first time, a 'recognized' school district. In addition, the district passed a $67 million bond issue and the school board was voted Board of the Year for Region 19.

"There were lots of positive things going on at Clint," Syl stated, "but this job (San Marcos) opened up and it seemed a great opportunity to come to a Central Texas town. Proximity to family had something to do with it, but, more importantly I saw it as a promotion and a great opportunity for me."

I noted that this is his third superintendent's job in seven years.

"I think three years is around the average at any one place, unfortunately. Society changes and you see education taking on more and more societal issues and when things don't work out, people get into the blame game.

"The Superintendent answers to seven board members and board members change, which means that sometimes the goals of the board change. Therefore they may want to make a change at the top. Many variables contribute to the high turn-over rate."

Without regrets or apology, Sylvester Perez stated, "The buck stops here. Whether it be discipline, academic performance, dropouts, college preparedness, or whatever, the superintendent is accountable. Accountability and the system of accountability has been raised significantly over the years."

Part of his guiding philosophy is explained when he says, "We have to be very careful not to cater to special interest groups. The only special interest group that I want to cater to is the children of San Marcos. What's popular may not always be right and what is right may not always be popular.

"I believe if one is always up front with people, if you are open to others—your system and yourself—I believe you enhance your credibility and develop trust."

I asked what he brought from athletics and coaching to his present job.

"A lot," he responded. "But a paramount aspect of coaching or playing is that one needs to really stay centered. That means that things are not always as good as they seem, nor, conversely, are they always as bad as they seem.

"For example, as an old baseball player, I learned that if one day I was '4 for 4', there would be another day when I would be '0 for 4.' But I knew I had to stay focused, I had to keep swinging and not be overly influenced by the really good or the really bad. In addition, as a coach, I was exposed to the pressures of the media, parental pressures, the need to think on your feet, make decisions and live by those decisions.

"Work ethic is another characteristic I brought from coaching. In a three year stretch at Judson High, we played 45 football games. Our last season began July 17th and ended December 17th. The work days were 12 to 14 hours long and we did not have a day off during that period."

What is happening in the evolution of education?

"We have reached an interesting place. Years ago we were able to take electives and pursue many interests in school. Today, with the public outcry for accountability, high stakes testing has become a driving force in education. It is an interesting debate.

"I am from the old school and the old school tells me we need to provide and produce good productive citizens and there is a lot more to teaching a child than getting an elevated score on a standardized test. I believe attitude is directly responsible for success.

"My teaching philosophy is that we must teach children first, not math, or English, or science first. That child must be seen as an individual. Educators are engaged with society from the womb to the tomb; from day care to adult education classes. Grades and academic performance are important, but if we emphasize the *student*, the rest will follow."

So, how does one reconcile that philosophy with the pressure to produce high scores on standardized tests?

"This is not meant to be a politically correct response, but it might sound that way. San Marcos has the best staff I have ever been around. Perhaps that is the result of its proximity to the area colleges and universities. Whatever, I have the best group of principals ever. Everywhere I go, I see teachers enthusiastically engaged with the students. I see students learning.

"But…we really need to address the dropout rate; to address conduct; to address simple things such as manners. We can do that. I'm excited to bring in such things as Career Investigations and Career Connections. These programs give kids some exposure to professions they might like to pursue along with high standards of higher education. It also provides an opportunity for them to learn some life skills such as conflict resolution and that sort of thing.

"We are constantly told by business owners and managers that they look for people who can get along with others, so I think the more social interaction children are exposed to, the more activities they can be a part of, the more they will learn about dealing with life and their contemporaries. I believe we must develop the whole child."

What about San Marcos. Describe your picture of San Marcos.

"San Marcos is interesting," Syl answered. "First, it is quite diverse for a district of 7,000 students and one high school. The infra-structure and the interest in education is that of a much larger community.

"For example, there are three Lions Clubs, two Kiwanis Clubs, two Rotary Clubs, two Chambers of Commerce, an Education Foundation, a Chamber Education Committee, the San Marcos Manufacturing Association, Partners in Education, and a daily newspaper—well, almost daily. That makes San Marcos unique.

"The infra-structure resembles a large school system and the expectations are there as well. Interest in the students at San Marcos is phenomenal. The community and the civic clubs provided more than $100 thousand in scholarships to our students this year.

"It touches the heart to see all these community groups so interested in our students and to back up that interest with funds to jump-start them on the road to a college education."

The goal of this profile is to provide a portrait of the man entrusted with directing the education of San Marcos children. While he is as comfortable as an old sneaker, I can't begin to list the projects he has on the drawing board. And based on his history, don't bet against his getting it done. He may go '0 for 4,' but I assure you, the next day, he is going to be '4 for 4.'

Referring to the more than $100 thousand in college scholarships provided to San Marcos High students by the community, Syl stated, "It is overwhelming. I have never seen such an outpouring of interest, caring and investment in students by a community.

"Southwest Texas is involved as well. We have partnerships with SWT and I'm excited about enhancing those partnerships. It is a great time to be in San Marcos. We have a new SWT president, a relatively new mayor and some new city council members. I am just finishing my first year. We have the potential to do great things."

On the subject of a new high school: "We have hired Dr. Oates, a former superintendent at Brazosport and San Antonio's Northeast School

District, and a professor at Texas A&M University—I consider him a mentor.

"He has been asked to study our facilities and solicit from the community what we want and need in the way of facilities. Additionally, we are putting together a Facilities Advisory Committee that will come to the administration and the board and say, 'This is what we want.'"

Syl explains that it is important to listen to the community. Without community support, nothing is going to happen. The Facilities Advisory Committee, with assistance from Dr. Oates, will recommend the type schools needed, the desired locations and the size of the school.

"Our kids have every right to have the same state of the art facilities as other school districts and we should be the prototype for school districts in the state of Texas. We are a university town; we have the tremendous support of the community; and we have Austin Community College as well as Gary Job Corps.

"We should be an outstanding school district—and we are going to be."

He went on to point out that Bowie Elementary was built in 1953, Travis Elementary was built in 1954, and the high school was built in 1958. The life-span of a school building is generally considered to be between 40-45 years. So, infrastructure is a major concern.

Community education and involvement is one of Syl's major goals. He pointed to a four foot high stack of papers, binders, notebooks and folders and said, "There is the record of some of the previous bond elections. I have studied all of them. There have been a number of issues responsible for some of the bond failures.

"Among those issues, according to one study, was lack of unity among school board members. Another issue had to do with disagreements among staff of one of the schools and the planning committee.

"An earlier bond failed because of the perception that the community was not fully consulted and informed. We hope to look at it differently this time. We want to insure that we have adequate and balanced community and staff input."

Dr. Perez is a great believer in taking his message to the people. He explained that in former successes, small groups were addressed—coffees and community meetings— where individual issues were discussed in detail. It is important, in his opinion, to have an educated vote. He is quick to recognize negative factors, i.e., a sluggish economy.

"I don't want your article to sound like I'm lobbying for a bond There will be other opportunities for that when we know more—get Dr. Oates' report—and get farther down the road. But I want people to know I am looking to the future."

Speaking of the future, I posed 'the perfect world' and asked, where will SMCISD be in five years?

"I see some state of the art facilities. A new high school and a couple of new elementary schools. I think we may very well see some neighborhood schools as well. With the growth and development predicted for San Marcos, which I see as a pleasant problem, we must keep pace. I'm hoping, by then, the state legislature will have developed an equitable system for funding schools."

In the current legislature, with an almost $10 billion shortfall, how is education going to be affected?

"We are holding our breath. There will be cuts. We hope it will be minimal. One of the things I have in progress is the decentralization of the district. I am a strong believer in having maximum dollars in the classroom. I will explain my reorganization to the board in the next few weeks and I think the taxpayers will be pleased to see that we are going to be lean at the top.

"We are thinning out some of our top-level positions and focusing those dollars toward instruction and the classroom."

I asked about teacher morale in light of the turmoil in school financing at the state level.

"In San Marcos, we have great morale as indicated by low teacher turnover. I think it is below 14 per cent. Most of the people who leave us are leaving to re-locate. I see high job satisfaction and stability due to the low turnover."

I raised the issue of student services outside the classroom: transportation, and security.

"That is an area of real concern, especially transportation and maintenance. I have heard the Wonder World overpass contract will be let soon. That means we must relocate our transportation and maintenance facility. We have no money to do that. It is a real concern.

"The public is not overly concerned with support staff or central office administration. We have a lot of our support staff at the old Lamar school—goodness, when was that facility built? We need to centralize the support staff. We need to have a good ingress/egress of transportation. We need more room in maintenance and we have absolutely no storage."

He pointed out that moving the bus barn was a priority project on the last bond election and the problem could have been solved at that time, had the bond passed. Now, there are no options and there are no resources to do the job. However, Dr. Perez optimistically points out that interest rates are the lowest in decades and it will be possible to do more with less money.

"Regarding security, we have a good partnership with the San Marcos PD. Our Security Resource Officer (SRO) serves as a deterrent and as a pro-active resource. They do little citation writing or reacting. They assist us to educate the students in acceptable behavior.

"We are constantly looking to revise and improve our student code of conduct. Laws change, and we need to change with them. We feel certain that we have adequate administrative staff and SRO's to keep our campuses safe. However, we caution our staff to stay alert in that area.

Syl agreed that the high profile cases such as a recent murder on the campus of an Austin high school tend to create the impression that schools are a haven for a criminal element. His 'glass half-full' attitude surfaced again.

"You should go to Senior Awards Night and see all the achievements of these kids. Athletics, Ballet Folklorico, academic awards of all types tell us that we have a bunch of really outstanding kids."

Syl pointed out that he recently forced himself to listen to some rap music to help him relate to 'kids today.'

"What I heard was sexually explicit, demeaning to women, and promoted drugs and violence. But I believe kids haven't changed," he said. "Society has changed. We, as educators, have to address those issues on a daily basis. We have to ground the kids and bring them back to center before we can teach academics."

In discussing the effect of a statewide voucher system, Syl reminded me he went to private school through the sixth grade. However, he pointed out that the most recently proposed voucher system did not require the same accountability from private schools as from public schools.

"If we are to be compared, we need to be on a level playing field. The bill did not address ethnicity and gender and so that concerned me.

"I admit that public education does not serve every need of every student. And there are students who do better in private schools. But, don't take away public dollars to support that.

"I think a voucher system would promote less diversity, more special interest groups and you would see people leaving the public schools for reasons outside of education, per se."

Syl looks inward to needs as intensely as he looks outward. He will be implementing a drop-out prevention program next year. Achievement Via Individual Determination (AVID) will be resurrected. He also has a Student/Superintendent Advisory Council with which he meets monthly. Students at every grade level are represented.

He asked me to emphasize that he and his wife, Dee are San Marcos citizens and love being a part of this community. Dee is a cancer survivor and a school counselor in Comal County. She plays a major role in his personal and professional life. Syl says, "Every school superintendent should be married to a counselor."

If you want to know what is happening in SMCISD, spend an hour—that's impossible—spend two hours with Syl Perez. You will walk away hoping his stay in San Marcos. is a whole lot longer than the three year average tenure for superintendents. *Author's note: Once again, Syl Perez helped get a school bond passed. A new high school and elementary school will come online within the next couple of years.*

John Lee

John Lee is probably the most famous man living in San Marcos who is not locally well known. And he prefers it that way. His books have been on the New York Times best-seller list. And as I write these words, his most successful book, The Ninth Man, is under consideration by Hollywood as a starring vehicle for Harrison Ford.

"I don't get out much," John said, as he settled his huge frame in the easy chair and arranged the plastic tube which connects him to his oxygen. "Oh, I go to the grocery store, eat out once in awhile, and take in an occasional movie, and that's about it."

His hideaway is at 212 Hunters Glen Drive and he is still mourning Barbara Moore, his wife of 45 years. A writer in her own right, she and John were collaborators in every sense of the word. They even wrote a book together, Monsters Among Us: Journey to the Unexplained. She passed away in November 2002.

Lest you get the notion that John has folded his tent and gone into the wilderness to await his own demise, be reassured. He has book projects, magazine articles, and computer game reviews which keep him hopping—well, typing. In fact, he requires four computers to keep up with his projects.

"I'm really just an old Texas journalist," John began. "I grew up in Brownsville, went to Texas Tech and got a journalism degree in 1952. Spent a summer with the Lubbock Avalanche Journal before going to the Fort Worth Star Telegram. Stayed there for five years, met Barbara there and then we took off for Spain for a year.

"It was there I wrote my first novel which was terrible. In fact, I wrote three terrible novels before I ever sold one. My first almost sold. If it had, I would have never lived it down. It was awful."

John and Barbara returned from Spain and took jobs with the Denver Post. After two years at the Post, the public relations firm for Goodyear Tire offered them a job. Nothing about Akron appealed to them but the money was convincing. So, they spent a year in Akron before the vagabond itch led them to relocate in Mexico.

While in Mexico, John met Willard Marsh who was teaching creative writing at USC. Willard's life seemed especially attractive and John wanted to go back to school, get his masters degree and teach. Meanwhile, he was offered a job as editor of the Teheran Journal, an English language newspaper in Iran. Barbara was to be managing editor.

"Barbara was ahead of the rest of us," John said. "She was afraid of going to Iran and she was right. About six months later, the Shah kicked out all the English speaking journalist."

John found a teaching assistant's job at West Virginia University where he pursued his masters degree and began a teaching career.

He says, "Then I became an academic vagabond. I taught at American University for two years, 1965 to 1967. Next, I went to University of Arizona from '67 to '71. A stint at New York University and Cal State, Long Beach left me burned out and sick of teaching.

"Besides my books were doing very well and I wanted to write full-time. I was turning out a book every two years while teaching and I thought if I wrote full-time, I could do one every 24 months."

The last statement was accompanied by a knowing grin, verifying the Peter Principle that work expands to fill the time available.

After six years away from academe, John found himself getting stale and yearning for the company of young students. He took another teaching job at the University of Idaho. The location was not based on money this time. He and Barbara had a champion Doberman that was suffering from flea-induced mange and there are no fleas in Idaho.

A friend at the University of Memphis suggested he come to a warmer climate, so in 1984, he took a position at the Tennessee school where he stayed until his retirement from academia in 1996.

"All during my academic career, I continued my writing, turning out books and writing for magazines. I wrote for about 40 magazines, some of which were pretty sleazy. When I shared the cover of one magazine with an article titled, Mabel, the Makeout Motorcycle Queen, I knew it was time to use a pseudonym to keep my academic resume respectable."

John says he tried to write funny books during his first three efforts. They did not sell. "What the hell," he said, "if they want grim, I'll give them grim. In 1968, I wrote a grim book about a recovering alcoholic, living in Spain, chased by bad guys. He is running for his life. It was called Caught in the Act and they loved it.

"I wrote the follow-up to Caught in the Act, and sent the same protagonist to Algeria. My publishers titled it Assignation in Algeria. People would come up to me and say, I saw your book, Assignment in Algeria, or they might refer to it as Assassination in Algeria. They didn't read it correctly and that's just as well. Assignation means a lovers' tryst and my book was about two guys."

John was at New York University when he wrote The Ninth Man. The first two books had sold, but neither garnered more than $8,000.00. He describes The Ninth Man as an, 'of course' book. That means you can tell the plot in about two sentences and everyone says, 'of course.'

It is based on a factual event which occurred in June 1942. Two German U-Boats each deposited a four-man team on isolated beaches, one in Florida and one in New York. Their mission was to cause havoc through sabotage and prove American vulnerability to Germany's war-fighting capability.

The eight men were captured within two weeks. The ninth man, a fictional creation of John Lee, was not caught. He had a unique mission—assassinate President Roosevelt.

"Everybody liked it," John said. "My agent got a movie deal with Zanuck and Brown, two of the most powerful producers in Hollywood at the time. I had just moved to Long Beach, so I was on the scene. Went to the studio commissary and had lunch with them. People were whispering, 'Who's that with Zanuck and Brown' and I was sitting there looking goggle-eyed at Charlton Heston.

"Steven Spielberg, had just finished Jaws and when I met him, he said, 'I read your book. It is going to be the Jaws of WW II.'"

Though he was paid a huge sum for an option on the book and the director, Richard Mulligan, called frequently to confer with John, the movie was never made. A year later, the studio took a second option on the book, and paid John the same figure James Michener got for Centennial.

"The book came out in 1976. It has now been optioned six times and it has paid equally well each time. However, I would take less money if I could just see the book translated to film," John said. "About three weeks ago, I received a new contract from Dreamworks Apparently, someone there really likes the script and wants to do something with it. I am told there are four websites devoted to the movie and apparently Harrison Ford is seriously considering it."

The Ninth Man was a life-changing experience for John. His first two books brought in less than $10 thousand each. The Ninth Man, a best seller produced more than $250 thousand. It allowed him to buy homes in Colorado and San Marcos. The Thirteenth Hour was also a best seller, but Jon says it will never be made into a movie because it requires the destruction of a city the size of Berlin.

The Thirteenth Hour deals with the last hours of Hitler's life. John also tackled Mussolini's last days in Lago, (Lake). Stalag Texas is a book about a German POW camp in Texas (Yes, Virginia, there were German POW's in the US, during WWII.).

"I'm not getting a lot of writing done right now because I have lots of other stuff going on," John said. "My medical regimen requires a lot of time. I smoked too much and damaged my lungs. I quit two years ago and my specialist says there's hope that I will recover to some extent.

"I thought I would like to do model airplanes and recapture my youth. I have $500.00 worth of models that have not been opened."

A great deal of John's writing these days is occupied with his reviews of computer games. He provides the magazine, Mac Addict, with reviews of new games All this began when he was teaching at the University of Memphis. At one time he wrote reviews for three PC and two Mac magazines.

In addition to his novels, John has written six non-fiction books, two of which are text books on creative writing. Diplomatic Persuasion examines the information attaches in Washington. The Patriot Press is about English language newspapers in non-English speaking countries. He and Barbara wrote a book on how to judge Dobermans and the aforementioned Monsters Among Us.

This profile may not make John Lee more well-known, even in San Marcos, but when Dreamworks puts The Ninth Man on the screen with Harrison Ford, a few people in town can say, "I know the guy who wrote that! Well, I know *about* the guy who wrote that."

John Holtermann

John Holtermann's fiery blue eyes looked straight into mine as he said, "In 1998 on a Saturday morning I came out of the hospital with congestive heart failure; Sunday morning, my daughter died; Monday morning, we opened a session [of the legislature]. I had to be on the floor [of the House of Representatives] at eight o'clock. I drove myself to Austin while my daughter was lying in the funeral home. We were waiting for my youngest daughter to come down from Washington state."

That quote illustrates John's attitude toward work and commitment. Industry, dependability, volunteerism and community service are as essential to the life of this Silver-Haired Legislator as air and water.

Born in Sattler, Texas, in August1911, he grew up on a cotton farm where the day began at 4:00 AM and ended at 10:00 PM. That farm is now 100 feet under the waters of Canyon Lake.

He reached school age during the height of World War I. John says, "One morning we were met at the entrance to the schoolyard and told there would be no more German spoken at school. I could not speak a word of English when I started school. But in six or eight weeks, I had picked it up and was getting along just fine."

Eventually, John found himself at the Salt Creek Independent School District where he attended school in a one room school house with one teacher. "There were eight grades," John said. "I was the only person in the eighth grade, so I helped teach the lower grades. My school career ended in 1926 when my father was unable to work. My sister and I had to run the farm. We had crop failures a couple of years and so the family moved to New Braunfels.

"I went to work at Krueger Motor Company where Ambassador Krueger's father owned the company. I worked in the parts department and later in the shop, but the smell of oil upset my stomach so, I had to quit. I went to work at the Faust Hotel in 1929 as a bell-hop. It was called the Travelers then and I made good money there until the Great Depression hit. They made me the night manager and cut my salary. I made $28.00 a month. I worked there until 1934."

To illustrate life during the Great Depression, John relates that at the time he married Gladys Lehnberg in 1932, he was making that extravagant salary of $28.00 a month, and he had $42.00 in the bank. President Roosevelt closed the banks, preventing access to that money.

Meanwhile, John's father found work on a ranch owned by J.J. Strickland, who also owned an insurance company in San Antonio. One day Mr. Strickland came by the hotel and told John, he had a job for him in San Antonio.

Typically, he began at the bottom. He started with the insurance company as an elevator operator and in six months was the assistant purchasing agent. In a year, he was the purchasing agent, a job he held for 12 years. When the insurance company moved its headquarters to Springfield, Illinois in 1945, John took a job repairing and maintaining dictating equipment with an office supply company. In 11 months, he was promoted to a sales and management job on the floor. When the company, Maverick-Clarke, opened a branch store in Brownsville in 1949, he was chosen to be the assistant manager.

John says, "I could not get a manager's job with Maverick-Clarke because I didn't have a college degree. After a number of years as assistant manager, Litton Industries bought Maverick-Clark. They fired the manager and looked at my experience and said, 'This store's yours, starting tomorrow. So, I managed the store there for 16 years."

He was transferred to Corpus Christi to straighten out a problem store. He remained there for three years and retired to San Marcos in 1977 at age 65.

John Holtermann retired from business, but he engaged life with even greater energy. He intensified his volunteer activities. Much of his volunteer work was through the First Methodist Church. He says, "First, I got involved with Dr. Gusendorf. He was a professor at Southwest Texas State. I drove him wherever he wanted to go for a little over two years, until he died at 91 with leukemia. Some of the jobs I have held with the church are: Commissioner of Education for a number of years; head of the Evangelism Committee for 19 years. I put 500 new members in First Methodist Church. For a long time I went out three nights a week to visit prospective members."

Volunteering has always been a part of John Holtermann. While in San Antonio, he was a scout master and as he describes it, "We had a small group of 58 boys, 15 of whom became Eagle Scouts in five years. My wife and I were always involved with our kids in band, choir or whatever activity they were in at the time. We had a boy, an exchange student from Denmark, live with us for a year and a girl from Greece stayed with us for a year. Actually, I have been volunteering and involved in community service since 1942."

John is a fixture on Sunday mornings at the entrance to the First Methodist Church on Hutchison Street. He has been greeting church goers at 8:30 and 11:00 AM services since 1977. Asked how many Sundays he has missed, he said, "I never miss more than three Sundays a year. This year I went to Tacoma, Washington during the Christmas Holidays." He also assists in counting the offering on Monday morning.

Other locations where John can be found as regularly as the sunrise are the Central Texas Medical Center where he has amassed 3,900 hours of volunteer time and the San Marcos Visitor's Information Center where he has accumulated 2,500 hours. These activities are not included in the list of 58 offices held and honors awarded for community service over the past 60 years. The following, while far from complete, is a fair representation of his accomplishments. Scout Master, San Antonio, 1942 to 1947. Served on Scout Advanced Council until 1951. Honored in National Scouting Magazine in 1944 with a full page story on scouting. Head usher at Methodist Church in San Antonio for seven years. Voted Friendliest Salesman in Brownsville, 1961. Outstanding Christian Service First Methodist Church, San Marcos, 1986. Elected to Texas Silver-Haired Legislature, 1986. Reelected 1988, 1992, 1994, 1996. No opposition for the past three elections. Chairman of the Legislative Action Committee since 1990. Honored by the Texas House of Representatives and Senate with John Holtermann Day, September 17, 1998. "One of the great moments of my life," according to John.

With the Texas Legislature currently in session, I asked John to explain the Texas Silver-Haired Legislature. He began, "In 1985 the Older Americans Act was passed and created the Department of Aging. The department decided they needed representation during the legislative sessions and decided on the Texas Silver-Haired Legislature. When our AARP was asked to put forth a candidate in 1986, no one wanted to run, so I stuck my neck out and here I am.

"Most of the 160 of us had never been in politics and when we went to Austin in 1986, we didn't know what we were doing. But we are allowed to hold our own sessions in the even years and we are organized just like the legislature. The first two terms I did not hold an office, but I am now in my sixth term as Chair of the Legislative Action Committee. All our legislation is funneled through that committee. Last year, we put 19 bills on the governor's desk. We are the only group allowed to meet in and use the facilities of the House of Representatives. They provide us paper, copy machines, meeting rooms, etc.

"We check in on Sunday, go home on Friday. This is all volunteer now. No pay and no expenses unless someone makes a donation to me."

He handed me an agenda with 33 items sponsored by the current Silver-Haired Legislature. While many of the issues affect the older population, there are items which affect the general population, such as lowering the blood alcohol level from .10 to .08 as a standard for intoxication; opposition to school vouchers; opposition to deregulation of electrical power; and requiring state prisoners to work to earn their keep.

John's eyes brighten, his shoulders straighten and his voice becomes full and strong as he explains, "We have a 70 per cent success rate with our bills. That is 70 per cent get to the governor's desk and he has vetoed only one in the time I have been in this job."

I asked how he stayed in such good shape at 89 1/2 years of age. "Last week I walked about 10 miles through the halls of the state capitol, visiting senators and representatives," he responded.

John Holtermann is an icon, rarer than an appearance by Halley's comet. The Titanic will be raised, the Buffalo Bills will win the Super Bowl, and Harry Truman will return from the grave and vote Republican before we see another like him. ***Author's note: John Holterman passed away January 6, 2002.***

Liz Ferguson

Liz Ferguson, General Manager of Quail Creek Country Club, seems to have inherited a characteristic of the land where she was born. She dusted up her first whirlwind in Vernon, Texas, the center of the Texas-Oklahoma tornado belt. She was born with the boundless energy of those wind-driven dynamos of nature. But before she could develop a high plains drawl her family moved to Phoenix, Arizona where her father was editor of the Phoenix Gazette. For twelve years her family enjoyed the wide open spaces of the desert and the security of her father's day job. However, he, like many who are visited by the muses, decided there was a great novel somewhere in his psyche and he retired from the newspaper to write the book. Editor's rejection slips paved the way for the family to move back to Texas—Wimberley, to be precise. Liz was fourteen at the time.

After graduating from Hays high school, Liz went to college at Sam Houston State, majoring in music education to become a high school band director. After 50 credit hours in her major, she grew tired of the long practice sessions required for the clarinet, oboe and alto sax.

"I haven't picked up an instrument since I left college," she said.

"I quit college and got married, very young—19. My first husband was in the military, so we moved around a lot. However, both my boys were born at Fort Hood. During this time, I was taking courses wherever and whenever I could and I finally got a degree in accounting from Mary Hardin-Baylor.

"A few years later, my marriage was falling apart so I ended up in Buda in 1990. I had two boys, a pending divorce and was looking for a job. Life was edgy, uncertain, and a little desperate. I was working as an accounting temp in Austin when I answered an ad for office manager from Quail Creek Country Club. I was with the club six months when the general manager's job came open. Needing more money and lacking the good sense to know better, I applied for the job.

"There were 38 applicants and I was probably the only one who had never been an executive. But the club needed financial management a lot more than it needed an expert in tennis, golf, food service or social planning. A club member who was temporarily serving as interim manager, gave me an excellent recommendation. But when I was told I had the job, I was scared to death. In fact, my first day on the job John Ferguson, the golf pro took me out on the course and said, 'this is a green; this is a tee box; this is the fairway,' etc."

Little did Liz realize the magnitude of changes awaiting her. She not only faced a major challenge to her managerial skills, she was opening the door to a new life. She didn't find golf all that intriguing, but she did find the pro interesting. Almost two years later, she and John Ferguson were married. When asked to talk about the intricacies of being a wife and a boss to the same person, Liz was straightforward.

"I have heard there are those who don't think our personal and professional relationship is a good idea. But we work hard at making it work. It is probably harder on John than it is on me. It is occasionally difficult for him to accept me as the final authority here when there is a topic on which we disagree. That doesn't happen often, but when it does, we look for compromises and try to respect that each person has a different responsibility to the club and to the membership. I'm probably harder on him than I am on any other staff member."

When questioned about the need to separate one's professional life from one's personal life, Liz admitted there is some difficulty. "However," she said, "it is a lot harder to leave our professional life at the office than it is to leave our personal life at home. We have a lot of trouble at home letting go of the day's work. We need help with that."

When asked what she would like this profile to say about her, Liz answered, "I want people to appreciate how hard I try to do what I say I will do. I have a habit of taking on too many projects—overloading myself. I have to remind myself I am not Superwoman."

She was reminded that she had another baby in 1996, and that she served as the chairperson of the San Marcos Chamber of Commerce in 1998-99.

"The Chamber job was wonderful," she explained. "First it gave me a social outlet I don't get [at the club]. Maybe that sounds ironic since I work in a facility devoted to promoting social interaction, but when I'm here I'm always at work. The chamber activity allowed me to have that socialization that I really enjoy while at the same time, I'm giving back to the community. And I'm representing my place of business to the community. So, I get a three-fold return from my involvement with the chamber. I had such a good time as chair I had trouble giving it up. It really makes me feel good about myself."

With respect to the new baby, Liz pointed out that while she and John were preparing for a major addition and renovation to their home, the club was getting ready for similar changes.

"I had my daughter, Lindsay, on March 11, 1996. Three days later, March 14, we had the ground breaking ceremony for the club house renovation. I was present for the ceremony. It was like the birth of two babies. Lots of pain, lots of inconvenience, but overwhelming joy with the addition of each. As for the rest of my family, my son, Justin will be graduating from San Marcos High School in May. Ryan, 14, is an avid tennis player on the high school team and plays in tournaments all over the state. And Lindsay, now four, is in control of the entire household."

When asked what no one knows about her, Liz, responding to some genetic coding said, "*I* want to write the great American novel. I love to write, and some day…"

Don't be surprised if this whirling bundle of perpetual motion turns out a tome that makes us forget John Grisham and William Faulkner.

Cliff Caskey

"Lots of people wonder where I got my accent "says Cliff Caskey, as the words roll out of his mouth like cold molasses. "Well, I grew up in Plainview, Texas where the wind blows 60-70 miles an hour on a good day—some days it blows hard—and when you are trying to talk with a mouth full of dirt, you develop a strange accent."

Cliff can go way back with his genealogy, relating that his maternal great grandfather came from Tennessee and farmed in Eastland, Texas before purchasing about 3,000 acres of land northwest of Plainview. His father came from East Texas during the Great Depression and met his mother while working for her father.

Cliff was born into agriculture and grew up on a farm on the High Plains of Texas. He relates helping his father milk 20 Guernsey cows by hand. They would sell the cream and give the milk to the hogs. That weekly creamery check would tide them over until the crops started coming in. "We went to town on Saturday, with our eggs and butter. "Cliff said. "It was 16 miles into town and it was a grand deal. The co-op creamery gave Daddy a check every Saturday and that check almost always got endorsed to Mr. Seago's grocery store where we bought our groceries, which were mostly staples like coffee, tea, sugar, and flour, because we grew everything else we ate. In the winter-time we bought coal because you don't have wood to burn on the high plains.

"The last place we stopped was the ice-house where we would buy a big chunk of ice—about 50 pounds—and try to get home as fast as we could before it melted."

"I took four years of vocational agriculture in high school, and I participated in Future Farmers of America and the Four H program. The day I graduated from high school, I went on the wheat harvest. We combined wheat all the way from Plainview to Bowman, North Dakota. I had my 18th birthday and registered for the draft in Perryton, Texas on the way to North Dakota."

Cliff points out that was important because Viet Nam was beginning to heat up a bit and he expected to be drafted. For that reason he did not enroll in college when he returned from the wheat harvest. Meanwhile, his dad had begun building homes and had a connection with a local lumber yard. He told Cliff the lumber-yard had a job for him.

As Cliff tells it, "I went up there and wore the title of assistant manager and I found out that's the guy that scrubs the floors, cleans the toilets, unloads the trucks, and does the accounting at the end of the day because the manager goes back to his office and sits there with his feet propped up."

The family moved to Tyler in January 1959 and Cliff worked for his dad building houses. He describes his decision to go to college: "I was working on a house by myself. It was August, I was in the midst of the tall pines, there was not a breeze. I was sweatin' so bad, I couldn't hang on to the hammer. A friend of mine came by and said he was going out to Tyler Junior College and enroll. I put my hammer down and said, I'm going with you. I told my dad about it later. East Texas heat and humidity put me in college."

After completing Tyler Junior College, Cliff went to Stephen F. Austin University to complete his degree in Agriculture and Biology. The draft notice never came, so after graduating from Stephen F. Austin, he was hired as an assistant county agent at Crockett which is in Houston County. Cliff started working on his master's degree at Texas A&M shortly after going to work.

After three years in Houston County, he was assigned to Hudspeth County near El Paso as the County Agent where he stayed for almost two years. "It is 130 miles wide, east to west and 160 miles long, north to south. The population is less than 3,000 people. They found water out there, though, and we had 70, 000 acres in cultivation. We had 5,000 acres of tomatoes, grew all the chilis for those commercial sauce makers in El Paso and produced all the corn silage for the dairies that supplied milk to El Paso."

Cliff then transferred to Rockwall County, near Dallas, where he stayed for a couple of years. "A guy talked me into quitting and coming to work for him," Cliff says. "I didn't know it at the time, but he didn't have the money to pay me, so I had to get a job teaching biology at Rockwall. First, thing I knew, I was driving the school bus and taking care of all the athletic fields. At this point, I finally took the opportunity to finish my masters degree in biology at East Texas State University, now Texas A&M at Commerce.

"I got tired of that school teaching pretty quick and it wasn't paying as much as a county agent job, so I found an opening in Gregg County at Longview. I liked my job in Gregg County. There were three Ag agents. I was the Extension Agent for Four H and the horse program in the county. Things were good. The pay was good, the taxes were low and I enjoyed my work."

So, what brought Cliff to Hays County and San Marcos? "When the head county agent retired, the Extension Service would not promote me or my colleague to the job. They brought in another man. And I told myself I wanted to get back to a rural county, so I applied for the job here. Boy, did I get fooled. When I moved here in 1977, I bought ten acres where I thought I was out in the country. Man, I got neighbors everywhere. I live out on the Seguin Highway and the traffic has gone from about six cars an hour to about six cars a minute. My father-in-law counted them."

Cliff recounts his days as the County Agent of Hays County. "I watched the county double in size while agriculture declined and horticulture increased in importance. From about 1982 on, oak wilt was a common problem and I was spending most of my time working in the towns. Wimberley was growing, Dripping Springs was growing and that was taking a lot of my time."

I suggested he must have gotten lots of calls about lawn insects and diseases from urban dwellers. "The last year before my retirement, we were running around 1,200 to 1,400 calls a month. My eight hour days disappeared. I was putting in 60 to 80 hours a week and I was visiting the chiropractor every week to ease the pain between my shoulders. I didn't know it was stress. He told me to quit burning the candle at both ends and I would quit having the pain. In addition to all the telephone calls, I was responsible for over 100 Four H kids. I helped put on the stock show and the horse show. I had to get volunteer help to get it all done. At one time I had over 100 volunteers working with me on projects. Of course, I had to constantly recruit and supervise those volunteers.

"That's why, when I came to the city in 1995, I told them I'm not taking a full time job." What does the city horticulturist do, I asked. Cliff used the recent ice storm to illustrate the scope and importance of his job. He pointed out that there were limbs down and damaged trees all over the city. In the parks, as a result of a pruning program begun when he came to the job, the city lost only one tree, a tree which had been earmarked to be removed. Other projects on which he is working include, an oak wilt ordinance which has not yet been passed, flower beds are planned throughout the city, he is responsible for the prize-winning athletic fields of the city. "We won Best-in-State for our softball complex, Cliff said, "and, with mostly volunteers, we are slowly converting Crook Park into a real park."Since he is the first, I asked why we need a city horticulturist. "Three hundred acres of park land is the main reason," Cliff immediately responded. "And that's growing. We are probably five to six men short on our crew right now. We been three weeks trying to clean up Veteran's Park over near the Little League fields."

I mentioned his 10-12 grass plots near the Activity Center last summer and asked why. "Twenty-Seven," he corrected, and proceeded to give me a 20 minute dissertation about grasses and how to select them, and how he got the major grass companies to donate a pallet of sod to use as a sample so he could select the most appropriate one.

"My job here is more or less education. When I started here, I was just a horticulturist, but now I'm over all the crew. Every time I try to tell Rodney Cobb, director of Parks and Rec, I'm just a horticulturist, he says, 'and whatever else I need you for.' For instance I have been very involved in rebuilding the walk-way bridge across the river to City Park. I was also very involved in building the stage for Sights and Sounds of Christmas."

Though he does not volunteer as much for the Lion's Club, Summer Fest and the dozens of other activities, of which he has long been a part, Cliff Caskey, at 60, has lost none of his enthusiasm for growing things, for helping others, and for the City of San Marcos.

Bruce Bush

Even at 55, Bruce Bush looks as if he could strap on pads and a helmet and hold his own with the 15 to 18 year olds who fill his days. It should come as no great surprise because football and coaching has literally been his life.

"My dad was a football coach," Bruce begins. "I grew up in a football coaching family. I was born in Center, Texas where my dad played and coached football. My earliest memories are standing on the sidelines of a football field and running out to retrieve the kicking tee."

To understand Bruce's deep ties to his father, one need look no further than the pictures on his office walls and to know that his only son, Travis, is named for his father.

Football coaches, by the nature of their jobs, tend to be a nomadic group. Bruce's father was no exception. After a playing career at Stephen F. Austin University, and a successful stint coaching at Center, Bruce's father ran for school superintendent. In those days, that is how it was done. He was defeated and decided he needed to move on.

The Bush family moved to Nederland, Texas in 1958 where Bruce went to Jr. high and high School. Naturally, he played football. His high school talents as a defensive back led to a football career at Blinn Junior College and later at Lamar University.

Upon graduation, Bruce, naturally, went into coaching. His first job was at Sweeney, Texas. "Because the head coach, at the time, was a former player for my dad," Bruce said.

"The next year I moved to Port Neches Grove where I had done my student teaching. I was on Doug Ethridge's staff there for six years and in 1975, we won the state championship."

During the week of the state championship game, Bruce's plate was pretty full. Port Neches Grove defeated Odessa Permian in Texas Stadium on December 20th. "When we got home, the team was paraded around town on the fire trucks with sirens blaring and we were celebrating until 2:00 AM. I go home and my wife, Ida, is in labor with Travis. I got her to the hospital and he was born December 21st.

"When I brought my wife home from the hospital two days later, we didn't even have a Christmas Tree. But I had a great year. And that is how it has been for more than 30 years. Ida has been a patient, understanding woman who has made it possible for me to do what I do and be successful at it. She is an equal partner in all I have accomplished.

"At that time I was 26 years old and after winning a state championship, you feel as if you have reached the pinnacle of coaching.

"I thought I was ready for a head coaching job. I wanted to see if I could do it on my own. I took a head coaching job in Dimmit. Dimmit is in the Texas panhandle, 722 miles from Port Neches Grove. We made the trip in a U-Haul Truck with Ida, two children and a dog in the front seat. It took three days.

"It was quite a change for me. I had never lived in the Panhandle, but it was a fun year. We played two games in the snow. In the district championship game against Littlefield, the snow was blowing horizontally. Toward the end of the game, the snow let up enough to see the opposite bleachers. There were about four people huddled under a big fur cover. I told my assistants that they were either coaches wives or they have frozen to death. The temperature was around 10 degrees."

Though there were few witnesses, that game would presage Bruce's football coaching career. Dimmit won the game and the district championship. His first year as a head coach resulted in a championship, though they would lose to Floydada in bi-district.

After a year in Dimmit, Bruce was contacted by the superintendent of the Livingston school district.

As he puts it, "The winds and the sandstorms in the Panhandle are rough. The kids were great, but Livingston is in East Texas where I grew up and thought I always wanted to be."

The football program was at a low point—they had not won in two years. But Bruce credits his experience in Livingston with much of his growth as a head coach. "I learned a lot about how to turn things around. I had to deal with a staff which was accustomed to losing; we had limited facilities; and we were in a tough district," Bruce said.

"The first year, we won three games. In my fourth year, we were 8-2. I thought I had done all I could do there and I had an offer from Pharr-San Juan-Alamo (P-SJ) a big 5-A school in the Rio Grande Valley. My wife is from that area and so it was appealing."

The facilities were far superior, funds were more plentiful and Bruce had an assistant athletic director, two secretaries and a large coaching staff. He managed the football program for three jr. highs, 1,500 kids in a ninth grade school, and a high school with over 3,000 students.

Bruce goes on to say that he learned something from each place he coached. He learned to recognize and manage talent in one place, while he learned how to make the most of limited resources in another place. Instilling confidence and self-esteem in kids who saw themselves as losers was always a challenge. Working with different minorities in the various locations was important in his success. But at P-SJ, organization was paramount.

At P-SJ, the pressure was immense. The three towns shared a common interest through the high school and the football team was a major focus of that interest. Huge crowds attended the games. P-SJ won district the first year and lost to Alice in the playoffs. The second year the school lost to Corpus Christi Carroll in the playoffs.

Won-lost is what people want to hear when talking to a football coach. Very few people outside the game are interested in how that is achieved. Coach Bush's success comes through organization, attention to detail, incorporating every resource and unwavering discipline.

Among his organizational tools is a booklet Coach Bush publishes each year. The San Marcos Rattlers Coaches Organization 2002-2003. It contains everything you ever wanted to know about San Marcos athletics, including who is responsible and what his responsibilities are. Examples of its contents include details of a football scouting report, the Rattlers' weekly football work schedule, and the roster of each football player with his parents' name address, home phone and work phone. It contains dozens of other lists and sets of instructions.

Parents are a major resource to Coach Bush. During July, he and his staff visit the home of the top 50 or 60 kids who are out for football. The parents are provided a home-visit booklet, titled No Excuses, which contains, among other things, Ten Commandments of Football Parents; What We Expect of a Rattler Football Player; and Study Suggestions That Work.

Discipline is another important aspect of any Bush team. Each football player signs an Athletic Discipline Covenant when the season begins. It is co-signed by the parents, the Athletic Director and the Assistant Principal. It explains in detail what is expected and the consequences if the Covenant is broken.

Everyone in his organization knows what is expected and what the consequences are if expectations are not met. I have served in highly trained military organizations around the world, but compared to the precision of Coach Bush's football program, most of them resemble a gathering of the Officer's Wives Club.

Two years at P-SJ and Bruce was on the move again. He was offered and accepted the head coaching job in Alice. Six years of success in Alice, including Regional finals against Holmes, San Antonio saw him ready to move again.

"In 1989, I went to Gregory Portland. Travis was in the seventh grade and during my tenure there, he finished high school and played quarterback for me. During those six years we were 59-19-2 and went to the state semi-finals twice.

"Gregory-Portland is a high pressure town. When I went there, I was only two or three games away from winning 100 games. At the Booster Club, I was congratulated on winning my 100th game and I remarked I didn't know if I would ever win 200 games. Someone in the crowd said, 'If you stay here 10 years, you better win 200.' Nobody laughed. With my son as the quarterback, the pressure was even greater."

When Travis graduated in 1994, Bruce moved to Donna to work in an environment with less pressure. Travis came to SWT to play football and Bruce found himself driving 600 miles round trip to watch him play.

"Watching my son play was a lot more fun than coaching him," says Bruce.

"We fell in love with San Marcos and driving 600 miles was beginning to get to me. I told Ida, I would like to give San Marcos a try. I wrote a letter to Mary Gafford and was invited to interview. I got the job, not knowing how far down the San Marcos program had fallen. But we have no regrets."

I suggested his arrival and the ensuing success of the football team had made a significant difference in civic pride of San Marcos.

"Our team represents the school and the community. A coach must be a competitive person and take pride in his work. The team he produces is a part of himself, a part of the school and a part of the community and that is the feeling we want our kids to have. We want them to take ownership of that pride and understand that they are building tradition."

Bruce Bush, with Ida's support, is a winner. Since coming to San Marcos his won/lost record is 52-18. Lifetime as a head coach, it is 216-88-8. But those numbers have never been his goal. His goal has simply been to be the best coach he can be and to make every kid he coahes a winner. ***Author's note: Bruce Bush retired from San Marcos High School in 2005.***

Gloria Suarez

From behind the sewing machine, facing the front door, she peers up from her work when you enter unless there are a number of customers at the counter. Then, she can be seen assisting with the intake of clothes, exchanging pleasantries or measuring someone's garment for alteration. Gloria Suarez's dark brown eyes and pleasant smile has been a trademark behind the counter at Victory Cleaners since she was five years old. At that age, her mother, Isabel Martinez, began bringing Gloria and her brother, Armando, two years younger, to work with her. They often slept under the counter.

In the early 1950's Gloria's father, Aurelio Martinez, opened Victory Cleaners on West San Antonio Street in partnership with Mr. Gomez. He bought out Mr. Gomez in 1958 and since then it has been strictly a family operation. Gloria's tenure in the business may have been foretold by the coincidence of her birth. She was born two years before her father bought out his partner. "I was in high school when I began working in the shop," she reports. "It was about 1972 when I began working regularly.

"After I graduated from high school at mid-term, I took a medical assistant's course with the idea I would become a nurse. There was a break in school and I was home for the summer and Dad said I could help him in the shop. At the end of the summer he suggested I just stay with the business. I thought, 'Well I might just do that for a couple of years until he retires.' He never retired."

When asked about her father and mother, Gloria responded, "He still comes in at 6:00 every morning. He is eighty years old and he comes in every day. My mom who is seventy-five is the lady you see at the far sewing machine. She still works every day, but Dad leaves at noon."

Queried about her temporary job which turned out to be anything but, Gloria admitted she really wanted to be a nurse. "But," she says, "I like my work. I like sewing and I like dealing with people. Our parents never encouraged us to go to college. They insisted we finish high school, but additional schooling was not that important at that time."

Armando is a relative newcomer to the business. After high school, he had plans to attend Texas State Technical Institute to become an undersea welder. However, TSTI did not work out for him and after working for Wuest's Grocery Store for 10 years, he also joined the business.

In discussing her childhood, Gloria points out that things have changed a great deal in the way parents relate to their children. "Our parents never had the time to read to us and encourage us in school. I was not introduced to the public library until I learned to drive. In those days my parents focused on making a living and they didn't have the time to focus on their kids the way we do. Today, we are more involved with our kids, especially their education. All my children will expect to go to college and I hope one of them may choose to become a nurse."

Asked how this small family business can deal with all the competition in town, Armando replied, "We welcome competition. But we like to think we have a special relationship with our customers. When they come in the first time, we may not know their name, but by the second or third time, we always try to call them by name and to remember their special needs. We avoid treating people like a number."

At this point, Gloria pointed out that the staff always tries to take care of clothes as if they were their own. "If we find a button missing or a hem is loose, we make repairs without being asked. Even if a zipper is broken and I know the customer, I will replace the zipper. We do everything on site and so if someone has a complaint, we don't have to send the clothes back to a cleaning plant or another location.

"Many of our customers are from out of town. They may have known us while they were here in college. After they moved away, they still come back to us. We have customers from Canyon, Luling, Seguin, Austin and other towns. Another major contributor to our success is our people who do alterations. I believe this aspect of our business has helped our reputation as much as anything. It seems to be a lost art and it is not easy to find people who can provide this service these days.

"Because we are a family business, the same people are always there and our customers get very comfortable with us. I have been working since I was 14 and I have a personal relationship with many customers." This can sometimes be a problem as well as an advantage, Gloria explained. "When I am away—for instance, when I had my children—people come in and because I'm not there they don't want to leave their cleaning."

Speaking of having children, Gloria and her husband, Edward, have three girls and a boy, Maricella, 12, Veronica, 11, Daniella, 8 and Joseph 5. Gloria is proud of all her children and spends as much time as possible with them. At present, she is especially proud of Daniella's selection as first runner-up in the recent Miss Cinco de Mayo Pageant.

Though she and Edward were high school sweethearts, they did not marry until she was 30. When asked the reason for her rather late commitment, Gloria said, "Edward asked me three times to marry him. I finally agreed the third time he asked. Daddy did not want me to get married and in those days, you listened to your parents. But it wasn't all bad. Living at home allowed me to save my money, so Edward and I had a good start financially and we were able to buy a house fairly soon."

Apparently Gloria's financial acumen has served her well. "When I started helping dad," she says, "we had two racks for hanging clothes and we folded most of the shirts. I remember we put in another rack and then Dad moved the counter forward to gain more space for clothes. In spite of Daddy's doubts, we decided we needed to expand. My brother and I, with help from one sister, purchased the present location from my uncle Henry and built the plant and store at 418 South LBJ. My Dad did not want to spend the money. He was afraid we would not make it."

The company is now incorporated. Aurelio owns most of the stock, but Gloria is president and Armando is vice-president and they get along well. The greatest conflict she experiences is when she has to choose between business and children. She says, "Daddy doesn't like me to leave the business. And he is getting older and I may not have him much longer, so it is important to please him. But at the same time, my children are growing so fast, and I won't have them very long. I have to make some very hard decisions sometimes."

But Gloria pointed out she has plenty of extended family to help with her children. Her mother is one of 18 children and almost all of them live in San Marcos or within a 50 mile radius. Her father is one of seven, all of whom live in San Marcos. Asked how many people show up when they have a family reunion, Gloria replied, "Half of San Marcos."

When Gloria acquiesced to the desires of her father, the medical profession lost a great smile and a deeply dedicated person while the San Marcos business community gained a familiar, comfortable and highly valued trademark.

Randall Reid

Artists are a breed apart. That is what makes them artists. They do not see the world as most of us see it. Thankfully, they show us another way to view the ordinary, the mundane, the common, the difficult. They show us the complexity of life and the simplicity of living. They heighten our awareness of the glory about us while forcing us to view the squalor in which we sometimes wallow.

Writers, painters, sculptors, actors, and photographers interpret the world around us and bring us to a more civilized place in the universe.

Randall Reid is a visual artist who sees things you and I don't see. Ordinary pieces of rock dug from a tree planting are the material of a sculpture housing a mail box. Snippets of a tape measure add mystery to a mixed media work. The juxtaposition of geometric shapes represent permanence while suggesting the transience of nature. He internalizes the world in a special way and emits a captivating vision of the space in which we live.

"I was born in Fort Worth in 1956," he said as I steered the interview toward a more linear conversation. "I lived there for only three years before my family transferred to Amarillo. My father was with an oil company and we moved around a lot.

"My mother was always interested in art. When I was around 12 or 13 she took painting classes at Amarillo College. She kept art magazines around the house. My older brother had a lot of talent and my dad took ceramic classes. While I was interested in art, I never imagined I would pursue it full time. Everyone in my family seemed more talented than I."

During his high school years the family moved to Houma, Louisiana. As a high schooler, Randall was interested in everything. He imagined he might study ecology or architecture or archeology or English.

As Randall explains, "It was different from Amarillo. My brother and I looked through the phone book and couldn't find any names we could pronounce. It was full of Boudreauxs, Thibedeauxs, and L'Enfants. But I liked high school there. Geometry was my favorite subject. That type of thinking and problem solving—relationships and connections of shapes and space were interesting and challenging."

He took the art classes offered in public schools and his senior year at Houma, he decided he might pursue it further. His art teacher recommended Louisiana Tech.

"I loved that school and the art teachers," said Randall. "When I was a sophomore, my sculpture teacher got me a studio. That was a real accolade. All I did was work in my studio, I never went to art class. Of course, I took all my basic math and English—I took 21 hours of English and got into writing poetry. It's pretty abstract."

1) adieu, I don't; 2)Opelousas Eggplant Grows Gregariously. That is not one line of a poem, it is two poems.

"One of the significant events at Louisiana Tech was when my basic design professor bought one of my paintings for $200.00."

Randall has allowed his life to be relatively free of structured plans. To a large extent, he has allowed the vision of the moment to dictate his career pattern.

"I thought, 'What do you do with art after college?' I was pretty sure I wanted to go to graduate school and maybe I would teach.

"To get back to Texas, I chose Texas Tech for grad school. I found it wasn't quite the same. I had become accustomed to the seafood, the huge oaks and the Louisiana climate. I forgot about the dust storms and the wind of the high plains."

Randall says grad school was all art all the time. At Tech, he got his introduction to teaching when he became a teaching assistant for two years. He taught basic drawing.

"Though I had a studio there, it was smaller than the one I had when I was a sophomore at Louisiana Tech," Randall said.

After graduate school, Randall applied to teach at a number of universities and colleges. He was always competing with 200 to 400 other applicants, and at that point in his career, based on his work, it was difficult to determine if he was a sculptor or a painter.

"It was difficult to find that first job," Randall said.

He returned to Metarie, Louisiana, just outside New Orleans, where he lived with his parents. While he focused on his art, and entered lots of art shows, he worked a number of jobs. He taught tennis at the Jefferson Parish Recreation Department and art to kids at the YMCA.

"I did all kinds of little jobs," he said. "Meanwhile, I made connections with the Contemporary Art Museum in Houston . In addition, I got a two week job team teaching at Loyola University and in New Orleans I worked in the Artist in Education Program. I then got a chance to go to MacMurray College in Jacksonville, IL for one semester."

Following MacMurray College, Gadsden, AL called and invited him to do a year as artist in residence in the elementary schools. That was followed by a two year stint in a similar position in Monroe, LA. A couple of summers, were spent in Wisconsin teaching art at summer camps.

By 1988, he was back in New Orleans, working in the public schools, still trying to land that college job. He made the last cut—number two or three at several interviews

"But, I always wanted to work at the college level. I had a show here at SWT when Eric Weller was the gallery director. A couple years later, he had an opening and he contacted me for an interview. I came here for a three day interview and was hired in 1988. Been here ever since. I was originally on a six year contract, but when the department saw my work, they put me on a tenure track. "

Five years ago, Randall reached full professor with a studio on campus and again,…"It is not as big as the one I had at Louisiana Tech, but I do have windows."

So, what is happening in art on the SWT campus, I asked.

"It is hard to say, overall. But we have real quality among our staff. There are probably 30 full time professors and 45 or 50 adjuncts. There are perhaps 800 art majors.

"There are so many sections we can't keep up. I have been bombarded with requests from people who want to get into my figure drawing class this summer. We are bursting at the seams and the money crunch exacerbates that situation. It is incredible the amount of quality work coming out of the art department. We are having four senior shows beginning this month. That is a fantastic place to get quality art work for a very reasonable price."

Randall's list of juried shows, prizes won and cash awards presented are too numerous to list. His work has been displayed throughout the United States in more than 200 shows. Listing only shows where he has won cash awards would exceed the space allotted to this article. A representative sample of his cash award shows include: The 14th Annual Watercolor Exhibition, New Orleans, LA; Hoyt Institute of Fine Arts National Drawing and Painting Exhibition, New Castle, PA; Print, Painting and Drawing Juried Competition, Parkersburg, WV Art Center; National Watercolor Exhibition, Edgewood College, Madison, WI; National Art Exhibition, Barnwell Art Center, Shreveport, LA.

I asked how some artists, whose work seems crassly commercial, command prices in the thousands while his widely acclaimed pieces are much less.

"I have wondered that myself," Randall replied. "I could probably have a garage sale with a lot of my art and it might not bring five dollars. People don't understand it. They are more likely to pay $500.00 to $1,000.00 for something much more ordinary.

"I took some of my work to a gallery in Austin and the owner was extremely impressed, but her reaction was, 'I'm not sure my clients are ready for this. I don't know if it will sell.'

"Last semester, a student wanted to buy one of my drawings. He couldn't afford it, but I wanted him to have it. So, I gave him a price he could manage. Sometimes I create a piece I don't want to sell—for any amount of money."

Randall explains his many parts. "There is a part of me that is the teacher. One part enjoys doing service. Another part is doing art work. I love being a father. And with golf and tennis, I have a life apart from all that. I think you would have a hard time identifying me as a stereotypical artist."

To verify that, it should be noted that he has won the Quail Creek Country Club tennis singles championship a couple of times and his golf handicap hovers around 10, but it is not unusual for him to be a lot closer to par.

Listening to Randall discuss golf helps one understand him as an artist. "I love the game, the creative aspect of it. Watching the flight of the ball fascinates me. It is incredible how it travels through space and gets to the hole. The beauty of the golf course attracts me and presents intriguing problem solving opportunities. The tennis, the golf and all these little things that are so much a part of me helps me make sense of who I am and what I do. I am blessed with the ability to focus, to become one with what I'm doing.

George Gilbert

George Gilbert had already decided he would be a professional soldier. He had his commission in the regular army. He had completed army flight training and was preparing to go to Korea. At the time he was stationed at Holloman Air Force Base, New Mexico where he bowled with a fellow soldier and old friend of his from Griffin, Georgia which is near George's home town of Thomaston.

George describes his change of plans, "This friend of mine and I belonged to a bowling league. We enjoyed it and bowling was popular at the time. It was featured on TV, a number of new developments—automatic pin setters, for example—were just coming out, and we started talking about going back home and building a bowling alley."

Before he and his friend could get their bowling venture underway in Georgia, the friend 'chickened out.' George was relating his situation to Mr. Bob Pollard, executive director of First National Bank in San Marcos, when Mr. Pollard suggested, "Why not San Marcos." It should be noted here that Mr. Pollard was George's father-in-law.

Time to digress. After completing college and receiving a commission from University of Georgia at Atlanta, George had entered the military and found himself at Fort Sill Oklahoma, the army's artillery training center. Being an artillery forward observer did not especially appeal to his sensibilities, so at the urging of one of his barracks mates, he applied for army flight training. His barracks mate did not pass the flight physical, but George was sent to Camp Gary to receive his basic flight training.

His experience working in a bank in Thomaston convinced him he needed to open an account in a local bank. Bobbie Pollard, a clerk at First National, helped him open that account. She has been overseeing George's finances since. They were married in 1956.

Though the shooting war in Korea was over, the prospect of going there for a year without his family held little attraction for George. With Mr. Pollard's encouragement, he and Bobbie built the first and only bowling alley San Marcos has ever had.

"We opened an eight lane bowling center in January 1959," says George. "I thought we had a big bowling center, but when the boys from Austin would come down to bowl with us, they said it was like bowling in a closet. In four years, 1963, we added four more lanes. That proved to be too small also.

"I had always been told that 16 lanes was the optimum size alley. Maximum return for your investment, labor, and equipment. In 1968 we added four more lanes, so now, we are at the magic number. That was a pretty good year. I went in the mobile home business that year, enlarged the bowling alley, built a new home and Bobbie had a baby. I was expanding on all fronts."

The development of the business was hardly a seamless effort of constant growth and expansion. As George explains, "When we opened, Gary Air Force Base was full and one crew of flight instructors worked mornings and one crew worked afternoons, so we had our lanes full all day. Just as I began my first expansion, the base closed. It got pretty dark (financially) for awhile. It got so dark we used both sides of our cash register tape. I quit all my bad habits—smoking, drinking, chewing—I had no money."

George and the family persevered and Sunset Bowling Lanes remained open. By 1968, things began to get better and recovery was underway. In 1976 eight lanes were added to bring the total to 24, its present size.

What has the bowling business been like since 1959? "The biggest change has been in the equipment," says George. "In 1959, you could get a black bowling ball or a black bowling ball. You could get a ball from Brunswick, AMF, or Ebonite, but they were all black, they were all rubber and all drilled the same way. They were basically the same ball.

"Someone got the idea you could drill those finger holes shallower and get more roll on the ball. That led to the question, 'What would happen if you changed the surface of the bowling ball?' and so plastic came into use. Today there are probably ten different surfaces available. Then someone saw the ball as a gyroscope and began to dally with the weighting of the block inside the ball and it seems that each week there is a new placement of that weight.

"The lanes have changed also. The surface we bowl on today is a synthetic called High Pressure Laminate, or HPL. The beauty of this is that we don't have to resurface it. Hardwood had to be completely stripped every year and a totally new surface applied.

"I had planned to open the facility with pin boys setting pins. At the Brunswick management school I attended in Chicago, I was told it would be a horrible mistake not to go ahead and get automatic pin setters. Even the pins have evolved. In the 50's they were wood, solid maple. Then came a plastic coating, then mesh and plastic, then the weight and balance were modified. The change in the equipment, as in tennis or golf, has made the game easier and people can have more fun at it."

When asked why, after 42 years, no one has ever built another bowling alley in San Marcos, George related a series of economic factors, then said, "In the mid or late 60's I heard that someone was seriously considering putting up a new bowling center. I went to see him and said, 'If you want to be in the bowling business, come see me. I can save you lots of trouble.' I just thought the town could not support two facilities and I didn't want to see both of us fail.

"San Marcos has really been good to us as far as supporting us. When we first opened, we had a big percentage of the people in town involved in bowling.. In fact, the manager of the Chamber of Commerce would call me and say, 'I need to have a meeting, but I don't want to call a meeting on the men's bowling league night.'"

George related that leagues are essential to the economics of bowling. He points out that he has leagues of all ages, gender, interest, skill-level, work related, very competitive, and purely social.

In response to what happens during the summer when San Marcans are largely outdoors, he said, "It was a problem until a few years ago when Parks and Rec began a summer program of bowling, swimming, skating, and movies one day a week. That has grown so that now we have kids filling the place four days a week during the summer. Our slowest season is the fall when we must compete with football, Thanksgiving, and Christmas "

What made you think you could run this business? Laughing, George replied, "About three weeks into it, I was wondering the same thing. Looking back, I see that I was really naive. Fortunately, the day we opened the salesman from National Cash Register stayed behind the register from 9:00 AM till midnight. The men's and women's bowling leagues from Gary AFB came and helped me that day. The bowling was free and the people from the base put someone on each lane to help score and assist in any way they were needed. I couldn't have made it without them. But I don't know. I don't know why I thought I could do that! I don't know who I thought was going to run it!"

What was San Marcos like to a Georgian who married a girl who came this close to being a BISM (Born In San Marcos)? "Well, the first few years, I was Bob Pollard's son-in-law. The next few years, I was Bobbie Pollard's husband, and then I became Gary Gilbert's father, and now I'm Terry and Sherry's grandfather. I have never had an identity in this town."

George is still acitvely involved in the operation of the business and at 70, he shows few signs of slowing. His sense of humor is ever present. He is passionately a people person. When asked what's the best part of his job, without hesitation, he responded, "The people. I enjoy the people. I especially like to help people enjoy bowling. People need to have something they can look forward to during the week which gets them out of their daily rut. They need to have something they can get passionate about. I like to see people do it well and enjoy it. I told Bobbie once I was called to do this."

Asked what this article should say about him, George responded, "I once had on my bill boards, 'Bowling Is Inevitable.', and I meant it. I do not understand a person who does not have a weekly outlet for himself or herself. In bowling, you can start younger—we have kids from nursery school—and bowl longer; we have 80 and 90 year olds, and you could have those two categories in the same league and they could have fun."

Cathy Dillon

If you are looking for a head cheer leader for San Marcos, look no farther than the Crystal River Inn where Cathy Dillon hangs out most of the time. Even though by San Marcos standards she is a relative newcomer—it is only 16 years since she arrived—Cathy loves to extol the virtues of our River City. First, she will admit she is "fatally attracted" to hill country rivers and small towns. Second, she agrees San Marcos rescued her from the treadmill of a highly successful, but self-consuming corporate life in Houston.

She became addicted to the hill country's charm early. According to Cathy, "We spent most of our summers in the hill country when I was a kid. Most of my relatives, aunts, uncles, cousins are in the area and I just never got it out of my system, so once I got out of college, I got engaged to a guy who ran a summer camp in Kerrville and came back here to Texas. The rest is history."

Though Cathy was born in Tyler, Texas she spent most of her school years in southern California. Her father was a physician, but her mother was a Hollywood actress, so when Cathy was in the third grade, her family moved to California. According to Cathy, "It's weird because when I can't sleep, I get up and at 3:00 AM I can watch my mom playing a nun in The Bells of St. Mary's on TV. I have been accused of inheriting some of her flamboyance and I guess I did."

Cathy went to college at Chico State in Chico, California which she describes as "very much like Southwest Texas. In fact," she says, "Chico is very much like San Marcos—a college town with a beautiful river running through it and not far from a major metropolitan area, Sacramento. I loved it there and my folks liked it so much, they moved there my senior year and now they run Dr. Coats Nut Farm in Chico. He raises almonds."

Between Chico State and Mike Dillon, Cathy's profession was nursing. With a masters degree in cardiovascular nursing, earned from Texas Women's University, she worked at the intensive care unit at Methodist Hospital in Houston where Dr. Michael DeBakey was the chief heart surgeon. Later she ran the pacemaker clinic and found herself entangled in the corporate world.

"The pacemaker clinic was my own private business," Cathy explained. "Initially, I ran it for the hospital, then a partner and I took it over and wound up with a company with more than twenty employees. A company from the east coast bought it and I found myself flying all over the country training nurses to do what we were doing. I got worn out being a corporate gadfly and traveling all the time."

By this time Cathy had married the guy who came over to repair the window she broke in her apartment when she locked herself out one day. He happened to be Mike Dillon who happened to live in an apartment near her in Houston. She had a major contract which she was servicing in San Antonio and Mike was involved in real estate management in Austin, so they looked on the map to decide where they might go to get out of Houston. San Marcos was a natural choice.

Cathy explained, "We came up and looked at houses one day, including this one [The Inn] and my thoughts about it were, 'I loved the house, but how can we live on a main street, no way.' We had a baby coming—Sarah, our daughter is adopted—and I didn't want to raise a child on a main thoroughfare."

Fate seems to have a way of having its way. The next morning during her shower Cathy's unconscious revealed to her the answer to achieving her goals of staying home with her daughter, staying in business and scratching the creative itch that has always been a driving force for her. This idea of getting into the fledgling industry of bed and breakfast facilities popped into her head. That was the answer she decided. She and Mike closed on the house at 326 West Hopkins Street in December of 1983.

"All our friends thought we were nuts," Cathy explained. They saw us as the corporate types. They couldn't believe we would go into something requiring domestic skills. They thought this was the stupidest thing they ever heard of. And the truth is, I could not *even* cook oatmeal. My initial plan was to serve a continental breakfast—orange juice and a roll—but it didn't take long to realize people wanted more than that. So breakfast has become a high point here."

Catering larger affairs has become a major activity at the Inn and this came about in much the same way as the Inn itself, by accident. People booked the Inn for parties and special events and after watching the caterers for awhile, Cathy, in her typical fashion, said to herself, 'I can do that.' "Sometimes, I think we are more a restaurant than an inn."

Cathy describes her last sixteen years as an incredible career. "Inn-keeping is not brain surgery," she is quick to admit, "but it is so multi-faceted and you have to be aware of so many things to make this work, including gardening and design and psychology and marketing. The Internet has made marketing a whole new challenge. I have been keeping a diary since our grand opening in September 1984. Some day I want to do a book, titled <u>Guerrilla Kitchen Warfare</u>."

When asked to relate some of the events that might be in the diary, Cathy told about the man who was eating his sausage at breakfast with a spoon because he had no fork. She immediately offered to get him a proper utensil, but he responded not to bother, he was accustomed to being deprived. That made no sense until she went upstairs to discover that a housekeeping oversight had left the man with no sheets and no pillow cases for his overnight stay. Another interesting and equally embarrassing story is about the man who showed up with his presumed wife-to-be to reserve a room for his honeymoon. However, on the day of his honeymoon, he showed up with a different woman.

"The most enjoyable part of running the Inn is the opportunity for creativity," according to Cathy. "When I reach the burnout stage and get in the dumps what brings me out of it is the opportunity to do something creative."

She went on to explain that the murder mystery weekends are a good example of the need for creativity in the inn-keeping business. "Winters," she said, "are a different animal here in central Texas. You have to think up something to fill the rooms during those months. Murder mysteries were our 1989 winter special event. We have been doing them ever since. We have conducted more than 200 murder mystery weekends, and we have six or seven plots, some of which we have written. We improvise on those from time to time. We were especially blessed with our first one. It was attended by a travel writer. We had a storm that night and the lights went out and it was perfect for our weekend. The writer wrote up the weekend and it was published in Continental Airlines magazine. Our phone was ringing off the hook for awhile.

"Gourmet dinners were our special for this winter and they have been so well received, we will be continuing them on the first Friday evening of each month."

When asked about some of their real trials since 1984, Cathy said the flood of October 1999 washed the foundation from under the house. That required a complete redoing of all the rooms, wallpaper, floors, everything. "And now the Inn is on the Tours of Distinction this week. It has been a hassle getting ready, but they needed some houses for the tour this weekend and it promotes San Marcos. So I agreed and I always feel so good when it is over. "

So, with all her accomplishments and overwhelming success in the inn-keeping business, what makes Cathy happiest about her life in San Marcos? "In a word, Playscape. The way people came together as a community and achieved so much. It was just a phenomenal experience. And that is typical San Marcos. Mike and I had a recent discussion about where we want to live the rest of our lives and we decided we want to stay in San Marcos."

Naomi Medina

"I was fat! I had always been fat. Well, not obese, but chubby. Fat is *not* a four letter word, so I can use it. I know some people hate the word, but it is a fact of life. I was a cute, chubby baby. I was a cute, chubby first grader. In the seventh grade I was even chubbier."

This is how Naomi Coleman begins her explanation of how she became involved in the fitness business. Today she has a body Cindy Crawford would kill for. Naomi is five feet, five inches tall and weighs 112 pounds with every pound exactly where it is supposed to be. She is the founder, owner and sole operator of *Heartbeat, San Marcos*, a fitness firm at 166 South LBJ.

"In seventh grade I went through what all girls at that age go through. I wanted to wear cute clothes the smaller girls could wear. I hated gym class because the outfits made me look even worse. I wanted to look like the petite girls, but, oohhh, I loved to eat! I still love to eat, for that matter.

"I probably reached my heaviest weight in my late teens and I was at least 25 pounds overweight. In my early 20's I tried aerobics, but I hated it. I couldn't catch on to the moves. I went home crying. I was *so* embarrassed. At the time I was working in a law office part time. Each morning I would get up and bake cookies or make bread or prepare some sort of food and then watch television most of the morning and comfort myself with the food. *Love Boat* was among the programs I liked to watch and one morning when this girl walked across the screen in a bathing suit, it was like…I had been hit by a bolt. I don't know what it was, but right then, I decided 'I've had it!'

"I stood up. I turned off the TV and said to myself, 'I'm sick of watching TV every morning. I'm sick of being fat. I'm sick of looking bad.' I went outside and began walking. While on the walk, I promised myself I would walk an hour every day, rain, shine, sleet, or snow. And I would eat nothing but tuna and raw vegetables."

Naomi followed through on the promise. She admits the diet was not the healthiest in the world, but she began to lose weight with the diet and the walking. She still refuses to watch daytime TV because it reminds her, she says, "that I was fat, I was lazy and I was unproductive."

One day during her walk, Naomi was overtaken by a woman who was jogging, at which point she said to herself, 'Why can't I run?' She began running instead of walking and, as most runners do, a short time later she entered a race. It was a 5 kilometer course. There was an award ceremony following the race and she decided to, "go and check it out." Surprisingly she heard her name called. She had finished second in her category.

She says, " I was so proud of my little medallion. I showed it to my father and I still have it today. It did a lot for my mental attitude. I decided to try aerobics again because I really loved the music. I was still just as big a klutz as I was the first time, but I felt better about myself and I had a different instructor. I came to love aerobics. It was changing my life.

"One of the greatest highs I have ever experienced was the day I was asked to substitute teach that aerobics class. My feet didn't seem to touch the ground for about eight hours. It was literally a turning point in my life. I began to think of aerobics seriously and think about it as a career. This was 1983."

Naomi and her husband, at the time, moved to San Marcos in 1984 from Brownwood. Initially, she worked for a law firm in Austin and pursued her aerobics as a hobby because she was limited to participating in the evenings in Austin. The long drive to Austin, the traffic and the long hours of the commute convinced Naomi to take an administrative job with the San Marcos police department as secretary to the chief of police. Meanwhile she pursued her passion by teaching aerobics for Jim's Gym.

In 1987 she encountered personal turmoil in her life and decided she needed to be on her own, completely independent.

"I didn't want to work for anyone. So, I opened *Heartbeat.* I went to the director of Parks and Recreation and asked if I could use city facilities in exchange for a percentage of my earnings. This was in May of 1987. He said yes, so June 8, 1987 was my first day of business as *Heartbeat Aerobics.*

"I was at the old recreation hall on the river. Every day for six months I opened those gigantic garage doors, lugged a 100 pound stereo out of my car, set it up in the building which had no air-conditioning—maybe that's why I don't like air-conditioning today. If it was a rainy day I would have to get there an hour early to mop up all the water. I don't know how I did it, but I had quit my job by this time and I had to make it work. I was really dedicated to it at the time. I doubt if I could do it now.

"Eventually, the Dunbar building became available and so I moved my classes there. But it soon became obvious that I needed another place for *Heartbeat.* For instance, we were often preempted by other functions. I found myself apologizing to my classes for missed sessions. I would try to make it up by giving a free lesson. It was just too difficult to manage. It wasn't a money maker because I didn't have a system. People would come in and hand me a whopping check for $18.00 and I would say, 'Oh, is it time to pay?'

"I needed an identity. I did not want to be known as a city aerobics program, so I approached Jim Neuhaus of Jim's Gym and rented the upstairs studio in his place on McCarty Lane. That worked out for about two years before I moved here. I reached a point where I really needed my own space. I moved to my present location in 1991.

"I really can't explain why I have made this a successful venture. It seems to me it is like a baby. You can't make a baby grow. You just nurture it, love it, care for it, give it all your attention and somehow, it grows. I have had and still have competition, but I like to think I can be a little better than most others because when a person walks in here I usually know them. I know what they drive; I know where they work' I know what they do; I know when they're not here, I'm going to call them. They get my personal attention.

"When the SWT Student Rec Center opened, I lost practically all my college clients, so I am making it without relying on the students and I feel good about that.

"I have begun to branch out and provide more services. I provide corporate programs now, I have a number of clients for whom I am a personal trainer, and I am an instructor provider for other programs. Exercise is evolving. The large aerobics classes where people just sort of dropped in are not happening any more. That no longer meets the needs of people. They are getting outside and going to the weight room and diversifying. Consequently, I am emphasizing my role as a personal trainer."

Naomi was asked about the fitness competitions in which she has participated. "Bobby Warren of San Marcos Athletic Club asked me one day if I would be interested in participating in a fitness competition. I had certainly never seen myself doing that, but he kept after me and finally after considerable resistance from within myself and outside sources, I agreed to try.

"Bobby put me on a diet and outlined a program for me and two years ago I entered Muscle Beach Fitness Competition in Galveston. To my amazement, I won second place. A month later, I entered the Lackland Classic in San Antonio. It is the biggest competition in Texas. Again, I placed second."

The next year she entered her third competition and placed third. That was sort of an eye-opener for Naomi. She said she looked in the mirror and it was apparent why she did not do better, "I didn't do my homework."

"I got back on my program and worked at it and went back to Lackland last year and I won my class which was for shorter girls. They divide the classes by height, rather than age, so I had to compete against these 20

261

year olds and I had to compete against the taller girl. I beat her and won overall.

"I will be 40 years old in January, and yes, you can print that. But I want to tell all women, no matter what age. Don't let yourself gravitate to the couch. Get off the couch and get out there, doing whatever you choose, but don't let yourself vegetate."

Naomi not only walks the walk, she talks the talk. Ten minutes with her and she will have you shopping for an aerobics leotard and a pair of training shoes.

Tom Partin

Tom Partin, arguably, gets more phone calls than any other person or business in Hays County. He gets over 7,000 calls a year. What makes Tom such a popular fellow? He heads the Hays County/San Marcos Emergency Medical Service (EMS). And no, he doesn't personally answer all those calls.

Like so many San Marcos residents, he came here to attend [Southwest] Texas State with the intention of becoming a high school agriculture teacher. That was in 1967. Thirty-seven years later, he is still here, serving San Marcos and Hays County in one of the most crucial and sensitive jobs in the area.

Tom came to San Marcos from Priddy, Texas, which he laughingly describes as being between Democrat and Indian Gap. After working for the Brown School a short while for $1.45 an hour, he sought to improve his circumstances and took a job with Hays Memorial Hospital for $1.63 an hour.

I asked him to recount the evolution of EMS.

"In 1971, I started working in the old Hays Memorial Hospital, which was located on the property where we are sitting right now (on the west access road at 1305 IH 35 North). When I started, the ambulance service was under the supervision of the head of hospital maintenance. We were orderlies assigned to patients on the floor, and ambulance drivers when needed. Until 1968, ambulance service was provided by the funeral home.

"From the hospital, we covered the entire county. There were three ambulances, but only one ambulance had a crew assigned to it. When there was a need for more than one ambulance, we just rounded up hospital staff and sent them to the scene."

According to Tom, it was not unusual for the maintenance director, the hospital administrator, the assistant administrators and accountants to man the extra ambulances. Tom said when he began at the hospital, one of the ambulances was a hearse, donated by the funeral home. It contained an oxygen bottle, splints, stretcher and a suction device. Theoretical or practical knowledge of first aid was the only requirement for personnel. In the early 70's EMS began to develop a life of its own.

"It wasn't long before Don Beeson was given responsibility for scheduling ambulance crews and supervising the operation," Tom said. "He was also still an orderly on the hospital floor. But we began to get some specialized training from the state. It was a precursor to the Emergency Care Attendant (ECA) course. Later that same year, money became available for a few of us to go to Austin for Emergency Medical Technician (EMT) training."

Those who became EMT qualified began working in the emergency room rather than tending patients on the floor.

Near the end of 1973, Don Beeson left and Tom Partin took over the ambulance operation for the hospital. He remained in that position until 1983, when the hospital moved to Wonder World Drive and declared that it could no longer subsidize an ambulance service for the city and the county.

"The city and county appointed a blue ribbon committee that came up with a non-profit corporation to run the ambulance service," Tom said. "That corporation remains our governing body today.

"The corporation's board of directors consists of a city council member, a county commissioner, a citizen appointed by the city and one appointed by the county. Those four members then select a physician for the board. Ex-officio members include the medical director, the fire chief and a hospital rep if the hospital chooses to appoint one."

I asked Tom about the operation of the service and the changes he has seen.

"We can do things in the field today that could have only been done in a good emergency room when I started with EMS. Over the years, I have seen emergency rooms that were not as well equipped as one of our Mobile Intensive Care Units (MICU) is today.

"We carry a lot of sophisticated equipment and our people are trained to do many critical procedures prior to a patient's arrival at the hospital. The basic ambulance runs about $90 thousand and then it is upgraded with about $30 to $40 thousand worth of equipment."

"Major trauma patients need to go to a trauma center," Tom explained, "not necessarily the closest emergency room. We refer to the golden hour with major trauma. What happens in that first hour often determines whether the patient lives. We are fortunate that we have the Star Flight helicopter from Breckenridge in Austin, Critical Air helicopter at Central Texas Medical Center (CTMC), and Baptist Air Life from New Braunfels."

Among the procedures that can be performed by the paramedics with the ambulance equipment are fluid replacement, airway management, including creating a surgical airway, and stabilization of fractures. The MICU crew is also capable of defibrillation and 12-lead, pre-hospital EKGs as well as monitoring of all vital signs. Medications, which may be administered, include cardiac drugs, diabetes medications, beta-blockers, and fluid expanders.

In addition to a staff of 45, the Hays/San Marcos EMS also has a medical director. All services performed by the paramedics and EMT's are performed under the license of Dr. John McNeil, an emergency room physician who practices full-time in Victoria, Texas. He worked for Tom for ten years before obtaining his credentials as a physician.

Tom explained the reason Dr. McNeil was selected. "Many doctors are not real familiar with the pre-hospital world. This one is. He comes here occasionally to ride with the crews. He meets with us monthly to do call reviews and provide us with standards of care. His job is to oversee and review our performance from a medical standpoint."

From a serendipitous organization at the old hospital site, covering the entire county, the EMS program has grown to seven manned MICU's stationed throughout the county. There are three ambulances in San Marcos, one in Kyle, one in Buda and two in Dripping Springs. There are two reserve vehicles with a third expected to arrive within the month.

His units team with the various fire departments throughout the county and provide first responder services in their various areas. The fire department is charged with the rescue mission—that is, they carry the Jaws of Life and other rescue tools. It is after the rescue that EMS takes over patient care. He pointed out that many of the firemen are trained as EMT's or paramedics and his people are experienced in crisis situations. Teamwork between the fire departments and the EMS is very close and well coordinated.

While the fire department and EMS each has a specific set of responsibilities, Tom made it clear that, if needed, a patient might be treated inside a wrecked vehicle while firemen worked to extract the individual.

Two paramedics man the first responder ambulances in San Marcos, Kyle and Buda. Paramedics have more training and experience than the basic EMT, so when the EMS ambulance arrives, it is a mobile ER and ICU manned by highly trained technicians. A paramedic and an EMT may man the reserve vehicles.

"Last year, we had 467 calls where we had to dispatch reserve vehicles in the San Marcos/Kyle area," Tom said. "All our first responder ambulances were already busy. If we have to organize a reserve crew during the day, I might go on the call myself.

"We are on duty 24/7, 365 days a year. In our last fiscal year, we responded to 7,200 calls in the entire area. About 700 of those calls were in the Dripping Springs area. Only 600 were in the Buda area. The remainder was in the San Marcos/Kyle area."

Tom admitted to a certain level of frustration in his job because not every call is a true emergency and often people with true emergencies do not call. He gave the example of a person who might call an ambulance because he/she believes it will help avoid a long wait at the ER. On the other hand, there are those with real emergencies who could be stabilized before they get to the ER, but fail to admit the seriousness of the situation and are reluctant to call.

How quickly the ambulance arrives depends entirely on where it has to go. However, Tom said that EMS has an 80 per cent response time of less than seven minutes. The size of the Dripping Springs area makes that response time less likely.

Officially, Tom Partin is the Executive Director of the San Marcos/ Hays County EMS, Inc. He is also a paramedic and an ambulance driver, plus he answers lots of phone calls.

John Huffman

John Huffman is a man comfortable in his own skin as he illustrates with a self-deprecating anecdote.

"While attending one of the numerous functions required by the consort to the President of Texas State University, I was approached by a prominent San Marcos lady with ties to the university," John said. "After a short conversation, she looked me over and said with a certain air, 'Well, I guess your are all right, but you are no Cathy Supple.'"

Though he may be no Cathy Supple, he is a first spouse with impressive academic credentials who has willingly deferred to the talents and ambitions of his wife, Denise Trauth. Actually, they are a team and John's role is and has been essential to the success of the team.

He has a Ph.D. in Mass Communications Law from the University of Iowa. John is quick to point out that he is not a lawyer, though his discipline had a number of lawyers on the faculty.

"I never had any ambition to be a lawyer," he said. "My real interest was in journalism. I worked as a journalist before going to graduate school. I wrote an education column in the Black Hills region of South Dakota for several newspapers in the area. And during the time I was in the Air Force, I wrote for various base newspapers."

Education for John was not a given. He was the first high school graduate in his family. After graduating in 1960, he enlisted in the navy and following boot camp, he was stationed at the Naval Auxiliary Air Station in Kingsville. His job was cleaning bugs from hangar doors. That convinced him that he needed a college degree if he were to succeed. It was in the navy that he got his first college credits.

"I was going to school and the navy was paying for it, but I did not want to stay in the navy" John related. "I knew there was a long cruise in my future and that was not very appealing. I was able to transfer to the air force and retain my rank of sergeant. In the air force, I became a crewmember on the flying command post of the Strategic Air Command. I was stationed at Ellsworth Air Force Base where I enrolled in Black Hills College in Spearfish, South Dakota."

After his discharge from the air force, John enrolled full-time and finished his under graduate degree at Black Hills. Following graduation, he was offered a job as a reporter on the Rapid City Journal, but his Graduate Records Exam was high enough that a friend suggested he should go to grad school.

"I applied to the University of Iowa for what I thought would be a masters program," John said. "They responded with an offer of a teaching/ research fellowship. I would do some teaching, a little research and I would pursue a Ph.D. My first job there was associate editor of one of the magazines in the school of journalism."

John had an interest in law and journalism and the university offered a program in mass communication law. After pursuing academia for a couple of years, he decided to give industry a try. He took a job with Digital Equipment Corporation in Maynard, Massachusetts where he worked as a technical editor for one year.

"They told me they would hold my fellowship at Iowa and when I returned in 1972, a new crop of Ph.D. students had arrived and one of them was named Denise Trauth. I was the old seasoned student because I had been in the program a couple of years. Denise was fresh out of a masters program at Ohio State, so I took her under my wing—all the way under my wing, as it turned out.

"The Daily Iowan was the student newspaper and the Iowa City daily. I became publisher of the paper and that's where I met Denise. She was the features editor. It was the first time she worked for me.

"Under my influence, she decided to pursue communications law. She chose broadcast communications while I was more interested in libel, invasion of privacy, copyright, that sort of thing. Our areas are slightly different, but we had a lot of the same professors."

In 1973 John finished his Ph.D. and went to the University of Tulsa for his first teaching job. Denise finished her course work in 1974 and came to Tulsa where they were married. She finished her dissertation, received her doctorate and joined John at the University of Tulsa.

As an assistant professor, he taught undergraduate courses in libel, invasion of privacy, copyright, and pornography law.

As an amateur journalist, I asked where does one separate law from ethics in journalism?

"You don't," John replied. "They are very closely attuned. My Ph.D. education consisted of a large helping of ethics as well as law. Courses in some journalism schools are often entitled, "Communication Law and Ethics."

John and Denise stayed at the University of Tulsa four years. Denise had her first administrative job there as assistant to the Dean of Arts and Sciences. By this time, neither could see much chance of advancement. Each applied for jobs at other universities.

John took a position at Pepperdine University in California, while Denise went to Bowling Green State University. At this point, the marriage involved a long commute. But the plan was for Denise to seriously look for a position on the West Coast. Seemed reasonable since she had experience in teaching and radio, TV and film production.

"As it turned out," John explained, "I became a rare breed in academia. I had my contract bought out. I was paid not to teach. Happens to football coaches, but seldom to professors.

"One of the hats I wore at Pepperdine was Director of Student Publications. Students in a magazine production course put out a slick publication at the end of the year as a part of the program. They came to me and said they wanted their lead story to expose the hypocritical attitude toward gays on campus.

"There was a large gay contingent among both students and professors, but Pepperdine, a church supported school, had official policies which condemned the practice and denigrated the gay population.

"When the story appeared in print, there was a fire-storm of controversy. My boss was an elder in the church. He came to me and said, 'Freedom of the Press does not mean total freedom at Pepperdine. I don't want any more of your liberal philosophy in your classes.'

"We had quite a discussion about philosophy and freedom and he finally said, 'You look for another job and I will continue to pay you.'"

The story became a national issue. Major newspapers, including the Los Angeles Times, covered it and so, John's firing at Pepperdine became, for many other universities, a highly desirable entry on his resume. Coincidentally, a journalism position came open at Bowling Green shortly after the dust-up at Pepperdine.

He joined Denise at Bowling Green, where he was given a raise and tenure and in a few years, became the director of the School of Journalism. Meanwhile, Denise had risen to Department Chair of Radio, Television and Film. Because many of their classes were similar, they initiated the idea of a School of Mass Communications.

The president and faculty approved the idea and John became the Director of the School of Mass Communications. As such, he was once again Denise's boss. To avoid charges of nepotism, John had no say over her promotions or salary.

John and Denise spent 14 and 15 years, respectively at Bowling Green. After so many years of administrative duties, John was eager to get back to the classroom and research. Denise, meanwhile, was enjoying her success in the administrative side of academia.

"We were marketing ourselves as a couple," John said. "A graduate deanship came open at The University of North Carolina, Charlotte. Denise applied and was hired. I was hired as senior professor in the communications department with tenure and a nice pay raise. That was 1991."

John taught 10 years at UNC, Charlotte. Meanwhile, Denise became Acting Provost, then Provost. In those positions, she became John's boss. In 2001, John retired when Denise, after encouragement from her colleagues, decided to seek a college presidency. His retirement would allow her to seek a presidency with no strings attached.

If you haven't already come to appreciate the teamwork and cooperation responsible for the phenomenal success of John and Denise, it is worthwhile noting that they have co-authored 80-100 professional papers and book chapters.

This teamwork continued in the process of her quest for a university where her vision and considerable skills could be fully realized.

"Once she decided she wanted to seek a presidency, I was the one who went through all the chronicles of higher education and found the advertisements and information about the various possibilities. We then talked about our desire to live in a particular part of the country; we talked about whether the school fit her vision; we talked about size, history, and goals of the various institutions.

"The discovery of [Southwest] Texas State was probably more the results of my efforts than Denise's. She interviewed at several schools and turned down two offers."

What have you learned as First Spouse, I asked? "It has taught me empathy for women in responsible positions," John said. "When we are introduced, even though it is clearly stated that Denise is the president, people—men and women—will look at me, shake my hand and say congratulations."

John points out that he is by no means a shadow president, but the teamwork is still there. His many years in academia make him an informed and understanding sounding board for Denise. He is an avid tennis player and manages their stock portfolio. He also mentioned that he does the cooking.

Neal Kinlund

Milton Jowers is Texas State University's legendary basketball and football coach. A huge athletic edifice bears his name. His was the first name enshrined in the recently initiated Society of Champions (won a national championship) of Texas State University. Milton Jowers is deserving of every honor Texas State University has bestowed upon him. Only problem is, he is, arguably, the second most successful coach in the university's history.

Neal Kinlund's tennis teams won 333 matches and lost 185 from 1973 to 1998. They were NAIA National Champions in 1981 and 1982. He coached 10 conference championship teams. From 1979 to 1985, he had seven consecutive undefeated conference seasons, an unheard of feat. And that was just the men's teams.

When I visited Neal in his office in the aptly named Jowers Center, I wondered how he occupied his time, now that Texas State no longer has an intercollegiate male tennis program.

"I teach nine classes," he said. "I have five tennis classes, three basketball and one badminton class. Sounds like a lot, but it isn't that bad. I really do enjoy those classes. As I think of the time I was coaching, I also taught nine classes. The position called for halftime teaching and halftime coaching. There is no such thing as halftime coaching. But that is how my salary broke out.

"I look back and I don't know how I did it. It was a brutal thing for 25 years.

"My background is really in basketball. Coach (Vernon) McDonald hired me to come here from SMU as an assistant basketball coach in 1973. Basketball is my strength, but I had a little background in tennis."

Neal grew up in the small Kansas town of Tribune. The newspaper owner had the only tennis court in the county and with no television, movies, or other recreation, Neal spent many hours on that tennis court teaching himself to play the game. When he wasn't on the tennis court, he was dribbling a basketball.

He describes himself as a basketball nut. Though he played all sports and appeared in the one-act plays in his small high school—32 graduating seniors—basketball was his favorite sport. He played at Hutchison Junior College and then at Fort Hays State.

His first job after completing his bachelors and masters degree was at Wilmer-Hutchins High School, near Dallas. It was an extremely poor school district.

Neal says, "Every teacher should have to teach one year at Wilmer-Hutchins just to appreciate wherever they are. I did everything—coached basketball, track, tennis. I knew nothing about football. The talked about an umbrella defense, I had no idea what they meant. In the classes I taught, we did not have money for paper to mimeograph the finals. I had to write my tests on the blackboard and make the kids use their own paper.

"Junior High kids are the best in the world to coach," Neal said. "Tell them to run through the wall, they run through the wall. I taught the kids ball handling drills, some rather complicated, and they loved it. I contacted a publicist for the old Dallas Chaparrals (a long gone pro basketball franchise) and we put on a demonstration during halftime."

"Meanwhile, one of my teaching colleagues, Kay Pinkham, was married to an assistant basketball coach at SMU. She told him what I was doing with these Jr. High kids. Mike Pinkham occasionally came to our practices and began inviting me to go with him to scout Southwest Conference schools. That was a thrill for me.

Mike knew all the high school coaches in the Dallas area and suggested he would help me get a high school coaching job. He called me one day and asked how I would like to have a coaching job. I thought it was a nearby high school.

"Of course," I said. "Then he asked if would like to be an assistant at SMU. I almost fell over. I couldn't believe it. I went from an eighth grade coach to an assistant coach at a major university and took a thousand dollar cut in salary. But I was furnished a car and an apartment. That helped.

During his tenure at SMU, the team was co-champion, with Texas, of the Southwest Conference. However, the team fell on touch times and the entire coaching staff was fired.

But Neal's unemployment was short-lived. Vernon (Coach Mac) McDonald, at Southwest Texas State offered Neal a job as his assistant basketball coach. As a relative newcomer to Texas, Neal was unfamiliar with little towns in the state, so when he began looking for San Marcos on the map, he began in the Uvalde/Junction area.

"I am living proof that the university was misnamed," Neal said. "I had to ask a friend where San Marcos was located and when he told me between Austin and San Antonio, I realized I had been nowhere close. The name change was appropriate."

When he arrived a Texas State, he fully intended to coach basketball. However, one of the more senior coaches who coached football, basketball and tennis was eager to give up the tennis job. Neal had tennis on his resume and Bill Miller, the Athletic Director (AD) assigned Neal to coach tennis.

"I took over the men's tennis program in 1973. They had not won a conference championship since 1939. In two years we were conference champions. I began by recruiting junior college players. Initially. I had four half-scholarships. A half-scholarship meant tuition and fees—no room and board.

"I took a gamble on a kid name Manzoor Syed from Pakistan and gave him a full scholarship. He became the conference singles and doubles champion and an honorable mention All-American. I then asked for another full scholarship.

"AD Miller said, 'I'll give you another scholarship, but he better be good.' I recruited Gary Seymour. He was an NAIA national singles champion and an NAIA All-American."

And as Neal says, things continued to get better. That is parallel to saying that from a little oil well near Kilgore, H.L. Hunt made a little money. Neal's accomplishments surpass whatever superlatives one might assign them. In addition to the accomplishment listed earlier, here other significant accomplishments of Neal Kinlund and his teams.

Five times his team was runner-up in the NAIA or NCAA division II national tournament.

Two times his team garnered fourth place in NAIA or Division II national tournament.

Among individual player honors, he produced 27 All-American selections, 52 all-conference players, four national tournament Most Valuable Player awards, three national singles champions, and 92 percent of his players graduated.

He was NAIA coach of the year in 1981; Lone Star Conference Coach of the Year in 1983; Gulf Star Conference Coach of the Year in 1985.

From 1982 to 1985, he served on numerous organizations and competition committees of the NCAA.

He was the NCAA Division II National Tournament host director in the 1983 and 1984. He was the Lone Star Conference tournament host director in 1975, 1990 and 1995.

He is the only coach ever to win championships in three separate conferences, Lone Star, Gulf Star and Southland conferences.

In 1988, he was inducted into the Texas Tennis Coaches Hall of Fame.

His name is alongside Milton Jowers and Bill Woodley (golf) in the Texas State University Society of Champions.

If this is not enough, I remind the reader that Neal also coached women's tennis along with the men from 1980 through 1989. The accomplishments of the women's teams are no less spectacular than his men's teams. They won six conference championships and in 1981, finished ninth in the AIAW National tournament.

When the men's tennis program fell victim to Title IX requirements, Neal was devastated. No matter that his life became less complicated, he was reluctant to give up something he loved. Today Neal is busy as a tennis umpire and referee. He often officiates major college conference matches.

There may never be a Kinlund Building on the Texas State University Campus, but when tennis is mentioned, Neal Kinlund should be remembered in the same legendary terms as Milton Jowers.

Ed Kuny

"Thomas is very intelligent," Ed Kuny said, as he began this interview. "He is reasonably fluent in French and he does wonderful art. He has done more than 30 pictures and we are planning to take them to San Antonio to a 'starving artist' exhibit and see if he can sell a few."

Thomas is Ed Kuny's 44 year-old son who suffers from schizophrenia. Ed says Thomas was around 15 when they began to realize something was not normal, but he was not positively diagnosed until age 20.

"Because of Thomas, my wife, Sally, and I became very involved with the National Alliance for the Mentally Ill—NAMI. It literally saved our family. It is very active organization in Texas. For two years, I served as the president of NAMI, Dallas. It has some 600 members, and is the largest affiliate in Texas."

Ed is currently the vice-president of the state affiliate, NAMI, Texas. He is slated to be the president next year. The organization's mission is to educate and provide support to families of persons with mental illness. It is also active in lobbying government entities to enact legislation to improve the life of persons with mental illness and to provide support to their families.

Ed describes some of the frustrations encountered by families dealing with mental illness: "In the early stages, we went through psychiatrists, one after the other. I became so discouraged. I didn't know whom to trust. I didn't trust any of them, actually. But the profession has gained a great deal of experience and now realizes that mental illness is biologically rooted and they treat it as such. Today's medications are fantastic compared to the early tranquilizers that were used to treat the disease. But it is still a lot of trial and error."

He pointed out that a medication could work well with one person while another person may have marginal or unsatisfactory results. Body chemistry, diet, life-style and other variables affect the results. Adjusting dosages is also a major factor in achieving appropriate results from the medicines.

"That is why the community mental health facilities, such as Scheib Opportunity Center, are so important," Ed said. "Sally and I have spent more than 30 years with Thomas and coping with this illness and we know that it is a family issue."

Ed pointed out that health insurance for the mentally ill is generally inadequate. The care systems, over the years, have evolved, but the prolonged nature of the illness and its debilitating effects set the illness apart from all others. Without the public health system and the community centers there is no place for many of these people. Houston, for instance, is a horrible example of inadequate care for those who have no family and can't care for themselves. San Antonio, he says, is not much better.

"The state legislature has enacted laws that put all the responsibility of caring for people with mental illness back on the counties and the cities. It was an un-funded mandate and if these entities are not willing to pick up the load, then we will have the old revolving door—from the hospital to the street, to the jail, to the hospital, etc.

"It costs about $40.00 a day to keep a person in jail and about $20.00 a day to maintain a person in treatment. Hospital costs are much more expensive."

One of NAMI's local projects is establishing a connection between the mentally ill people who come to the emergency room of Central Texas Medical Center with mental health staff at the Scheib Center. In addition, Ed lauded the local law enforcement agencies for their efforts in training officers and supporting the efforts of NAMI.

"At our February 2, support group meeting, we will have Commander Bill Glasgow of the San Marcos Police Department and Deputy Steve Cunningham, a specially trained officer of the sheriff's office, present their programs.

"The police department is initiating a program to train officers in crisis intervention and they have asked NAMI to assist in their training. What is exciting about this is that the departments realize the need for these specially trained people and we will then have jail diversion. It will not only save lives, but it will also save money."

The purpose of the NAMI support group that meets the first Monday of the month at the First Presbyterian Church is to give support and education to the families of persons with mental illness. One of the ways they will do this is to train peer counselors from among clients of Hill Country MHMR, of which Scheib is a part. Ed is bringing Cliff Gay from NAMI, Dallas to do the training. He has recruited 19 persons, all clients of mental health centers, to participate in the training.

"They will organize peer to peer support groups along the lines of our family to family support groups," Ed said. "There are 19 counties in Hill Country and we plan to have a trained facilitator in each of those counties to start these groups.

"My immediate dream for San Marcos is to have a drop-in center. We must find a location—my next project—and it would be open from around10:00 AM to 5:00 PM. It would be an all-volunteer facility and open to any adult with mental illness. We would have crafts, reading material, and other diversions available. But, the main purpose will be to provide a place for them to get off the street and interact with their peers. Eventually, we will have a hot lunch. If they can pay, fine, if not, fine."

Ed Kuny is literally immersed in making life better for persons with mental illness. He described last year's lobbying efforts that were aimed at passing House Bill 2292 passed. It separates mental health from mental retardation.

"The system was broken," Ed stated. "We think the bill will help fix the system. Texas Department of MHMR will no longer exist. Mental Health will be a program under Health and Human Services and Mental Retardation will be under another department.

"We have seen a system work in the Dallas area. Called North Star, it is based on cooperation between providers, HMO's and insurance companies. The providers are private for profit concerns and the system provides services for 22,000 mentally ill people in the seven-county Dallas area.

"We had great trepidations about leaving that system and coming here where we would once again subject Thomas to the public mental health system. But after I looked around and visited with the people at Scheib, I felt a lot better. It was just beautiful to come in and see the care that was given the patients. Thomas's life is better now than it has ever been.

"In fact, HB 2292 mandates that urban mental health care will be patterned on the North Star system and rural, public systems will be patterned on Hill Country MHMR."

Ed sees Hays County as a fertile place to plant seeds for new programs and provide new treatments. For example, he and wife, Sally are qualified teachers of Family to Family, a 12-week course that meets weekly for about two and a half hours each meeting. It gets deeply into the family dynamics of mental illness and teaches people how to live with it. They also teach a second course called Visions for Tomorrow for families with children or juveniles who are mentally ill.

Since Hays County does not have a NAMI chapter, Ed is affiliated with the Austin chapter and when he mentioned his goal for a drop-in center in San Marcos, he was encouraged to establish one in Austin.

"I am going to concentrate my energies in Hays County," he said. "We need to walk before we run, and so I want to get the word out about the support groups to families who have loved ones with mental illness. We want to get out the word that help is available. The more people we can get involved the more good we can do."

Ed Kuny actually has a life outside NAMI. He retired from his post as Vice-President for Development of Director's Investment Services a couple of years ago. The company owned 70 funeral homes and an insurance company. In this position, he was able to hone his golf game and plays to a seven handicap.

In addition, Ed is a commissioned lay pastor of the Presbyterian Church and preaches each Sunday at the First Presbyterian Church in Luling.

Families in Hays County that have been touched by mental illness can be thankful that Ed Kuny chose San Marcos for his retirement home. He can be reached at 512-353-4339. He would welcome any calls concerning mental illness or NAMI.

Susan Hanson

I was a bit intimidated when I undertook this profile. Susan Hanson was winning statewide awards for her Daily Record features and essays when I came to San Marcos nearly 25 years ago. In fact, she has compiled a book of her unique writings. In April, Texas Tech Press will publish *Icons of Loss and Grace: Moments from the Natural World*.

She attempted to put me at ease by announcing that this interview… "is very weird because I'm on the other side and I'm not used to this. I'm accustomed to asking the questions, so if I start asking *you* questions…"

In 1971, Susan came to San Marcos, like so many others, to go to school. That led to marriage and a teaching career at the University. She came here as a transfer from a community college, near her home in Bay City and obtained a degree in English. She got her masters degree at Texas State and began her teaching career almost immediately. With a few minor interruptions, she has been teaching English at the University since 1975. She teaches freshman composition and advanced reading and writing. She also teaches an honors course in nature writing.

I reminded her that she also had a journalism career with the Daily Record.

"Seventeen and a half years," Susan said. "That started by accident. In fact, everything I have done has been by invitation. Teaching, for instance: Lou Ann Brunson, chair of the English department, heard from a mutual friend that I was eager to get back into teaching. It was October, but a situation arose and I was asked to teach and I said sure."

"As for my career as a journalist, it began when I was the editor of the St. Mark's newsletter and Betty Medford, Neighbors editor of the Record, was a member of the church. I did a few interviews and wrote some small pieces for the newsletter. One day, Betty called, said she had a little bit of extra money, and asked if I would be interested in doing something for the paper. Initially, it was a very, very, very part-time job. It finally evolved to about three-quarter time. I did one or two features a week, the stranger the better, and a column on Friday."

Susan also did book reviews—of books she liked. Otherwise, she said, it would have been a waste of her time. And like her features, the book reviews were a little off-center. She also won a number of awards.

"I don't know how many I got," she said when I mentioned them. "I received the Jack Douglas Sweepstakes award for a column I wrote. And

I won the writing award at the state Associated Press convention one year. That shocked me.

"I made a special effort to interview people I admired and wanted to meet, or whose work I teach. Wendell Berry, Bill Moyers, Matthew Fox, a theologian, and many others. Berry is an essayist and novelist. He writes a lot about nature and that is what I'm interested in."

When asked what motivated her to write, she said, "My second grade teacher complimented me on a sentence I wrote on the blackboard, using the spelling words. I remember the sentence was something about butterflies. Writing is what I have always. done. Others encouraged me. I am an introvert and it is easier to write than talk. So I write."

If you have read any of her writing, you know she is fascinated with nature and that she is a deeply spiritual person. I remember her essays extolling the virtues of digging in the soil and turning up earthworms; marveling at the beauty and grace of a red-tailed hawk circling in search of prey; sharing with her readers her unique memories of her mother.

You have met two parts of this complex, busy woman, but there is a third part. She is a lay Episcopal chaplain; the three parts are as interwoven as the plaited strands of a braid of hair.

"I started coming to St. Marks when I first came to San Marcos. I was raised a Baptist, but I began looking into the Episcopal Church when I was in junior college. I had a teacher who was a priest. He was from the north and knew nothing about Southern Baptists. We had lots of interesting conversations.

"When I came here (St. Marks) I knew this is where I wanted to be."

How did she happen to become a lay Episcopal chaplain, I wondered.

"The chaplain left in 1996 and there was no one to take the job. I was already working with students in the church and again, I was asked by the diocese if I would be interested in giving the job a try—just to see how I liked it. Obviously, I liked it.

"We were doing some things in conjunction with the Lutheran campus ministry because we are both small groups and our efforts are similar.

"We became closer when we had the fire in St. Marks. Both groups met at the Campus Christian Community building. Lou Flessner, the Lutheran campus minister, and I wanted to consolidate much earlier, but it wasn't until St. Marks decided to relocate to Ranch Road 12 that we really started thinking about an official partnership.

"It became obvious that my campus ministry would be homeless when the church moved to its new location, unless we built something or bought something. At first, we tried to purchase land from the University. We talked for about a year before they turned us down.

"A campus ministry must be near the campus. For most, it has to be within walking distance. We started looking at this building. The diocese said no. The bishop said no. It is too much building for a campus ministry.

"But I kept nagging for about three years. Finally, it came to me that what we had in mind was too small. We needed to enlarge our scope. What we settled on was The Center for Spiritual Formation and Religious Studies. It will not be just a campus ministry. A lot of things will take place here."

Susan said that the Lutheran and Episcopal campus ministries have now joined completely. She foresees a hybrid Lutheran-Episcopalian congregation, but readily admits she has no idea what that would look like. Looking to the future, it appears it will be at least three years before the St. Marks congregation will be relocated.

In the meantime, to purchase the building, the Lutheran and Episcopalian campus ministries must raise at least a million dollars each. It will then be known as Christ Chapel and will host a variety of activities. A board of directors is in place to over-see the fund raising and other activities. According to Susan, it is planned to have workshops, seminars, lecture series, speeches, classes, mentor programs, and community groups, e.g. Weight Watchers, can meet at the building.

"We want a full slate of activity every day," Susan said. "We want this to be a place that celebrates the humanities. Art will be a part of it. It should also be a place that connects the community and the university. Given our geographic location, we should be able to draw from the Presbyterian, Lutheran and Episcopal seminaries in Austin, and then the six universities. Eventually, we may offer courses for credit.

"It has been fun dreaming. Lou nor I have ever done anything like this—raising a million dollars, but we keep talking as if we know what we are doing."

We came back to her book. Susan mentioned that she began putting the book together some years ago. It generated some interest among publishers but no one knew what to do with it. Like its author, it is not about any one thing. It does contain many of her writings that appeared in the Daily Record over the years.

From the publisher's press release: *Written as reflections, rather than full-blown arguments, Icons of Loss and Grace offers no final resolution to the questions it presents. Yet in these essays we may recognize that delight and sorrow are soul mates, that loss and redemption are a part of the same sacred ground, and that pain can evolve into grace.*

Susan Hanson is a shy, unassuming individual, gifted with a deep spiritual sense of being. But, I'm still intimidated. Her power comes not from any air of superiority, but rather, from her resolute convictions. She can truthfully be labeled an icon of vision and accomplishment.

John Ferguson

John Ferguson is this year's (2004) cancer survivor honoree of the Cattle Baron's Ball, San Marcos's principal fund-raiser for the American Cancer Society. For those who do not know, it is hard to believe that this healthy specimen and professional athlete, in 1998, did not expect to see his two year-old daughter's next birthday.

John Ferguson grew up with Quail Creek Country Club. As he explains it, "I was 11 years old when the club was built. I came out here with my parents and we watched the clubhouse go up and watched workers move dirt for the golf course. So, I was here from day one. I hit my first golf ball on the ninth hole, a 600-yard, par five. It was here that I began playing golf, but I never imagined I would wind up as the General Manager and Director or Golf."

While John witnessed the beginning and development of Quail Creek Country Club over the years, he had some interim training and development.

"I actually started golf seriously at the Aquarena course," John said. "I took lessons from Russell Scott and it was something my dad encouraged me to do.

"I played some baseball in high school as well as golf. We had two good golf teams. My golf in high school was not all that great. We went to a lot of tournaments and I was always scrambling for that fifth position on the team. I was competing against guys like Jackie Waldrip, Chuck Yarbrough and Bucky Smith. Fortunately, my golf got better after high school."

From high school, John enrolled at [Southwest] Texas State and played one semester on the golf team. However, a job prevented his pursuing a collegiate golf career. That job happened to be running the Aquarena golf course.

"I worked for the Rogers family during my high school years. One summer I worked at Texana Village and another summer I worked in the parking lot. When I was 16, I thought it would be great to work at the golf course. Scott McGehee gave me a job mopping floors and helping close the shop.

"My first day on the job, Scott left about noon and his assistant left about 2:00 PM. There I was, at 16, first day on the job and they just left me. I had a set of keys and I was in the golf business. I worked there for four years until Scott retired. Then I left for a while and went to work in the accounting business for Jack Schwartz. In the year I was there, I learned to keep books the old fashioned way—you know, ledger sheet, etc. before computers."

Still in college and 21, he heard about an opening for a manager at the Aquarena Springs golf course. In January 1979, John was hired and took over the course, where he says, "I had a beer license, owned the golf carts, mowed the greens, took in green fees, ran the pro shop and did it all. I was a one-man operation and my budget guidance was 'don't spend any money.'"

John remained with the Aquarena golf operation until November 1987 when, at age 30, he moved to Quail Creek to become the fourth golf professional at the club. He succeeded Steve Veriato who served in the position for about two years.

While running the golf operation of Quail Creek Country Club was a huge challenge for a young man of 30, John's biggest challenge would come eleven years later when he was diagnosed with colon cancer.

"I was diagnosed with a characinoid tumor in April 1998," John said. "I was forty-one years old. Liz and I had been married five years, and my daughter Linzy was two years old. In addition, I had two stepsons. It was not a good time for me to be sick.

"I had the warning signs for a couple of years, but I just didn't want to go to the doctor. I ignored the signs. I thought it couldn't be serious. I'll worry about that later. I might add, I don't stop and ask directions when I'm driving.

"I knew I should have a physical at around 40, but I put that off for at least a year. But when I did have a physical, my doctor referred me to a gastroenterologist. He did a colonoscopy and told me I had a tumor.

"My first thought was, 'Well, they will just go in there and take it out.' However, when I talked to the surgeon, he told me he was going to remove one-third of my colon. Suddenly, it hit me that all this might be a little more serious than I thought.

"None of the doctors ever used the word *cancer* during this time. I had no idea I had cancer until shortly after surgery. My primary physician came to my room with a worried look. There was no one else in the room. He was the first to tell me I had cancer and there was a good chance I would not survive."

The surgeon removed the tumor and several lymph nodes. About half the lymph nodes showed signs of malignancy. Further tests revealed that John also had cancer of the liver. He says the liver cancer developed as a result of his failing to visit his doctor early enough to prevent the cancer from metastasizing.

Nevertheless, John says he was in denial to the point he was thinking he needed to get out of the hospital and get his situation remedied right now.

"But, things don't happen that quickly," John said. "It took me a week to see the oncologists. I was on pins and needles. I don't think I got two words out of my mouth. I just cried the whole time. I went through the 'Why me?' the bargaining, the denial."

Next, he saw a liver specialist who removed the malignant section of his liver and at this point, there has been no recurrence of the cancer. In fact, his liver has regenerated completely. But the treatment was not over.

"I took chemo for one year. Fortunately, for me, I was able to take it as a shot once a month and the doctors told me that its purpose was to mop up after surgery. Unlike so many chemo procedures, I never suffered any debilitating effects. I would get the treatment and come right back to work the same day."

I wondered how this close and unexpected brush with death affected John's family.

John said, "We were in shock. It was a nightmare. As I mentioned, I kept asking 'Why me?' There was major denial, especially on my part. But as I began receiving treatment, the medical people were so attentive and concerned, I began to realize they really cared what happened to me. The doctors who performed the surgery made it clear that they were planning to save my life, that it was not a band-aid procedure they were performing. That helped a lot."

John has continued with his check-ups, which, at this point, are now conducted annually.

"I continue to keep my appointments and do what the doctors tell me to do. I have an MRI on April 16th and I expect it to be negative. But I am nervous every time I go for my check-up. I know the cancer can come back. I look for that doctor's expression each time and recurrence is very much on my mind."

John explained that new treatment procedures are developed at an amazingly rapid rate. For instance, today, he might not even have surgery for his type cancer. Instead a radioactive dye that locates the cancer can be injected. That is then followed by chemo that isolates the cancer and destroys it.

I asked what he wanted to tell people about cancer prevention.

"That's interesting," John said. "When word got out that I had cancer and was in treatment, I had lots of people my age tell me they were scheduling an appointment with their doctor, or that they were going to get a colonoscopy. Many of my friends said they didn't realize cancer attacked young people. They thought it was an old person's problem."

A Cure is in the Air is the theme for this year's Cattle Baron's Ball. Let's hope the motto is prophetic. In the meantime, listen to John Ferguson's sage advice.

John warned, "I can tell you, it is an equal opportunity disease. Listen to your body. Don't panic, but don't take any chances. Go to your doctor. And support cancer research through the American Cancer Society."

Nettie Serur

Nettie Serur is a fixture in San Marcos. She came here 65 years ago from Bartlett, Texas as a 16 year-old farm girl to be a student at [Southwest] Texas State University. In many ways she bridges the gap between old San Marcos and the new.

San Marcos High School has almost twice as many students as SWT had when she came. There was virtually no commercial activity that was not located on the square. River City claimed a population of about 6,000 citizens.

There have been some changes in her time, but as she prepares to move to Mobile, Alabama to be closer to her daughter, Sherry, Nettie is still as enamored of this "wonderful place" as when she first arrived.

She began this interview with, "I came here in 1939 and I met Dempsey," as if that was her sole purpose in coming to college. It was not. It was simply one of the first and most important things she did when she arrived.

"Myrtle Tarbutton introduced us," she said. "I was a freshman and Myrtle was a sophomore. She was a 'town girl' who had a car. She sort of took me under her wing."

"I started dating Dempsey in 1940 and we dated for several years," Nettie said. "I lacked only ten hours to graduate, but I married instead."

Nettie was somewhat ahead of her time. She came to [Southwest] Texas State to major in business when most women of that era sought one of three career fields—teaching, secretarial, or nursing. Though she did not get a degree, the training she received would serve her well in future ventures with Dempsey.

"When I met him, he was a football player at the college," Nettie said. He was four years older than I. And so he went in the Air Force in 1941, before Pearl Harbor, and became a pilot through the cadet-training program.

When Nettie told me she and Dempsey married in 1942, I assumed it was because she was concerned that he might be sent overseas. "No," she said, "you know, it just seemed that everybody was getting married. When he graduated from cadet training as a second lieutenant, he was stationed at Hyannis, Massachusetts on Cape Cod, and I rode the train from Texas to get married. It took three days to get there.

"We lived there for two years, then we were transferred to North Carolina where Terry was born. When Terry was one year old, Dempsey was sent overseas. In those days, we didn't know where he might go and I did not know where he was for a number of months. As it turned out, he went to London and later to Paris and on to Germany."

When Dempsey went overseas, Nettie returned to Bartlett with her new baby to await the end of the war. In 1946, she returned to San Marcos with Dempsey.

They, with Dempsey's brother, Edmund, purchased the clothing store, which was located on the east side of the San Marcos square, from Dempsey's older brothers, Ellis and Tom. For the next 56 years, they would continue a family tradition of doing business in downtown San Marcos. When Nettie's son, Terry closed the Varsity Shoppe at 326 North LBJ in 2003, it would end 110 years of continuous family business.

"We built our first house on Holland Street in 1948," Nettie said. "During that time, I went back to school (SWT) for awhile, but I still did not get a degree. When Terry was five, I started working as a stenographer at Gary Air Force Base. I was there for two or three years.

In 1956, Dempsey and Nettie bought out Edmund. Nettie then put her education in business to good use. She became an integral part of the store operation as she managed the women's clothing side of the store and did all the bookkeeping. That particular store was sold to Bealls before Dempsey opened the Varsity Shoppe on LBJ. Nettie continued to do the bookkeeping for the next 10 years.

"I finally freed myself of that job and I was back to being a housewife," Nettie related, "When the Bluebonnet Belles were organized. The Bluebonnet Belles were sort of a precursor to the Heritage Guild. The Heritage Guild is responsible for the Cottage Kitchen.

"The Heritage Association and the Heritage Guild are related but serve separate functions. The Guild operates somewhat independently under the overall umbrella of the Association.

"I was the first treasurer of the Heritage Association and a past president of the Heritage Guild. The Guild is the one that made the money. We organized the Friday lunches at the Cock House.

"When we started, all we had were folding chairs and card tables on which to serve people. As we began to make a little money, we began to purchase furniture for the lunches. Helen Van Gundy and I did most of the furnishing of the Cock House as we see it today."

Nettie and Helen were instrumental in the phenomenal success of the Cottage Kitchen. For the first three years, they did all the scheduling of volunteer groups who prepared and served the lunches. They were such a success that nearby New Braunfels requested they make a presentation and explain their program.

According to Nettie, "We succeeded through perseverance, hard work, and 'doing it ourselves.' There were times when we could find no one to do the luncheon. We had to round up some help and do it ourselves. Generally, people were willing to help.

"However, we started out washing our own dishes, and cleaning up the whole thing. It got to be so popular we just had to hire some help. I don't know what it does now, but it wasn't unusual for us to serve 100 people for lunch."

Nettie, when asked, did not remember exactly how long she played a major role in the Heritage Guild and Heritage Association. She suggested it was probably 15 years—"until I just couldn't physically do it any more." She is a lifetime member of the board of directors of the Heritage Association.

Proudly, she informed me that, "They named a room in the Cock House for me and one for Helen.

I asked Nettie to elaborate about the changes in San Marcos since she arrived here as 16 year-old in 1939.

"San Marcos had about 6,000 people. There was one car on the Hill (at SWT). Parking lots were the least of our worries. San Marcos was a wonderful town in which to rear your children.

"I would take Terry down to the theater on Saturday morning for the showing of cartoons. I would leave him there and Mr. Zimmerman, the owner, would take care of all the kids until the parents came back to pick them up."

Nettie explained that there was no garbage pick up. There was almost no commercial activity beyond the square. She and Dempsey bought their first car from the Scrutchin dealership.

"When we came back after the war, there was no Sessoms Drive. When we built our house here on Rogers Ridge, there was no Mimosa Circle; there was just a barbed wire fence behind us. Aquarena Springs was the biggest thing in town.

"One of San Marcos' defining moments was the organization of the country club. We were really a country town that had never had a country club. When the organizers got together and succeeded in getting it started, it changed a lot of things about this town. My family had never played golf. We water-skied. We used to water-ski at Five Mile Dam. So, when the country club became a reality, we started playing golf."

What's the biggest change she has seen in her 65 years, I asked? "The University," Nettie immediately replied. "From 1,200 to 26,000 students is a big change. Traffic is probably next. Before IH-35, Hopkins Street was the main road to San Antonio. We had three theaters and a big Duke and Ayers, a five and dime store. A defining event in the history of the University was the organization of the Strutters by Barbara Tidwell in 1960. They put SWT on the map."

Nettie Serur is part of the Greatest Generation, a vanishing group whose footprint is inordinately large. While most of us think of the Greatest Generation as those who went to WWII with the military, there were thousands like Nettie Serur who served silently, patiently, faithfully, asking nothing special in return, while devoting a lifetime to creating and giving. She will be missed.

Ed Lee

If have ever used a back yard gas grill, or if you have ever owned a recreational vehicle (RV), you have probably used one of Ed Lee's patented inventions or adaptive appliances. Ed's career has taken him from sharecropper to Senior Applications Engineer for Marshall Gas Controls, a multi-million dollar international manufacturing company, located in San Marcos.

He is credited with at least 12 patented inventions or adaptations. All this from a man with no college degree and no formal training as an engineer.

He was born in Noble, Arkansas, a little farm town "about like Martindale used to be when it had businesses," Ed said. "I was about three years old when my mother died. My sister was about a year old. My grandparents reared her, but I lived with a series of aunts and uncles.

"I moved from one family to another. They all had kids. Times were really hard, and they couldn't afford another child. I would stay a year or so with someone, then I would move on. That was my life until I was about eight years old. Eventually, an aunt and uncle took me in and I stayed with them until I finished eighth grade."

As a sharecropper, Ed's uncle moved almost every year from one farm to another. He provided the labor for the landowner and in exchange received half the income from the cash crop, which was cotton. The sharecropper's house normally consisted of little more than a front room, a bedroom and a kitchen. Ed and his three male cousins slept four to a bed in the bedroom.

"My uncle never went to school, couldn't read or write. However, he was the most honest, hardest working man I ever saw. And he showed me how to be the kind of man I thought I ought to be," Ed said.

"I quit school at the end of sixth grade and found myself perfectly content to work on a farm because I thought that was all there was or ever would be. Owning my own place never crossed my mind. I never considered it a possibility."

Ed described grocery shopping in those days. "My uncle would walk to town, do the grocery shopping and the store owner would bring him home. It was all on credit until the cotton was harvested.

"Cotton was the core of the economy. If we had our crop in, we could go out and work for another farmer. I picked cotton for three dollars a hundred pounds. It takes a ton of cotton bolls to make 100 pounds."

After WWII, Ed's uncle took the family to California in search of a better life. In California, school was mandatory until age 16 or until completion of the eighth grade. Ed entered and completed eighth grade without ever attending seventh.

After a year, California offered an economic picture no better than the one in Arkansas, so the family returned to Arkansas. Meanwhile, in 1947, Ed's father remarried and he finally claimed his son. He took Ed to Michigan to live with him. Again, he encountered mandatory schooling so he graduated from Marshall, Michigan High in 1951.

In spite of severe doubts about his ability to do college work, Ed entered Western Michigan University in Kalamazoo where he studied airport management. The military draft supporting the Korean War was a constant threat, so after one and a half years of college, Ed joined the Air Force in 1953 to avoid the draft.

He spent a large part of his Air Force tour in Germany where he met and married Josephine Kratz. He also learned something about mechanics.

"When I returned to civilian life in Marshall, Michigan, the economy was in a recession and jobs were difficult to find," Ed said. "I spent a few years working as an auto mechanic with a friend of mine. Then I bought a service station in a great location—until the interstate highway rerouted all the traffic.

"After selling the service station, I worked for a Ford tractor dealership until, in 1961, a friend, Eugene Kilborn, Chief Engineer of the S.H. Leggitt Company, suggested I might like to work for the company. He was the Chief Engineer because he was the only engineer.

"I had no idea what the company did, but Mr. Kilborn gave me an orientation tour and at the time, they bought and sold plumbing supplies and made two regulators and water lines for the RV industry. It looked promising to me."

Installing a large air compressor to enhance production was Ed's first job at the company. Mr. Kilborn, meanwhile, was working on an LP gas operated pulsator for traffic/construction warning lights. When he received the prototype parts, he asked Ed to assemble the gadget and make it work.

"That was my first experience with anything related to engineering," Ed said. "I finally got it working, but it was not very dependable. A friend of Mr. Kilborn's came up with the idea to use mercury to open the pulsator and so we began an effort to make it reliable enough to go into production in 1963.

"We called the devices Spot Guards and Michigan recognized it as the product of the year, but we could never get a patent on it, because several years earlier, someone in England had devised a similar product."

Shortly afterward, a Leggit salesman informed Ed that the mirrors, used when towing travel trailers, were no longer compatible with the new automobile designs.

"He asked if I could design a mirror bracket that would work on all automobiles. I said sure. I was too dumb to know better. After a few experiments, I concluded that I would never be able to make one bracket to fit all the new cars. I had to change my approach. What common feature do all cars have?

"I came up with the front wheel well and the top of the fender where it meets the hood. I went to a junkyard, purchased the front end of a car and began work on the bracket. I developed a complete mirror that really worked well.

"Two months after we went into production, an identical mirror, showed up on the market. It had the same tubing we were using. Our tubing supplier had stolen our design and began producing mirrors. We were in the process of getting a patent and after going to court, I ended up with five patents on it. Though we no longer produce it, that mirror is used all over Europe today."

Soon after designing the towing mirror, Ed designed a pressure fill cap used on RV water systems. To create pressure in some RV water systems, it was necessary to use a tire valve in the top of the lid. After partially filling the tank with water, one created pressure by introducing air into the tank through the tire valve.

"The problem with that," Ed said, "was that, when removing the cap on the water tank, you might take off a sizable portion of your forehead and brain if the tank were still pressurized. It could blow the cap across a four-lane highway.

"I designed a cap that would lock unless the tank was completely depressurized. It was unique enough that I was able to get it patented. We were going great guns with the product until trouble developed in the field because of the material we used to make it."

In 1970, Ed transferred to Waco to open a new plant for the Leggitt Company. The new plant was to make bathtubs and lavatories for RVs. The bathtubs were made from plastic and fiberglass and initially, were not very stable. Again, Ed devised a solution by reinforcing the bottom of the tubs with plastic strips.

The 1973 oil embargo and competition from cheaper steel tubs made it impractical to continue production of those products and the plant closed.

"I was offered the chance to return to Michigan with the company, but by that time, I had become a Texan. So, I left the company for a few years," Ed related.

The San Marcos plant was built in 1979 and in 1981, Ed received a phone call from Mr. Leggitt, asking him to return to work for the company at the San Marcos plant. He did and since that time, he has developed or helped develop a number of devices to improve the safety and efficiency of gas barbecue grills and LP systems on RVs.

Almost all of Ed's innovations have been designed to improve the safety of a product. Space limitations prevent my providing a comprehensive list of all his work, but in addition to those mentioned above, among some of his more successful developments are the Integral Two Stage Regulator, the Automatic Change-over Valve, The Type I Connector for BBQ grills (it is on all gas BBQ grills sold in the U.S.), and a Heat Regulator on the popular fish/turkey fryers.

Ed Lee is almost 10 years past the age of retirement. I asked him when that event might take place.

"When they put me in the grave," he said. "I enjoy what I do. I get five to seven calls a day from RV techs and people around the country needing help with some problem and it makes my day when I can help them out."

Charles Johnson

Charles Johnson sees himself as an innovator. "Innovation" is his favorite word. He describes himself as "a very eclectic type person." And he says his eclecticism is one of his strengths. His variety of backgrounds has been useful in his career and has contributed to his seeing the world on a wider screen than he might, had he concentrated on a narrow specialty. Another insight into Charles is a set of rules posted above his office door: *1) Do the right thing. 2) Do things right. 3) Do things better.*

As the developer, designer—and department head until August of 2004—of the Department of Health Sciences Research at Texas State University, he has employed all facets of his character to create a unique organization.

Charles grew up in the Bay Area of California, but family roots in Texas brought him to East Texas State University for his undergraduate work. While a college student, he was exposed to the medical profession as an x-ray lab tech and a surgical assistant. As he describes it, those were full-time jobs while he went to college part-time.

With a degree in biology/chemistry, Charles says, "I decided to leave medicine and went to Texas A&M to get a masters degree in oceanography. So, I am a geo-chemist as an oceanographer. I was building upon the strengths I acquired as an undergraduate, but I was taking it in a different direction. As I spent more and more time at sea, a lot of the glamour wore off. So, I switched fields again."

Charles chose educational psychology this time—instruction, specifically. "It was, again, a completely different field, but I enjoyed statistics and computers as an oceanographer, so once again, I got into a field where I could use an acquired strength and build on it. I further developed my knowledge of statistics and my skills with computers in pursuit of my PhD in education."

In 1976, Charles came to [Southwest] Texas State University. His computer skills, at the time, made him a uniquely qualified assistant professor. Consequently, University President, Dr. Lee Smith, chose Charles to head the Management By Objective (MBO) program. The MBO program was an innovative management system that met a fair amount of resistance on campus.

"I learned a lot," Charles said. "I can't think of a better position for a new assistant professor to learn about higher education. I learned about evaluation, planning, and implementation at the highest level. And not just about academics. I worked with the campus police and the bookstore, as well as administrative and maintenance people.

"Before I worked for the president, I had begun developing our Health Services Research Program which is a quantitative, computer based health program. Health care is a major industry, but it is far behind when it comes to adopting industry's management tools. The goal of the program, then and now, was and is to bring new techniques to health care by measuring those things that can be measured.

"It continues to amaze me that health care, even today, has not adopted industry's standard practices of seeking improvement by measuring production and outcomes. That is the goal of our department—to develop innovative techniques that will improve the delivery and lower the cost of health care."

Of particular interest to the Health Services Research Program are patients' length of stay, errors in medication, time required for the patient return to work and pain management. The department provides tools, i.e. computer programs for doctors and medical facilities to collect and analyze their own data. The programs allow the health professionals to look at what they are doing and to improve their services. This, according to Charles is an innovation in the medical profession.

"The practice of medicine has often been considered an art, rather than a science," Charles said. "What we are trying to do is bring the science of measurement to health care. And, yes, we have run into resistance. But, we are making headway. We are now able to report the number of deaths each year from medical mistakes. Preventing those deaths is a part of what we are trying to do."

Charles showed me one of his student's masters thesis. The research was done at Central Texas Medical Center emergency room. In conjunction with Sigma Breakthrough, a local company, computer simulations of emergency room procedures were conducted and resulted in changes that brought great improvements in quality of services. M.D. Anderson hospital in Houston has adopted some of the same techniques.

"We are the only university in the United States teaching this program," Charles said. "I borrowed a lot of ideas—or stole them, if you wish—from other people. I have no problem using other people's ideas. But I applied them in an innovative way to the medical profession. We produce graduate students who are specialists in researching quality improvement, computer applications, epidemiology and medical practices.

"In addition, we have two other programs in this department. One is human resources; the other is a gerontology specialist program. When our graduates go out into the world of work, they don't have to be trained. They know what to do and they bring a lot to any employer."

When I received a call about Charles Johnson, the caller informed me that he was very active in scouting. I asked him to elaborate.

"Once again, I am looking at adding value. I work with college students, so I want to improve and produce the best graduate I can. For 15 years I have been the advisor to the Medical Explorer program. This is an all-volunteer college age Boy Scout program. We meet weekly and present medical type programs. I have physicians talk about things that excite them; there are admissions people who talk about the latest developments in their field; health administrative folks bring us programs. I try to get programs where I learn something."

Charles explained that the local medical community has cooperated exceptionally well in exposing his Explorers to real life medical settings. The Scouts are committed to service. Central Texas Medical Center allows Explorers to volunteer and to observe. Local doctors have taken as many as two Explorers into their offices to observe, learn, and assist within their capabilities.

Charles continued, "They ride with EMS and respond to emergencies. Some have even been certified as EMT's. They work in emergency rooms. I have had some students decide to become ER physicians as a result of their experiences with the Explorer program. Their volunteer work set them on a career path.

"But the icing on the cake," Charles said, "is the medical missionary work we do. We have teamed up with the Christian Medical and Dental Society in San Antonio for the past 10 years. There are about 45 undergraduate students in Explorer Post 4077—A student with a sense of humor chose the number in honor of M*A*S*H—All of them have indicated a desire to pursue a career in health services.

"We go three times in the fall semester and three times in the spring to Mexico on border trips. These are weekend trips because that is about all the time the medical students from San Antonio can afford. The Explorers serve as aides and assistants to the MD's who perform the medical and dental services. And they pay most of their own way."

Charles related a story of a young woman (yes, some of these Boy Scouts are girls) who was a pre-physical therapy student. She was assigned to assist an oral surgeon on one of the trips. After two trips, she decided to become a dentist. Another female student became so enamored with the missionary aspect of their work she joined the Peace Corps and spent two years in the Amazon region, living in the most primitive conditions with the Indians before attending medical school. She is president of her freshman med school class.

He had many more similar stories and I had to remind him of my space limitations.

"We do other trips. In the summer we go on longer trips to the Copper Canyon region. And during Spring Break, we go to Monterey."

Besides innovation, Charles's second most favorite word is service. While he is a passionate believer in promoting both, he is reluctant to elaborate on his accomplishments. However, the plaques on his office wall give testimony that he not only talks the talk, he walks the walk.

Kiwanian of the Year, 1982-83, catches my attention, then I notice Kiwanian of the Year 1993; Outstanding Service Award, San Marcos Noon Kiwanis Club 1993-94; State Award, Outstanding Effort Assisting Students with Disabilities; Professor of the Year, 1988, Texas State University; William Spurgeon Award for Explorer Scouting; Outstanding Service to San Marcos Noon Kiwanis Club 1991.

Eclectic, innovative, passionate, dedicated, religious—are words that give some insight into Charles Johnson, but the real Charles Johnson defies description.

Printed in the United States
28922LVS00005B/1-48